Eric Grounds

THE QUIET
AUSTRALIAN

The story of Teddy Hudleston, the RAF's
troubleshooter for 20 years

Eric Grounds

THE QUIET AUSTRALIAN

The story of Teddy Hudleston, the RAF's
troubleshooter for 20 years

MEREO
Cirencester

Mereo Books

1A The Wool Market Dyer Street Cirencester Gloucestershire GL7 2PR
An imprint of Memoirs Publishing www.mereobooks.com

The Quiet Australian: 978-1-86151-478-3

First published in Great Britain in 2015
by Mereo Books, an imprint of Memoirs Publishing

The address for Memoirs Publishing Group Limited can be found at
www.memoirspublishing.com

The Memoirs Publishing Group Ltd Reg. No. 7834348

The Memoirs Publishing Group supports both The Forest Stewardship Council® (FSC®) and
the PEFC® leading international forest-certification organisations. Our books carrying both the
FSC label and the PEFC® and are printed on FSC®-certified paper. FSC® is the only
forest-certification scheme supported by the leading environmental organisations including
Greenpeace. Our paper procurement policy can be found at
www.memoirspublishing.com/environment

Typeset in 11/16pt Bembo
by Wiltshire Associates Publisher Services Ltd. Printed and bound in Great Britain by
Printondemand-Worldwide, Peterborough PE2 6XD

CONTENTS

Introduction

Acknowledgements

This book is dedicated to the memory of
Teddy and Nan Hudleston, for the benefit of their
children, grandchildren and great grandchildren.

INTRODUCTION

I first encountered Teddy Hudleston in 1949 when he was an Air Vice-Marshal aged 40, already with five years of experience as a two-star commander. I was a babe in arms, the son of an American wartime sailor and an Australian mother. I have a picture of Teddy standing in the Davis family group outside Holy Trinity church in Sloane Square on the day of my christening. Heaven only knows why I was flown from Missouri to England for this ceremony: my grandparents lived in Australia, my mother lived in America, my uncle with his wife and children in England, and the group of Jewish maternal great aunts who attended were all originally from New Zealand, although they had lived in a nest of apartments around the Dorchester Hotel for several years.

In 1953 my mother and I moved from St Paul, Minnesota to post-war London via Honolulu, Auckland, Sydney, Marseilles and Paris. Her drinking was fuelled by an anger which no child could comprehend, but age has taught me that it had much to do with her perceived injustice of being young, without money and saddled with me. She would beat, kick, bite, threaten, starve and imprison the cause of her ills. In many ways it was a relief when she was comatose. But it was also frightening, for hours - sometimes it felt like days - would go by with a silence broken only by the hiss of a gas fire and the snoring of my mother. The net curtains which protected the two or three windows of the modest South London council flat smelt of dust and sweat, leaving a dull half-light to illuminate the bedroom, bathroom, small sitting room and kitchenette. I still hate net curtains. There were no books, no games and certainly no television: just imagination, isolation and fear.

I have no idea what it was that triggered the alarm, but there came an evening when Nan and Teddy Hudleston, accompanied by their daughter (my pal) Sal, hammered at the door. There was no way my mother was going to respond. She was out for the count. I can remember the concern and controlled impatience of my aunt and uncle as they tried to motivate me to open the door. My hesitation was not a lack of desire, but a lack of stature. I was five years old, very frightened and unsure how to reach and deal with the lock mechanism. Sal's vital role was to keep me calm, which she did by the novel device of promising to give me a bread rat which she had acquired on a recent trip to Hamelin with her parents.

As she was to do many times over the next thirty years, Nan took control of the physical management of her sister. Teddy took control of the mental and spiritual management of the children. Sal, he and I went to a small café yards from my recent prison where I was offered my first-ever English omelette. I never lived with my mother again.

For the next forty years Teddy Hudleston treated me as his son. I make absolutely no apology for larding his professional and private story with the insight which that gave me. A biography must look at every aspect of its subject, and my attempt to write about Teddy is tinged with the sadness that I believe I understood him, and that he understood me somewhat better than his own children. The roots of that lie in his own childhood, which is one of the reasons why I have started this story with a candid introduction of my own early challenges. It is to his eternal credit that he ensured that I became a law-abiding and productive Englishman.

Another man played a most important role in my upbringing. Johnny Collingwood fell in love with Nan Hudleston in 1948. For more than 25 years he was Nan's lover, willingly accepting the burden of supporting her sisters and children. I was fortunate to be part of that parcel, so I owe my productivity and confidence to two men who were not my blood relatives, who shared one woman, and who went through the entire emotional scale from friendship to fiendship in the years of their acquaintance. Johnny was commissioned into the Queen's Bays in 1925. Through his influence, Teddy Hudleston's son, Tony, and I, both colour-blind and therefore unqualified for the RAF, joined the same regiment, which became 1st The Queen's Dragoon Guards in 1959 when the King's Dragoon Guards amalgamated with the Queen's Bays.

This book does not attempt to evaluate or dissect major historical events in great detail. I do not seek to define defence policy or military performance. There are plenty of excellent books, memoirs and archives that cover the territory. Instead, this work sets out to do what Teddy himself intended when he drafted the framework of his biography, which is to study his own role as he took part in some of the defining moments of the 20th Century.

ACKNOWLEDGEMENTS

Many individuals have been extremely kind and supportive with this project. In thanking them, let me include:

Lieutenant Colonel Patrick Andrews, OBE

Malcolm Barrass, whose website, Air of Authority, has been absolutely invaluable

Lulu Benson

Colin Cheshire

Sebastian Cox, Head of Air Historical Branch (RAF)

Squadron Leader Tim Cripps

Peter Devitt, RAF Museum, Hendon

Wing Commander Gerry Doyle, RCDS Executive Officer 2013

Isabel Drummond

Air Commodore Sir Timothy Elworthy, KCVO

General Sir Charles Harington, GCB, CBE, DSO, MC

Nick Hudleston

Annette Hudleston Harwood

Air Vice-Marshal Ernest Hey, CB, CBE

Air Vice-Marshal Bob Honey, CB, CBE,

Lady Brenda Hudleston

Air Vice-Marshal Sandy Hunter, CBE, AFC, DL

Robin Kernick

Air Chief Marshal Sir Michael Knight, KCB, AFC

Air Chief Marshal Sir Peter le Cheminant, GBE, KCB, DFC

Wing Commander DG Lucas, AFC

Captain Leigh Merrick, RN

Vera Merrick

Dr Gregory Pedlow

Air Chief Marshal Sir Thomas Prickett, KCB, DSO, DFC

Air Commodore Henry Probert, MBE

Kerry Ray

Air Commodore MJ Rayson, LVO

David Rosier

James Scarlett

Staff Sergeant Morris Scott

Major Michael Sender

Air Marshal Sir Frederick Sowrey, KCB, CBE, AFC

Rosalie Spire of Spire Research

John Strafford

Mrs RC Sturtivant for permission to quote sections of Hawks
Rising, notably pages 55 and 56

Group Captain Ian Tapster

Rick Thomas

Sally Usher

Tim Usher

Field Marshal Lord Walker of Aldringham, GCB, CMG, CBE, DL

Mrs Rosemary Waller, Guildford Grammar School Archivist

I want to pay a particular tribute to Vincent Orange, who is an Olympian in the field of biographical writing. Years ago he said to me 'don't be hesitant: just do it. And remember that you are writing about one subject; if he is not mentioned on every page, you have to ask yourself why you have spent time on that information.' I also want to thank Air Vice-Marshal Sandy Hunter, who has offered solid wisdom and guidance on RAF matters for the many years that I have been engaged with the project. Air Commodore Sir Timothy Elworthy has added real colour to my understanding of the high offices of the RAF, for which I am deeply grateful. Tim Usher, who was Teddy and Nan's son in law, did me great honour by reading the penultimate version of the book and providing focused and informed criticism. And there are members of the family, notably Sally, Teddy and Nan's daughter, and Kerry Ray, Teddy's niece, who have provided fundamentally important personal insights.

CHAPTER 1

THE EARLY YEARS - PERTH, WESTERN AUSTRALIA

The temperature was just nudging 82 degrees in the late September afternoon as four teenagers from Guildford Grammar School completed their third set of energetic tennis. They stopped for a cool drink of lemon. Swimming was next on the agenda and the only question was whether it would be in the Indian Ocean or the Swan River. John Laver, John Lefroy, Wallace Kyle and Teddy Hudleston were all school sporting heroes, leading lights in the 1ˢᵗ XI, stalwarts of the football team, school prefects and good friends. Each of them would become Captain of Guildford Grammar School, with Hudleston followed by Laver, followed by Kyle and topped off by Lefroy. As they put presses on their rackets, their hostess, Caroline Drummond, appeared at the side of the court with her son, Roy.

Western Australia was a small place and it had lost the prime of its youth in the disaster of Gallipoli in 1916. In Teddy's words, anyone who survived was not only lucky but a hero. Roy Drummond was both. Having enlisted as a private soldier in the Australian Imperial Force in September 1914, he was invalided out of the Army in 1915, but managed to reapply and gained a commission as a 2nd Lieutenant in the Northumberland Fusiliers. By April 1916, he had transferred to the newly-created Royal Flying Corps and became a pilot with 67 Squadron. He won a Military Cross (MC) in August 1917, and then added the icing of two Distinguished Service Orders (DSO) in March and July 1918 for feats of astonishing bravery and flying excellence. By any standard, he was indeed a hero; to the young men meeting him beside his parents' tennis court, he was a form of god.

In 1923 Roy Drummond had proposed the notion of officer exchanges between the Royal Air Force (RAF) and the Royal Australian Air Force (RAAF). Gratifyingly, he was one of the early candidates and returned to his native Australia to serve as the Deputy Chief of the RAAF as a 32-year-old Squadron Leader.

The boys were itching to run off to swim, but good manners and a degree of awe dictated patience. 'I am giving a lecture on the air force this evening,' said Drummond. 'Would you like to come along?'

Teddy recorded his thoughts: 'What a choice! The wonderful swim, or putting on a heavy suit and sitting in a lecture hall?' But this was a great man and his invitation was the closest thing to a royal command. The lecture was about the Royal Flying Corps, the Royal Air Force and RAF Cranwell, which was apparently an English college designed to train pilots. Within the hour, Teddy Hudleston was completely hooked on the idea of a career as an airman.

School House notes in the December 1926 issue of The Swan reported:

'*The House has suffered greatly in losing Hudleston. He obtained, by gaining the Governor General's nomination, an entry into the RAF Training College at Cranwell. He has been in the House since it started, he played a great part on the sporting side - cricket captain, football, tennis captain, running; and he did splendid work as Captain of the House last year, and of the School this year. He sailed in November. Our best wishes go with him.*'

The selection had been subject to one proviso, that he should satisfy the medical authorities. This presented Teddy with no difficulty, but he did discover for the first time that there was a physical complaint called colour blindness. When the medical took him to an ophthalmist, he was invited to separate a number of coloured wools. He thought his interrogator was a trickster or mad. After all, everybody could tell red from green, surely? Curiously his son, Tony, born in 1938, was colour blind, thanks to the genetic codes inherited from his mother, Nan.

Teddy sailed on the SS *Hobson's Bay* on 18 November. He would not return to Perth for 32 years.

ANCESTRY AND PARENTAGE

The Hudlestons claim descent from Norman invaders who first arrived in England with William the Conqueror in 1066. Thanks to the work of Annette Hudleston Harwood, there is a verifiable

record of the family going back to one Nigel, who was alive in 1110.

The family seat became Hutton John, a Pele tower and manor near Penrith in Cumberland, in 1564 when Marie Hutton, a god-daughter of Princess Mary Tudor (later Queen Mary), married Andrew Hudleston, who was a gentleman in the Princess's household. The property was to remain in the family for the next four hundred years.

In 1861 Andrew Fleming Hudleston died, leaving Hutton John to his cousin, William Hudleston of Kelston in Somerset. William and his wife, Laura Taylor, produced eight sons and three daughters between 1856 and 1874.

William was a British colonial administrator whose career peaked when he acted for six months as the Governor of Madras in 1881. Several of his children were born in India, notably Cuthbert, the sixth child and fourth son of this fruitful marriage, who appeared in 1863.

With landed families it was a general convention that at least one younger son would go into the church. In the case of Cuthbert, his calling was natural and sincere. After his education at Wellington College in Berkshire, he went up to New College, Oxford before entering Wells Theological College in 1886. He spent eleven gruelling years learning his trade in the slums of

East and South London before deciding to emigrate to Perth in Western Australia in 1898.

The contrast with his earlier life could hardly have been more vivid. In the words of Kerry Ray, Teddy's niece, her grandfather moved from the damp, dank streets of a major conurbation to work his way around the gold mining towns of Norseman, Kalgoorlie and Coolgardie, some 600 kilometres east of Perth. It was remote, open gibber plains, clay pans, heavy loose sand, sparse trees with little or no shade and only the amount of food that could be carried. His diaries and notebooks became travelling maps of his journeys along tracks and unsigned trails to remote diggings where miners lived 'on the track' with a barrow and their belongings, powered by shank's pony. For six years, he was itinerant, a popular visitor to the remotest places in the region not only for his religious succour, but also for the link he provided with civilization.

He returned to live in Perth in 1904. Now aged 39, his mind was moving towards matrimony and he quickly met a suitable candidate. Julia Phillips was thirteen years younger and had travelled extensively in places as far afield as England, Morocco and Japan. With no living parents, she seemed to be sensible, well organised and highly presentable. Indeed, she was rather beautiful. They married in London on 13 November 1906.

Cuthbert became the rector of St Alban's, Beaufort Street, Perth from 1907 to 1919 and of St Patrick's, Mount Lawley from 1923 to 1929. He was appointed Archdeacon of Perth in 1910 and served as the acting administrator of the diocese from 1916 to 1941, quite apart from enjoying an enduring connection with Perth Girls' Orphanage as a governor from 1904 until he retired in 1941. Obituaries tend to be polite about their subjects but it must be said that the tribute to him in the West Australian Church News of 1 January 1945 was a compelling psalm of praise for a very special spiritual and administrative leader.

Cuthbert was generous to a fault and, with no real interest in material wealth, he literally gave the shirt off his own back to a man who arrived to beg at his house whom he believed to be in greater need. This did not always meet with the approbation of his bride, who was made of much sterner stuff and despaired of her husband's unswerving generosity and his eternal determination to give away his children's inheritance. Cuthbert was forever bringing home 'down-and-outers' for sustenance; Julia would have preferred to feed them a bone under a tree – and not her tree either.

Julia was the youngest of three daughters of George Braithwaite Phillips, who died in 1900 whilst still serving as the Police Commissioner for Western Australia. Policing was in the family tradition because George, who married three times, had taken as his second wife Annie Emma Hare, the daughter of an earlier Police Commissioner, Gustavus Hare. This was Julia's mother, who died tragically early in 1879 at the all too commonly youthful age of 32, leaving Edith (eight years old), Frances (five) and Julia (three). The only good news in this disaster was that George was one of six children, providing him with a large enough family to supply backup for his young family.

His older sister, Georgiana, had moved to Adelaide after her marriage to William Lavington Marchant, produced a number of daughters and died in 1866 at the age of 33. Mary, his younger sister, died in infancy, but Margaret, the youngest of the Phillips girls, survived and, as often happened in families when a child died young, she was known as Mary also.

George's brothers were entrepreneurial, notably his eldest brother, John Randall Phillips Jr, who was the driving force in the development of Kanyaka Station, some 25 miles from Quorn in South Australia.

In 1886, when Julia was 10, George married for the third time. Vittoria Ellen Jane Burges was a daughter of a colonial family who had emigrated from Tipperary in 1830. Vittoria was substantially younger than her husband, but he had little thought of producing a new family. He also failed to plan for his death and left no will when he died at 11.00am on 26 March 1900. His wife swiftly applied for, and on 5 April 1900 was granted, letters of administration for her late husband's estate. His daughters, now mature young women, were left with adequate funds and their stepmother's goodwill. Vittoria survived into old age, dying in 1933, apparently on reasonable terms with her stepchildren.

But Julia clearly lived a life without much parental affection. Her father was a distant, authoritarian figure; her mother had died when she was little more than a baby. Female attention in the family home was negligible through the most formative years of her young life, and her stepmother seems to have been more dutiful than loving. Julia could not be wholly blamed, therefore, for a degree of iciness in her attitude to her children. The fact is that she rarely mentioned her eldest son, Teddy, and left him a mere £200 in her will. Although she barely knew her daughter-in-law, Nan, she thought little of her and was known to comment 'she's a Jew, you know'. She was appalled when her daughter, Marjorie, married a divorced man and reduced her contact to the bare minimum until she was an old woman and spent some time living with her daughter in Melbourne. The youngest son, Bill, who was less academic and sporting than his older brother, was treated with little more than passing interest. The sadness is that this emotional vacuum left her children untutored in matters of love and affection. As a group of siblings, they were relatively shy and undemonstrative.

After their wedding in London, Cuthbert and Julia swiftly returned to Perth and ten months after the wedding their first child was born - stillborn. It was unnamed, unknown and is buried in grave number 0199A at Karrakatta. It is not clear even today whether Teddy and his siblings ever knew about their parents' first born child.

Undeterred, the young couple swiftly conceived another child and Teddy, Edmund Cuthbert Hudleston, arrived in the world with little difficulty on 30 December 1908. He was followed in 1912 by Marjorie and in 1914 by Arthur William, better known as Bill.

Julia was evidently a very complex character. When at home, she conducted her maternal duties with rigid discipline. Children were to be seen and not heard. They were to be obedient, diligent and thoroughly educated. And - to be fair to Julia - they were to be well informed and proud of their Hudleston heritage. It was from her that they learned of Hutton John and Julia's great affection for the house.

Sally Usher, Teddy's daughter, was amazed to learn from her father that he and his siblings had been tied - literally tied - to the kitchen table to learn their bible studies. Curiously this was to hold Teddy in good stead later in life, particularly when he was in the western desert in 1943 and trading bible quotations over the dinner table with Field Marshal Jan Smuts. Over the forty years of his service life, Teddy frequently embarrassed military padres who misquoted biblical texts in their sermons.

Whatever maternal instinct Julia may have had, it was no constraint for a woman who enjoyed enough personal wealth to do roughly what she wanted. There is a famous story of her leaving a note at home which read 'Look after Bill; I'm catching the *Orion* which sails this afternoon.' Without doubt Cuthbert was as bemused with his wife as were their children, and it is fortunate for them that he displayed the quiet parental love and support which Julia failed to apply.

Teddy proved to be all that an ambitious parent could desire. He grew up a thoughtful, determined child, consistently performing well in his studies and excelling in sport. His father described him in a letter to his brother-in-law, Sir Arthur Martindale, as 'a careful reliable lad, who has always been a bit old for his years.' He made friends easily and from an early age demonstrated a natural flair for leadership. It was small surprise, therefore, that he captained the cricket and tennis teams, his house and his school and topped it all with an appointment as the Company Sergeant Major of the School Cadets. The ambition to fly, which had been ignited by Roy Drummond, was swiftly endorsed by no less a dignitary than Sir William Campion, the Governor General of Western Australia, leading to Teddy becoming the first-ever Australian to be accepted for training at RAF Cranwell.

His move to England was difficult for his father, who loved his oldest boy dearly. Financially it was uncomfortable too, for he paid in advance for the cost of the training at Cranwell. This amounted to £250 (equivalent to £7,400 in 2012) for two years, comprising an annual educational fee of £75 and uniform fees of £100. In addition he deposited £50 in an account at the Bank of Adelaide in Leadenhall Street in the City for Teddy to use.

Teddy embarked as a first-class passenger on his voyage to England, a journey which cost his parents £45. The trip lasted four weeks and included a memorable stop in Colombo, where he and another seventeen-year-old from Perth, Bill Sutherland, decided to go window shopping. Gazing into a leading jeweller's shop, they were invited inside and shown many beautiful and expensive rings. Teddy wrote

'Clearly we were not buyers but the shopkeeper was insistent. He picked out a ring and said 'you take it to London, have it valued and send me what they say.'

Teddy never forgot the incident, because it was his first introduction to the utter trust created by the British men and women who lived in the East during the previous one hundred years. Not only did this singular incident stick with him, but it was reinforced when he served in India, and he always affirmed that he was intensely proud of the reputation for integrity established by the Indian Civil service and Britons on service in India.

Cranwell

The arrival in England was a grim transformation. It was 18 December 1926, twelve days before Teddy's eighteenth birthday. The air was cold and damp, with the acrid yellow murk of the time, which lingered in Teddy's nostrils for years to come. Despite the physical discomforts, the young man felt that he belonged in this strange land, largely because of the Hudleston heritage of Hutton John, which at that point he had never seen.

To his dismay, he quickly caught flu, which delayed his arrival at Cranwell for a week. He arrived on 20 January 1927, feeling that this was an inauspicious black mark on his service career. His commitment was tested further by the foot of snow that greeted his arrival at Cranwell in Lincolnshire. He hated it; it was the first time he had encountered snow and it convinced him that it didn't belong in England. The ex-Guards sergeant major who first briefed him on local conditions insisted that it was a mild spell.

Cranwell bore no resemblance to today's excellent campus. There was a collection of iron huts, tarred over and connected by catwalks, the legacy of the Royal Naval Air Service. Five cadets lived in a hut with a smoking iron stove for warmth. Each hut had a living room, a common bedroom and washroom. The hierarchy was carefully considered and each hut had a third-term cadet, who was in charge, two second-term and two first-term novices. The composition changed every term so that young men learned from the experience of their seniors (Teddy's notes actually say 'betters') and acquired some sense of responsibility beyond their purely military training.

Teddy's hut commander on arrival was Hugh (Connie) Constantine, who later became Air Chief Marshal Sir Hugh Constantine, KBE, CB, DSO and a lifelong friend. Other hut mates during his time at Cranwell included Lord Malcolm Douglas Hamilton, Hilary (Herbert) Dale, James Scarlett, Patrick Coote and GRA (Reggie) Elsmie. Teddy later wrote that Elsmie was 'possibly the most outstanding all-round cadet ever to enter the Services. He would almost certainly have become Chief of the Air Staff had he not been lost over Greece in 1941.' Elsmie was a Wing Commander with a DFC when he was shot down on 18 April 1941.

It was one of the great tragedies that all but Constantine and Hudleston eventually died in aircraft. Coote, who won the Sword of Honour in 1930, was killed in action on 13 April 1941; Dale was killed in action on 11 May 1941; Douglas Hamilton died in a flying accident in the Cameroons in 1964; Scarlett changed his name by deed poll in 1939, so his death was recorded under the name Scarlett-Streatfeild on 10 May 1945 when his aircraft flew into high ground ten miles north of Oslo. At the time he was also a 35-year-old acting Air Vice-Marshal, having beaten Teddy to two-star rank by twenty-three days. Actually, Scarlett-Streatfeild was walking on water, because he was the first of the team to make it to Air Commodore, in February 1943, ten days after his thirty-fourth birthday.

As an aside, Scarlett-Streatfeild's father was also an Air Vice-Marshal in the 1920s. Famously, he won a DSO for leading a bombing mission in 1917 while flying an unarmed aircraft. He also acquired some notoriety for conducting a tour of inspection of a naval carrier and stepping very smartly from the deck straight into the sea.

One other contemporary went on to great things, thanks to the curriculum at Cranwell. During their final term, students had to write a thesis on a subject of their own choosing, provided it concerned aviation. A young man called Frank Whittle wrote up his theory and concept of the jet engine, which was immediately recognised as 'the' revolutionary step forward by the aerodynamics professor. A year after Whittle graduated, he was taken away from his squadron and given a free hand to develop the first-ever jet engine.

The curriculum was far less academic than it is today and most senior officers regret the change. In general terms, cadets spent 20% of their time flying, 30% learning English, History and Mathematics, 10% on practical engineering, 20% on service subjects like navigation, armaments and electronics, and the final 20% on assorted team building activities ranging from drill to sports. Teddy readily admitted that he and his colleagues often resented the scale for each activity. In their judgement, they were there to fly, but the timetable limited the opportunity and the weather was a further impediment. With no bad weather instruments, they had to spend far too many hours on the tarmac waiting for the weather to clear.

Air Vice-Marshal Frederick Halahan CMG, CBE, DSO, MVO was the commandant when Teddy arrived at Cranwell. Commissioned initially as a Midshipman, he served as a Gunnery Officer on HMS *Dreadnought* and finished the Great War as a Colonel, withal as a serving officer of the Royal Navy. He even attended the Naval Staff College in 1923, three years after being awarded a permanent commission in the RAF. In what may now seem to have been a leap of faith, he was appointed as Commandant at Cranwell in 1926 in the rank of Air Vice-Marshal. Despite this roving example of a complex career, Teddy truly valued the skill and experience of his commandant and instructors, all of whom had served during the Great War.

But Teddy was particularly lucky to be tutored and mentored by a man who became one of the most outstanding military commanders of World War II. Squadron Leader Arthur Coningham, DSO, MC, AFC, was in charge of B Squadron and played a significant role in flying training. Renowned as a brilliant pilot, Coningham, who was commonly known as 'Mary', which was a bastardisation of his nickname 'Maori', acquired on his arrival in England from New Zealand, had an extraordinary flair for teaching people to fly. He was able to quickly identify why a pupil could not understand a specific action or technique. Having discovered this, it was normally fairly easy to settle the pupil. The instructor's log book would record 'smoothed him down.' Over the next eighteen years, Mary Coningham would prove to be the most important influence on Teddy's career.

In the draft of his biography Teddy recorded which aircraft the cadets learned to fly. There was the Avro 504K, a two-seater biplane with a rotary Gnome engine; the Bristol Fighter, a distinguished veteran of the Great War; the Sopwith Snipe, which arrived right at the end of the War, too late to make its mark; the de Havilland 9A, which was fitted with the Liberty engine, an Anglo-American venture which was allegedly designed by a team that was shut in a room and released only when they had agreed on the format; and the Siskin.

Engines were of real interest to the pilots. The Gnome radial engine had nine cylinders rotating around a fixed axle. It spewed castor oil as it rotated and occasionally it cast a complete cylinder, seemingly with no impact on its behaviour. There was no slow running control and slow revolutions were achieved by cutting the ignition with a switch on top of the control column, known as the 'blip switch.' Performance was inconsistent and Teddy recalled one of his colleagues taxiing into line in front of a hangar when, to the astonishment of all, the aircraft developed a Buster Keaton slapstick comedy routine and shot forward at full throttle into the shed.

The Rolls Royce Falcon engine in the Bristol Fighter had very close tolerances on every bearing, while the Liberty engine worked on clearances of several thousandths of an inch which continued to operate regardless of oil or temperature. The Bristol was a two-seater which had performed well in the Great War. In its combat role it carried a Lewis machine gun in a rotating mount, known as a Scarff ring, mounted around the edge of the rear cockpit. It also carried a forward-firing Vickers machine gun for which the firing rate was determined by an ingenious cam, which stopped the gun firing as the airscrew appeared in front of the barrel. This equipment, known as the Constantinesco gear, could perform inconsistently, so a steel plate was fitted to the rear side of the propeller to protect it from bullets fired when the gear was out of phase.

Both the Rolls Royce Falcon engine and the de Havilland Liberty engine were liquid cooled. The temperature was controlled by louvre shutters on the radiator and if these were neglected, clouds of steam would envelop the cockpit and, if the reaction was too slow, the engine would seize.

Teddy's flying began on the Avro 504 K under the instruction of Flight Lieutenant H.B. (Hab) Russell, a former RFC pilot, who was quiet, entirely likeable, calm and patient. Russell told him to climb into the front seat, where the cockpit only came halfway up his chest. Feeling extremely exposed to the elements, and with very mixed feelings about what was happening, he found himself in the air with the ground disappearing below him. His memory was of the calm voice of the instructor, the noise of the engine, the air stream whistling through the rigging, the relative silence of the glide with the engine just ticking over, followed by an even deeper silence on landing. Most students went solo after a mere nine or ten hours spread over ten weeks.

In his quiet, reticent Edwardian way, Teddy often alluded to the rough and smooth of life as a Cranwell cadet. The implication was that senior cadets never feared to use physical methods to apply a lesson and other 'justice' was often equally stern. 'We learned to accept it,' he wrote, 'we also learned to administer it and we benefited on both counts.' In his view, enshrined in writing in the 1980s, many of the problems with young people derived from a lack of firm treatment.

With a sense of certain inevitability, Teddy covered himself with great distinction at Cranwell and he was clearly an excellent pilot, even though he had two accidents. On 9 March 1928 when practising landing he misjudged the approach and undershot, hitting a ridge. Then on 14 April 1928, again during landing practice, he found himself across wind and as he implemented the correction a gust of wind under his starboard wing forced the port wing into the ground. Happily he was not injured and despite two errors in little more than a month, the fact is that he demonstrated a natural flair for machines in the air in a way that he never really mastered with motor cars on the ground. Indeed, he always treated his car as an aeroplane, which gave passengers an uncomfortable insight to the potential of travelling in three dimensions. He also shone as a student, both academically and as a team player. His final report summarised his performance thus: 'An under-officer whose work and games have maintained a standard of all round excellence. Very reliable. Representative colours in Cricket and Tennis.'

His boss, Squadron Leader Arthur Coningham, wrote to Archdeacon Cuthbert Hudleston on 8 January 1929:

Dear Archdeacon,
Will you permit me to write to you a few words of appreciation of your son's two years at Cranwell?

He was a great asset to the College and by force of example in all the various fields of activity did more good than any other Cadet who has been here during the last two years. But the outstanding thing about him is his exceptionally fine character.

Of course we all think he should have won the Sword of Honour but it was a case of choosing between two very fine lads and the AOC had a very worrying week making his decision.

But he has started his service career on a foundation of efficiency, respect and sportsmanship. These qualities, in addition to his character and the popular admiration he receives, should give him a brilliant career in the Royal Air Force.

He is flying very well and has been posted to the excellent station he selected.

Believe me, Sir, yours sincerely, Arthur Coningham.

This was supported by a letter in a similar vein to Teddy himself, exhorting him to do well, beware of the different quality of plane he would encounter, keep up his cricket and not to worry about coming second to another for the Sword of Honour. He pointed to one of the Beamish brothers, who had a similar experience but went on to break all records by becoming a Flight Lieutenant at 25, five years after leaving Cranwell. He was referring to Victor (1903-1942) who was killed in action on 28 Mar 1942 leading the Kenley Wing. As it happens, his brother, George (1905-1967), did win the Sword of Honour in 1924 and later became Air Marshal Sir George Beamish, KCB, CBE. The man who beat Teddy to the draw was Cadet Guy Pendrill Charles, whose early promise did not lead him to the highest ranks in the Air Force because he died in combat with 208 Squadron as a 32-year-old Wing Commander on 13 January 1942.

Teddy enjoyed Cranwell immensely and played his own part in the recruitment of Australians who became senior airmen. After only five months as an officer cadet, he wrote to his old school friend, Wallace Kyle, who had become the head boy at Guildford Grammar School. He strongly advised him to follow his example. Kyle did so and some 30 years later succeeded Teddy as Vice Chief of the Air Staff before retiring as an Air Chief Marshal and becoming the Governor General of Western Australia.

CHAPTER 2

THE LIFE OF A YOUNG OFFICER

No. 25 Squadron was a fighter squadron equipped with Gloucester Grebes, a post-war aircraft which never saw active service. In Teddy's judgement, it was a beautiful fighting machine, highly manoeuvrable with an astonishing all-round view. The cockpit was so shallow that the pilot could lean over the side and see under the fuselage.

Fighter Command did not exist in those days, so the Squadron was one of 11 fighter squadrons under command of Wessex Bombing Area based at Uxbridge. The AOC was Air Vice-Marshal John Steel, another senior officer who had learned his trade initially in the Navy and who rose ultimately to become Air Chief Marshal Sir John Steel, GCB, KBE. Teddy thought highly of him because throughout his life he never forgot a name or face.

Most young officers quickly discover that a commission is little more than a starting point. Appearing on parade at Hawkinge for the first time, proudly displaying his wings on his service dress, Teddy was sent back to his room to remove them until such time as his Squadron Leader judged him worthy of them. Of course this was totally unconstitutional, but the Squadron Leader's word was law and many victims of this harsh introduction to life as an officer later realised that it had probably contributed to saving their lives.

To his delight, the two next most junior officers in the squadron had been in the year ahead of Teddy at Cranwell. Charles Beamish was the third of four brothers from Ireland who all served with distinction in the RAF. They were all rugby players; George, the second eldest, played for the RAF, Ireland and the British Lions and was captain of the RAF team in 1933 when his brother, Charles, was in the team. Charles played in the RAF team for several years and won 12 caps for Ireland, but he was also a fine golfer and became RAF Champion in 1927. Cecil Beamish, the youngest brother, devoted his time to golf and was RAF Champion seven times between 1949 and 1973.

(Walter) Karl Beisiegel was another sporting phenomenon. He played hockey for England and as a schoolboy at Uppingham was judged to be the best cover point after Hobbs. Between 1928 and 1934 he played 15 first class games for Leicestershire, although his first-class record was not hugely distinguished. Teddy reported: 'He could have played both hockey and cricket for England, but he was so damn lazy.' On the other hand, Beamish and Beisiegel, commonly known as 'Bike', were fine pilots and were stalwart friends and mentors of their youthful colleague.

It was disconcerting when the ferocious squadron leader, 'Porky' Park, died of appendicitis shortly after Teddy's arrival. Park had a puckish sense of humour and by chance had lodged with his adjutant instructions on what to do in the event of his death. The adjutant duly honoured the order, which was to fill his CO's car with fuel, place a full bottle of brandy on the front passenger seat and bury the Bull-nose Morris close to the 'T; on the landing strip. This ceremony was carried out with the full squadron on parade and the Grebes arranged in a hollow square around the gravesite. At the signal from the adjutant, one of the Grebes opened fire and discharged all of its ammunition into the void as the final tribute to a much valued leader and friend.

He was replaced by Squadron Leader L.G.S. 'Lousy' Payne, MC, AFC, who was described as tall, languid and handsome. He had earned a reputation as a night fighter pilot in the Great War, yet was something of an intellectual with no false fear of senior officers or establishments. Backed by greater private wealth than most officers, he was always prepared to fight his corner for the squadron with respect but absolute determination. Teddy believed this to be an admirable and commonly-expressed characteristic of the RAF which meant that senior officers always knew what the troops on the ground were thinking. Payne retired as Air Commodore Payne, CB, MC, AFC, and became the highly-esteemed and influential Air Correspondent for the *Daily Telegraph*.

The operational team of 16 fighters was led by three flight commanders, each flight with five aircraft, leaving a single squadron reserve. The flight commanders were all Flight Lieutenants and old men in the eyes of the new young officer, who thought 32 was ancient. Unsurprisingly, they were very different in character and style: W.E. (Walter) Swan commanded 'A' flight and was Teddy's first boss: dour and meticulous, a strict disciplinarian; Hewson, slow of speech and action but always thorough; and Harcourt Smith, quick and intolerant of fools. But they made a good team and the leadership of 'Lousy' Payne was the binding ingredient.

Hawkinge was a single squadron station, so the family learned and lived together. Everyone knew everyone else, creating great respect and affection between officers and airmen. Flying and looking after their men were the main preoccupations of the officers. Very few men – no more than 2% – were married. Motor cars were rare (although Teddy did buy his first car in the summer of 1930 for £67), so the focus of life was the squadron. Every officer had a machine allocated to him, along with a rigger and fitter to look after it. It was entirely normal to find the teams polishing and tinkering with their aircraft over the weekend.

As a senior officer, Teddy regretted that it took so long for the modern fighter and bomber to prepare for a flight, something in the order of 30 to 60 minutes for a fighter and up to several hours for a bomber. In 1929 an aircraft could take off within minutes of the flight commander's instruction.

Pilots generally flew 'by the seat of their pants' and it was accepted that ex-cavalry officers tended to be good pilots. When they flew, they were always given a specific task, mostly involving map reading. This enabled them to enjoy endless cross-country flights to see other units, and created a network of bright young men who exchanged ideas on operational performance and made friends far and wide.

Teddy recounted a flight in formation under his flight commander, Walter Swan, to North Weald. The weather was foul with visibility near zero but Swan somehow found the destination, much to the amazement and relief of his admiring pilots. The weather was so bad that they had to stay the night but, before the decision, Teddy's old friend Hugh Constantine of 56 Squadron appeared out of the fog on the far side of the airfield. His Commanding Officer, Squadron Leader Alan (Nunkie) Lees, happened to be present on the scene and promptly challenged the young officer, 'Morning Constantine, what are you doing here?'

'I've just come up from Eastchurch, sir,' he replied.

'Did you receive my negative weather report?' barked Lees.

'Yes sir, I did, but I thought I would have a go anyway.'

'Very well,' said Lees, 'then you had better have a go getting back again!'

The company gaped. The weather was clearly getting worse. Tail between his legs, Constantine climbed back into his aircraft and took off into the gloom. Happily he made it back to Eastchurch.

In Teddy's view, this was an excellent lesson for all present. First, an order, particularly a flying order, is given to be obeyed. Second, a good commander must know his men and their capabilities. This was a calculated risk by Lees, which was all the more emphatic for its immediacy and effectiveness; better by far than any other disciplinary action.

But life was full of fun, as well as hard lessons. Soon after joining No. 23 Squadron at Kenley, a young pilot called Douglas Bader decided to do a low roll over his airfield. It was literally a step too far because he hit the ground and lost both legs. A little more than three months later, Teddy attended a Ball at Kenley and to his astonishment there was Bader, dancing.

In 1929 Gilbert Harcourt Smith responded to a general call for volunteers to go out to the Sudan, where trouble had erupted. For some reason, he began his journey by sailing from Dover to France by ferry. The Squadron decided to give him the best send-off from the quayside. One or two cars made the trip to Dover, while the remainder of the squadron caught the train in ample time. Indeed, there was so much time that it seemed appropriate for the company to repair to the bar on the ferry for a valedictory tribute. The drink flowed – and so did the ferry. It was only as the harbour wall disappeared past the bar room window that the Squadron realised it was on its way to France. Negotiations with the captain were completely unavailing, although he did agree to send a message to the Air Ministry informing them that 25 Squadron RAF, less the Commanding Officer, had embarked for the Continent. No airman could understand the demands of the tide and the ferry could not turn back. Hours later, having fully enjoyed the enforced confines of a duty free bar, a large group of dishevelled airmen disembarked and weaved its way back to base. In those balmier days, the Air Ministry took no action and HM Customs and Immigration treated it as a tremendous joke.

A major preoccupation of the Squadron in 1929 was to prepare for the ninth Hendon Air Display, which was scheduled for 13 July. 25 Squadron were teamed with No 1 and No 43 Squadrons, who were also equipped with Siskins. Based at Tangmere near Portsmouth, they were the local rivals who, in typical services fashion, were never given any overt credit for proficiency, although they were highly competent and professional.

No. 43 Squadron was commanded by Squadron Leader C.N. (Cyril) Lowe, MC, DFC, who won 25 caps playing rugby for England between 1914 and 1923 and set a scoring record of 18 tries, which endured for more than 60 years. In his notes for his memoirs, Teddy commented that Roy Drummond, the man who had transformed his life, was commanding No 1 Squadron. In fact Roy Drummond had not returned from Australia at this point, although he did appear as a Wing Commander at Tangmere some months later. Drummond's journey back to England with his bride included a very narrow escape. They travelled on Imperial Airways 'City of Rome', from Karachi, which they left on arrival in Alexandria. The following day, 27 October 1929, the aircraft crashed with the loss of all crew and passengers en route to England.

Teddy remembered the air show particularly because, in his opinion, it was possibly the first time 27 aircraft had drilled in formation. The three squadrons took off together and each squadron landed back in formation. This feat was all the more remarkable because the aircraft had no flaps or brakes, thereby demonstrating a very high degree of airmanship by the assembled crews. One of the highlights of their display was a downward spiral in line askew, which was captured on film by Pathé News and is still available in their archives. Teddy recalled that he was the 26th of the 27 aircraft and, although the formation leaders were flying at little more than 100–120 mph, the back markers were going flat out just to maintain their place.

The squadron became well known because of its competence at formation aerobatics, having launched its first tentative success when 'Bike' Beisiegel and Teddy Hudleston flew with their wings tied to each other with elastic cords.

Sport played an enormous part in the lives of the young officers of 25 Squadron. Both 'Bike' and Teddy would be away playing cricket for the RAF or Free Foresters whenever they could. With squash and rugby as additional interests, they secured access to many people of the same age in other walks of life, quite apart from putting them in the public eye with their lords and masters. Throughout his life, Teddy maintained that his rise to the top had been amply enhanced by sporting prowess.

While still at Cranwell, Teddy had made friends with J.G. (Griff) Llewellyn, whose parents generously invited him to their home near Exmouth during the summer holidays. He felt very much at home with the family and, in company with Griff's younger brother, Robert, and sister, Joan, they decided to enter all the tennis tournaments in Budleigh Salterton, Exmouth, Seaton and Sidmouth, invariably taking prizes at the end of each week of the summer over a period of three to four years.

In April 1930 the Squadron was informed that it was to be fully re-equipped with Armstrong Whitworth Siskins. This was probably the first, and certainly one of the earliest, all-metal aircraft to be built. In comparison with the Grebe, it was a heavy, big beast with a low altitude performance little better than the Grebe and none of the Grebe's good looks and all round visibility. Although the pilots did not like it, it did have a superior high altitude performance. But some of the older pilots absolutely refused to accept it because it was regarded as a retrograde step.

The excellent history of 25 Squadron, *Black Hawk Rising* by Francis K Mason, itemises the record of service of 42 Siskins between 1928 and 1932. Five were involved in ground accidents and eight crashed, with three pilots killed. One of these, Sergeant JW Pearce, was overcome by CO_2 poisoning and crashed at Godstone in Surrey.

In 1929 the squadron often practised battle climbs. With no hint of war in sight, all fighter squadrons maintained a flight of five aircraft on permanent alert, fully armed and ready to roll. The order to scramble as a practice was regularly given. The flight would climb to 20,000 feet in formation, manoeuvre around, then return to earth. Of course they were in open cockpits with no oxygen and thought nothing about it. They knew nothing about anoxia and survived largely because of the slow rate of climb.

In the autumn of that year, the starboard side of Teddy's undercarriage collapsed during take-off. He was unaware of the problem until he saw his flight commander gesticulating at him. There was no radio communication at the time, although experiments were being conducted with little success, much to the chagrin of the Squadron Signals Officer, Jo Stewart. Eventually Teddy realised that something was wrong with his plane and he understood that his undercarriage had broken. The flight returned to Hawkinge, leaving Pilot Officer Hudleston to fly around overhead as his colleagues landed. Some minutes later a line of airmen was strung out across the airfield together with a fire engine and an ambulance. Bracing himself, Teddy lost height, cut the engine, side slipped to the right to obviate drift, put his left wing down and landed at minimum speed. With typical reserve, Teddy wrote 'I had the good fortune to land successfully.' Clearly this was a notable flying success, for he managed to land and taxi at a sufficiently slow speed to allow ground crew to run beside him and support the wing. This incident reinforced the evidence of his natural flying skill and persuaded his squadron leader, 'Lousy' Payne, to recommend him for the Central Flying School.

Teddy was always able to laugh at himself. In addition to his normal squadron duties, he was also the sports officer and the officer in charge of the workshops, where second line maintenance on engines and airframes was undertaken. He remembered his rigging instructor at Cranwell hitting the wing of a Bristol Fighter, which rang out like a music box. 'There you see,' said the instructor, 'that noise tells you that the bracing wires inside the wing want tightening up.' One day at Hawkinge, he was walking around the workshop with his Flight Sergeant and suddenly remembered the rigging lesson. He gave the lower wing of a Siskin a hearty blow with his hand and produced a splendid musical return. Rather pleased to have the chance to show off his technical knowledge, he turned to the Sergeant and said 'Flight, the internal bracing wires need tightening up.' The Flight Sergeant was poker faced. 'Sir,' he replied, 'the wings of this all-metal aircraft have no internal bracing wires!'

Wherever you find groups of bright young men, you tend to find whizzbang ideas which do not always work according to plan. It was during Teddy's time at Hawkinge that the squadron conceived the notion of building a glider. History does not record who was ultimately responsible for the design, but the project had the enthusiastic support of the officers, NCOs and riggers. After weeks of devilling in the hangar, a small biplane glider was eventually rolled out into the open air. It was a single seater with a very small wingspan and very little load-carrying capacity. After much heated discussion, Flying Officer Fox Barrett was given the accolade of piloting the first flight, principally because he was the lightest officer in the squadron. The debate over the best launching site was energetic and there was a strong move to launch it off the cliffs of Dover, where a south wind would provide good up currents. Happily some wisdom prevailed and they resolved to tow the new glider across the airfield behind an ancient Bentley belonging to Flying Officer Richard (Revver) Ford. A tow rope was found, Fox Barrett climbed into the cockpit and the Bentley set off. To universal delight the machine took off, swiftly reaching a height of 50 feet. Unfortunately no one had thought of a release system for the tow rope. Within seconds the glider overtook the Bentley but, unable to let go of its launch system, the flight corridor was effectively barred and the only route was down. End of glider. Happily 'Foxy' Barrett escaped with no more than a broken nose and his face covered in blood. During the post mortem, the failure was attributed to the length of the tow rope, the adequacy of the control surface (the ailerons and tail plane), oh, yes, and the lack of a release system. All agreed that it was a lucky escape for the pilot, who might have fared rather worse if he had gone over the white cliffs of Dover.

The Central Flying School, Cranwell and the Air Armament School

The Central Flying School was established in 1912 and was widely regarded as the flying instructors' Mecca. It had a worldwide reputation for highly skilled and disciplined flying, not only in the RAF, but on a global scale. Many of the most successful airmen of the world's air forces graduated there.

The course which Teddy attended from February to April 1930 had no more than 15 pupils. Most knew each other, but on this occasion there was a member of the RAAF who was to later become their Chief of Staff, and 'Balu' Brown from the RCAF, who later served in Teddy's 84 Group in 1944. The new students arrived feeling pretty confident about their ability; indeed, they may have quietly claimed that they knew all about flying. Inevitably it took less than an hour for the entire course to realise that they were good amateurs, but very poor professionals. Certainly they were competent, but they did not really understand why aircraft responded to the control movements they made. That was what they were there to learn.

Wing Commander John (Jack) Baldwin, who had served in the Great War as a cavalry officer in the 8th King's Royal Irish Hussars, had been the commandant since 1928. He had gathered about him a team of superb instructors – 'brilliant teachers', in Teddy's words – who breathed inspiration into their charges. James Robb, the Chief Flying Instructor, was to play an important part in Teddy's life during the War; others included Johnny Johnson, who was largely responsible for the development of modern bad weather instrument flying, and Johnny Chick, another famous rugby player.

Teddy graduated with distinction, categorised A2, which was close to the best that one could achieve as a pupil. He was promptly posted back to Cranwell as an instructor. This was unusual. He was still only 21 years old, a Pilot Officer, and such a recent graduate of Cranwell that he was teaching senior cadets who had arrived whilst he was still a cadet himself.

The good news was that the RAF was constantly improving the quality of its training. During his time as a cadet at Cranwell, Teddy logged 75 hours of flying, half of it dual and half solo. During his two years as a member of the instructing staff, cadets were achieving twice that. The main instructional aircraft was the Avro 504N, which was a development of the Mono Avro but with a Lynx engine instead of the rotary Gnome Plane. It was a good flying machine and excellent for teaching. Bad and inaccurate flying were revealed immediately without any vicious results. The Bristol Fighter had been replaced by the Armstrong-Whitworth Atlas and the DH9a. The Siskin remained as the basic fighter trainer.

Looking back in later life, Teddy readily admitted that flying instructing was the most satisfying of all his service appointments. In his words, 'there are few jobs that you do and stay in long enough to see the results.' The better you worked, the better the returns. The instructors used to say 'what goes up must come down' and their principal task was to ensure that the pupil came down in one piece. For the instructors, the most exciting time was the moment when one of their pupils was sent off solo: both parties yearned for success. Another of the great life lessons that Teddy learned in this role was that sympathy between instructor and student was immensely important. Not infrequently a backward pupil would be assigned to a new instructor, almost invariably with beneficial results.

Even at this very early stage in his career, his key mentor was reappearing. Wing Commander 'Mary' Coningham was the Chief Flying Instructor and he was genuinely delighted that one of his close protégés would be able to prosper under his benign leadership. The Flight Commanders included Dermot Boyle, who was four years older than Teddy and had secured an exceptional A1 grade when graduating from the Central Flying School. He would later become Chief of the Air Staff and recruit Teddy as his Vice Chief. It was an important success for Teddy that he was re-categorised as an A1 instructor a few months after returning to Cranwell.

By good fortune, the Air Ministry had been drafting plans for a permanent RAF College to replace the hutted camp which had served from 1916. In Teddy's words: 'The RAF were fortunate that at this period the Ministry of Works contained the most enlightened architect, J.G. West, who was to create one of the most handsome academic centres built in England in the 20th century. While he was responsible for the main structure, much of the credit for the embellishments and high quality of the interior must go to Wing Commander P.G. Sayers, who started his military career as a cavalry trooper and secured a commission in his regiment before moving to the newly formed RAF.' Sayers became Secretary to the College and devoted his life entirely to Cranwell and its cadets.

There was plenty of time for sport and Teddy spent much of it playing squash, tennis and cricket. Already a member of the RAF Cricket team, he also served on its organising committee and spent many weekends with one of his fellow flying instructors, AJ 'Speedy' Holmes, who played for and eventually captained Sussex, travelling the country for weekend games and RAF matches. Teddy was also able to take weekends with his cousins, the Hudlestons at Hutton John and the Martindales at Merrow. Cranwell was roughly four hours of motoring from both places, even on the second-hand motorcycle which he bought for £27 (£800 in today's money). He fell in love with both places, where he received more affection than he had enjoyed from his mother at home, and where he was able to observe the curious behaviour of his father's brothers, who were notably eccentric. One of the few times he saw his mother after his departure from Perth was over Christmas 1929, when she appeared for a swift visit at Merrow. In Teddy's memory, the whole holiday was filled with dances and balls, dressed in white tie and escorting his cousin, Christine.

As Chief of the Air Staff, 'Boom' Trenchard's policy was to create a force manned by 'jacks of all trades'. He could not afford specialised branches in the Service in the way that the Navy and Army could. Instead he sent officers on various specialist courses, such as Armament (Gunnery and Bombing), Radio/Signals, Navigation, Photography and Engineering. These courses lasted for three months, or for a year, although Engineering took two years. Thereafter the graduate served as a specialist for two or three years before reverting to general duties. Many officers attended the three-month courses and a small selection completed the full year ones. The effect was to spread a strong thread of technical expertise throughout the service. The impact was immediate on the effective and efficient operation of equipment, but it also ensured that airmen were able to criticise existing methods and equipment in order to formulate ideas for improvement. Moreover, the rotational system contributed to a benign relationship between expert and user.

It was quite a shock to Teddy to go to ground school, because he really loved his flying. But the long armament course at Eastchurch in the Isle of Sheppey was going to do him no harm. The Commandant was Wing Commander Arthur Tedder, who would be important in Teddy's life in the western desert and would become Chief of the Air Staff in 1946.

Tedder was 'of a retiring nature', but he was wholly in control and a stern disciplinarian. The message was immediately clear to his new students: 'you work, or you go.' That did not prevent the course from being fun, principally because of the varying characters delivering the instruction. The senior RAF instructor was the aptly named Squadron Leader Eric 'Dizzy' Davies, who was commonly believed to be as mad as a hatter, but who was a real whizz on gunnery and bombing. Flight Lieutenant Wilfred Wynter-Morgan had won an MC when serving as a temporary 2nd Lieutenant with the Gloucestershire Regiment in 1916 and was an expert on small arms and machine guns. They were complemented by a range of distinguished civilian professors in mathematics, ballistics and aerodynamics. The course was small with just eight students, including Charles Beamish, Albert Dark, who would join Teddy at the Staff College in 1938, Claude (Cresps) Champion de Crespigny, for whom Teddy was to serve as best man on the occasion of his marriage during the course, and John Homer, who had been instructing with him at Cranwell. It was here too that Teddy acquired his first godchild, Michael Sender, who was the son of Douglas (Doug) and Barbara (Barb). Michael reported that his godfather did not really bother with the formalities, so he knew very little of the man whom his parents affectionately called 'Hud', although he did go to visit him in company with his mother when Teddy was living in St Leonards on Sea in the mid-1980s. The Sender family clearly played an important role in the life of the young airman because Doug's brother, known to Michael as Uncle Jack, had been a fellow officer at Hawkinge in 1929.

Most of the instruction was on the ground but they still had the chance to practise in the air because they spent many hours engaged in air gunnery and bombing, both high level with the Wimperis bomb sight, and dive bombing without mechanical devices. Their main aircraft were the Siskin, the Fairy IIIF and the de Havilland 9A.

Clearly Teddy was proving to be the sort of instructor who could establish a sympathetic relationship with his students. At the end of his long armament course, he was posted with Cresps in March 1933 to No. 1 Armament Training Camp at Catfoss near Hull. The camp was commanded by Wing Commander Percy Sherren MC, a Canadian by birth, who Teddy judged was the strongest man he had ever met. One of his party tricks was to lift an armchair by one leg using one hand.

There were three such camps, the other two being North Coates and Sutton Bridge in Lincolnshire. Squadrons would be attached for a month at a time during the summer, during which they did nothing other than practice bombing or air firing against ground and towed targets. At Catfoss, the camp majored on bombing and received Sidestrands, Virginias and Fleet Air Arms squadrons, two at a time.

The team was tiny. Squadron Leader L de V (Leonard) Chisman was the Chief Instructor, with another Flight Lieutenant, Howard Weblin, in support. Teddy and Cresps were joined weeks later by Flying Officers Frank Hayward and Alister Matheson. Their main task was to analyse results, point out the errors and recommend remedial action. They fought a constant battle against their visitors, who were intensely competitive and always treated the evaluation as extremely suspect. There would be acrimonious arguments, as every crew was utterly convinced that they had achieved a high percentage of bull's eyes.

The camp also provided mobile targets in the form of armoured motor boats based at Bridlington. One of the crewmen was TE Lawrence, Lawrence of Arabia, also known as Aircraftman Shaw, who had been seeking anonymity with very mixed success since he had first enlisted in the RAF as a humble aircraftman in 1922. Curiously, Teddy had met him at Cranwell on a number of occasions and saw him often at Bridlington. Teddy wrote 'he was a quiet, unassuming man, who kept very much to himself. I never got to know him. Indeed, few people did apart from his section commander, who didn't talk either.'

Teddy held the Fleet Air Squadrons in particularly high esteem, mainly because the fliers themselves were intensely enthusiastic. Few rose to senior positions, other than Caspar John, who became Director General of Naval Aircraft production in 1941, Naval Air Attaché to Washington in 1943, Vice Chief of the Naval Staff in 1957 and 1st Sea Lord in 1960. Teddy and Caspar John became lifelong friends.

Most senior naval officers regarded fliers as renegades and resisted serious debate about the value of air power. Teddy, who was not shy about recording his impression of his seniors, was convinced that their naval lordships could not bring themselves to believe the evidence of successful bombing against the Catfoss towed targets and the old warship *Centurion*. The same view prevailed in the US navy and it took the loss of *Repulse* and *Prince of Wales* in the Far East to Japanese bombers to effect a change of mind in naval circles.

Relationships between the Services and civilian fleets were not always straightforward. Because of the bombing, the target areas were prescribed Sea Danger Zones. Of course this incensed the fishing fleets, who immediately claimed that these were the most valuable fishing grounds which should be treated as native reserves, qualities which had not been imagined until the Government implemented restrictions. From time to time there would be fractious stand-offs between fishing boats that insisted on intruding in the Danger Zone when bombing practice was planned.

India

As the summer training season drew to a close, Teddy started to plan on a move overseas. The prospects were highly attractive for a young man, with the possibility of service in Egypt, Iraq, Aden, India and the Far East. He had tried on several occasions to secure a posting abroad, without success. Now, in September 1933, he discovered that a friend, Flying Officer Lionel Freestone, had been warned to prepare for a posting to India. They both had the same qualifications as flying instructors and armament specialists. The difference was that Freestone had just acquired a wife. Teddy 'offered himself' as a substitute, which pleased Freestone and his new bride. They wrote simultaneously to the Air Ministry, pointing out the advantages of sending a bachelor instead of a married man. The plan was approved and within weeks Teddy received orders to go to No. 1 (Indian) Wing at Kohat on the North West Frontier as the Wing Armament Officer. For the record, Lionel Freestone's decision led to a full career in armament and his final two appointments were as Director of Armament in 1949 and Director of Armament Engineering in 1952. He retired as an Air Commodore in August 1957.

Teddy was especially pleased with the idea of India because members of his family had served there for several generations and his uncle, Sir Arthur Martindale, KCSI, who was now a close friend and mentor, had enjoyed a distinguished career in the Indian Civil Service, ending up as Agent General, or Governor, of Rajputana. It was Martindale who had advised the young Teddy that he had to work at making himself more than a cypher in a large organisation. 'Apply for any job,' he was told, 'even if you don't want it. After a time people will begin to say, 'who is this fellow? He's becoming a terrible nuisance'. That's the moment that you will no longer be invisible.'

His orders were to sail on the troopship, SS *Nevasa*, in November. Before that he had to help clean up the camp at Catfoss and collect the clothing and equipment which he would need on the North West Frontier. He wrote to his new Wing Commander, Alan Lees, with whom he had played a lot of cricket, and who had been the fierce disciplinarian with Hugh Constantine, to formally 'touch his forelock' and ask if there was anything he wanted his new recruit to bring. The reply arrived a few weeks later, and was not entirely what Teddy expected. There was no mention of the Wing Commander's joy at Hudleston's future arrival, nor was he told to take his golf clubs or cricket bats. No, the important task was to go to Paxton & Whitfield in Jermyn Street to instruct them to prepare a Stilton which would be ripe on arrival in Kohat. To his eternal pleasure, Paxton's achieved their goal and the cheese was pronounced 'perfect' when it reached its destination.

When he embarked on his ship, Teddy discovered that he was the only Air Force officer on board. Accommodation for officers was very adequate, but this was not the case for the troops, who suffered terribly in bad weather. Teddy reported that he could remember being the officer of the day in ghastly weather as they approached Malta. The conditions down below were indescribable, with some 500 men eating, sleeping and being sick on their respective decks: a memory which he claimed cured him of seasickness forever.

They left Malta and pressed on uneventfully through the Suez Canal to Aden, which was then the responsibility of the RAF. The greeting party with the Harbour Master, landing officer and other officials coasted up to the side of Nevasa and Flying Officer Hudleston noted that the RAF contingent not only wore black ties, but black socks and shoes too. Clearly he had adopted the wrong sartorial order and kept out of the way until the visiting airmen had gone ashore. The next day, he casually appeared in the black outfit, only to be caringly questioned why he was suddenly in mourning.

Three weeks after leaving Southampton, Nevasa arrived in

Bombay. There to greet him and share his life for the next five years was his new bearer, Sohat Khan. He was a young, highly efficient Pathan whose task was to devote himself to Teddy entirely. It was to prove the warmest of friendships.

Khan helped to ensure that the landing formalities were completed without difficulty and the two boarded the Frontier Express for Lahore, Rawalpindi and Kohat. They travelled with some 50 soldiers from the Argyll & Sutherland Highlanders who were heading for Rawalpindi and, as he was the sole officer present, this unexpected liaison proved to be his first formal command of soldiers.

The steam engine puffed its way northwards over more than 2,000 kilometres with many stops to take on water for the engine. At Rawalpindi the detachment of Argylls left for their intended destination. They were some six hours from Kohat, having travelled for thirty-six hours across a featureless plain. The scenery now changed rapidly; cultivated fields gave way to a barren, rocky landscape with bare hills and little vegetation. Once across the Attock Bridge and the Indus River, the country became even wilder and more mountainous. The railway line snaked its way through the hills and as sundown approached Sohat Khan made his way to Teddy's compartment to tell him that they were very nearly at the end of their journey. It was three days before Christmas 1933.

The officer strength of No. 1 (Indian) Wing was thirty, of whom twenty lived in the Mess. In those days an officer was not encouraged to get married under the age of 30 and most of those at Kohat were in their mid-twenties. Here Teddy met for the first time one Flight Lieutenant Basil Embry, who had passed the RAF

Staff course the year before and was now a staff officer – a role which he did not much enjoy because he thrived on flying, leadership and action. As a tangible mark of his style, he was to win four DSOs and a DFC during World War II. Another of Teddy's new messmates was Flight Lieutenant Harry Wheeler, who would be his best man when he married Nan Davis in 1936.

The Wing comprised No. 27 Squadron and No. 60 Squadron, both equipped with 16 Westland Warspites, powered by a radial Bristol Jupiter engine. They were two-seater, open cockpit light bombers capable of carrying four 500lb bombs. There was a forward firing Vickers machine gun and a Lewis machine gun mounted on a rotating Scarff ring in the rear cockpit. The rear gunner was also the bomb aimer, equipped with a Course Setting Bomb Sight mounted on the floor of his cockpit. It was a simple and reliable machine.

This was a remote outpost of Empire. There was no effective public radio, no television, no reliable telephone service. As Teddy quickly discovered, all of the entertainment was created by those based in Kohat. So he was not hugely surprised on Boxing Day when he found ten or twelve camels lying on the Mess lawn with camel boys squatting beside them. These were the mounts for that day's polo match, in which Teddy was warmly exhorted to play. His knowledge of camels was based solely on visual encounters in Australia, the Suez Canal and assorted zoos. He had seen riders comfortably perched on camel backs and it was very clear to him that camels were both stupid and docile. Invited to select his ride, he unerringly chose the largest beast. This was a mistake. As the camel lurched to its feet, Flying Officer Hudleston was forced into a passionate embrace with its neck in order to prevent himself from sliding off the front end. Then as the front rose, it stopped him from being tipped out the back door. The camel turned its head and at very close quarters gave its rider the benefit of its foul breath, yellow teeth and supercilious disdain. The control system was a single piece of string attached to one nostril, which Teddy never quite fathomed. After a stately procession from the Mess to the airfield, the burgeoning confidence of the polo players was swiftly dissipated when the camel boys left the field of play. There followed a few moments of uncoordinated and uncontrolled scrummage around the football which served as the polo ball. Two players fell off and no one else seemed to be able to hit the ball. A draw was declared immediately.

Kohat was in the North West Frontier Province with its governor, Sir Ralph Griffith, based in Peshawar and a service of District Commissioners and Assistant Commissioners spread across the Province. The man at Kohat was Bertie Smith, a jovial but shrewd man who was widely respected by the Pathans, soldiers and airmen in his District. India had its own Army of some 60,000 men, supported by 20,000 men of the British Army. The RAF deployed three Army reconnaissance squadrons, four light bomber squadrons, and a bomber–transport flight. The latter was equipped with Victorias and the remainder with Warspites. The immediate Army counterparts to the RAF at Kohat were Probyn's Horse, a cavalry regiment, and 13 PFF, one of the famous Frontier Force regiments. Every Army outpost had a small landing ground and Miranshah, some 150 miles from Kohat, retained a permanent detachment of three aircraft, which were regarded with wonder and respect by the Frontier tribesmen who saw them as large birds which roosted on the rafters when they were pushed into a hangar at night.

Teddy took over from Flight Lieutenant Sandy Herd, who had completed five years in India. Naturally one of his first visits was to his new boss, Nunky Lees, whom he knew well from the sporting field, but hardly at all professionally. In the two and a half years they worked together, Teddy acquired considerable admiration for him and learned a lot. On one occasion, Teddy put a 'brilliant' suggestion to the boss, who listened politely and then asked 'why do it?'

'Because, Sir, because......' He quickly ran out of steam and realised that he had been taught the vital lesson that when presenting a case, all the arguments must be carefully marshalled.

Within weeks Teddy felt fully at home and decided that he needed to visit some of the outstations. The first port of call was Miranshah, which took him at a few thousand feet over barren, hilly terrain. Over his right shoulder he could see a couple of hundred miles along the Himalayas, and occasionally he passed close to or over small villages and one sizeable town, Bannu, near the Kurram River. He was relieved when he finally spotted his target and started to glide in to land. At that point he recalled that Flying Officer Wall had made the same landing with his goggles raised and lost an eye to a stone fired by a tribesman's catapult on the perimeter of the airfield. He kept his goggles on.

The garrison was manned by the Tochi Scouts, who like their counterparts, the Waziristan Scouts, were an elite unit of 200 Pathans and 10 British officers. They were all hand-picked and had established a superb reputation for professional skill, discipline and high morale. The officers prided themselves on being able to outstrip their men in terms of physical endurance and there was rigorous testing before anyone was considered for the unit. There was a famous story of a young Scottish RAF Flying Officer with a particularly unathletic physique who asked to be taken on patrol. The Scouts made every excuse but the airman was extremely obstinate and finally wore down their resistance. In due course, the patrol turned out for inspection, all immaculate in well-laundered drill, polished chaplis, leather belts and rifles. The mission would take them 25 miles at a fast pace with a brief halt every hour. As time went on, the well-pressed clothing would wilt with sweat and even the smartest, fittest Scout would look pretty bedraggled.

At the end of the first hour, the young RAF officer's kit was in exactly the same condition as when he started. Stung, the Scouts applied more pace. At the end of the second hour, everyone apart from the RAF officer was sweating heavily; his kit remained obstinately well pressed and not a drop of sweat shone on his brow. Five hours after they set out, they arrived back at their camp, tired, scruffy, and totally bemused by the novice airman, who simply never perspired and looked as if he had just come on parade.

Although Teddy was not posted to a flying appointment, both he and Basil Embry enjoyed the generosity of the flying squadrons who were prepared to lend them an aircraft whenever they wanted one and they managed to fly almost as often as the regular pilots. The cavalry were equally generous with their horses and Teddy managed to hire a good mare for 28 rupees a month.

By the end of May, the temperature was rising well up into the eighties and everyone longed for cooler air. It was important also to give the troops and airmen a break from the heat, so the Army and RAF set up a series of hill depots. The Kohat garrison was able to use one at Lower Topa, near Marre, north of Rawalpindi. Here they established a hutted camp among pine trees some 2,000 feet above sea level. They had good games facilities and courses of instruction. The few people who were married could take their wives with them and for four or five weeks at a time people would flow through the depot, which was commanded by an amiable Squadron Leader called Freddie Glass. Teddy 'lost his name' with said Squadron Leader when he introduced a dancing bear to his office while he was briefly absent.

It was while he was delivering armament and gunnery courses to officers and airmen that Teddy first met Flight Lieutenant WH (Willy) Merton, who became a lifelong friend and fellow member of the Air Council 30 years later. At that moment, Merton was the Viceroy's pilot, normally based in Lahore. The Viceroy was His Excellency Major the Right Honourable the Earl of Willingdon, formerly a Liberal politician and a career colonial administrator. Merton was a very keen and knowledgeable philatelist and an experienced big game hunter. The two resolved to undertake a joint trip to the United Province south of Lahore over the following Christmas in order to pursue big game.

Teddy himself was now a Flight Lieutenant, having been promoted on 1 February 1934. Even at this early stage in his career, it was evident that he was learning how to develop a good network, easily making friends and professional contacts wherever he went. One of these was Lieutenant Colonel William Penney, the CO of the Army HQ Depot at Upper

Topa. This link would be helpful in 1943 when Penney was the Signal Officer in Chief Middle East, then GOC 1st Infantry Division in North Africa and Italy.

Every officer was required to learn Urdu before he was granted leave, and Teddy was gratified to pass his Lower Urdu exam before Christmas 1934. Success carried with it a financial reward of 250 rupees, which amounted to £20, an important addition to the monthly pay cheque of £30. Interestingly, Teddy was not an acknowledged linguist but throughout his life he was able to astonish his family, who were all linguists thanks to the Davis genes, by being able to identify a French or German word thanks to his classical education.

During the late summer of 1934, Mirza Ali Khan, known as the Faqir of Ipi, started to stir up trouble in Waziristan. He was to conduct a low-level guerrilla war against the British for almost two decades and at one point nearly 40,000 British and Indian troops were reported to be in the field trying to capture him. His own force of armed tribesmen, probably not exceeding one thousand men, was armed with rifles and a few machine-guns. The Faqir of Ipi was always short of ammunition, had no radio communication, and relied upon a traditional network of informants and messengers for his intelligence.

Teddy flew the Group Commander, Group Captain Norman Bottomley, around the area so that he could work out for himself how to isolate his opponent. Despite all their best efforts, the Faqir was never captured. Years later *The Times* of 20 April 1960 described him as "a doughty and honourable opponent... a man of principle and saintliness... a redoubtable organizer of tribal warfare."

The region was eternally dealing with outbreaks of trouble,

normally in the winter months after the crops had been harvested. The truth was that the Pathans rather enjoyed fighting and took great pleasure in pulling the lion's tail. Life would be too boring without this sport and if things became too hot for them, they could escape to Afghanistan or the Tirah, which was a stretch of territory north of a line from Kohat to Peshawar. The land was extremely rugged and, in an example of natural pragmatism, the tribesmen agreed not to interfere with the British using the road linking the two towns in exchange for a small annual cash subsidy.

Halfway along this road the tribesmen had built a rifle factory. Here they constructed exact copies of the .303 Lee Enfield rifle, complete with identification number and a seal of the crown over the initials V.R. Teddy reported that they were beautiful replicas and extremely accurate, with the barrels bored by a foot-driven lathe, and with the grooves and lands of the barrel meticulously accurate. The only difference between these and the real thing was that they were made of softer metal and could fire no more than a couple of hundred rounds. Of course the owners were extremely proud of their weapons and guarded them jealously. And they were a proud people with a clear sense of honour and integrity. When they were your host, they would guard you with their life. If you were on the road which was agreed neutral territory, you were safe. But if you strayed off the road, you were fair game.

On one of his trips to other outstations, Teddy flew to stay with a company of Gurkhas at Arawali. He was tremendously impressed, both by their reputation and their immediate performance. Overnight he enjoyed the issue of the rum ration, a tradition which the Gurkhas had long enjoyed. At the appointed hour the Company Sergeant Major (Havildar) reported to the officer of the day with a kerosene tin half filled with rum. After a small ceremony, a small cup of spirit was offered to the officers and the Sergeant Major. The tin was topped up with water, then the same cup was passed to the senior NCOs. The can was topped up again with water before being offered to the Corporals. Finally it was topped up with a further ration of water and offered to the rank and file. Teddy gravely appreciated this subtle way of introducing inexperienced drinkers to a powerful tonic.

In the weeks leading up to his big game hunt with Willy Merton, Teddy read everything he could lay his hands on about the subject. Accompanied by Sohat Khan, he took the train to Lahore, where Merton was waiting to meet him. They transferred to the air depot and over a whisky and soda Merton confessed that the plan had gone awry and he would not be able to keep Teddy company on the expedition because the Viceroy, Lord Willingdon, had just had a new aircraft delivered to Karachi and he had to go and get it. Teddy was dismayed because he had fondly imagined his pal acting as his mentor and guide.

But there was nothing to be done about it and the next day he checked his own weapon, a .318 Westley Richards, and was pleased to accept Merton's offer of his own .470 double-barrelled Jeffrey. They went into town to buy some more rounds for the Jeffrey and the following day Teddy and Sohat Khan set off by train to Moradabad, where the two hunters had previously arranged with the Forestry Department to rent two blocks of 5 miles square, together with Forestry Department bungalows.

On arrival it was obvious that something wasn't right. There was a lot of human activity with a number of servants and several elephants nearby. A white man greeted them and apologised for still being in occupation and encouraged Teddy to spend the night in a tent which he had arranged to be pitched nearby, explaining that he and his wife would be leaving in the morning. He hoped that Teddy would dine with them that night.

When Teddy presented himself for dinner, he was astonished to see a small dining table set with silver and cut glass. His host, who turned out to be a District Commissioner, explained that he had to spend over half of the year touring his domain and with his wife had decided that they had become tired of the eternal picnic. They travelled with half their possessions, which were transported by two camels, three elephants and a retinue of servants.

Dinner went well and as Teddy prepared to leave for his overnight lodging, his host said that he had found a small deer during his round in the morning. It had been killed by a tiger, which would almost certainly return in the morning. He offered to lend Teddy one of his elephants to go out for it. Teddy demurred. Naturally he was thrilled with the offer but good manners dictated that he should encourage his host to follow through. No, said his host. He had shot several tigers and preferred to go after a black woodcock he had spotted earlier in the day. So at dawn, Teddy mounted his elephant, sitting behind the mahout and accompanied by two other elephants with a few beaters. In minutes they were into the jungle, sitting high enough to see all around, but also able to look straight down into the long grass, which was eight to ten feet tall. The line of march was entirely Roman in concept – dead straight, with no deviation for anything other than large trees; small ones were pushed over, leaving a trail of devastation behind each beast.

In due course they reached the site of the previous day's kill and lurked patiently for the expected tiger. After two hours it was clear that the tiger was not going to make the anticipated appearance and the team turned about to go back to the camp and return the elephants to their owners.

Teddy now had a problem. Because of Willy Merton's absence, he had two native hunters (shikaris), each of whom expected 20 rupees for their two-week contract. Not only did he not need two hunters, he really did not want to squander 20 rupees unnecessarily. This observation was noted in Teddy's own draft of his biography, and it is a telling reminder that money was an anxiety for him throughout his life. He was never less than generous, but he simply would not spend more than he needed to.

While he was considering the economics, a native runner appeared out of nowhere. It seemed that word had spread that there were two shikaris with a lone hunter. Another hunter some miles away was short staffed and would very much like to borrow the spare man. In his newly-acquired Urdu, Teddy questioned the runner to find out the name of the supplicant. 'He is Lord Sahib,' he was told. Swiftly he penned a note 'Dear Lord, herewith my spare shikari. Good hunting.' Curiously he never received an acknowledgement, although he discovered that it was Sir Herbert Emerson, the recently appointed Governor of the Punjab, who should have done better. 'No sense of humour,' noted Teddy.

Building a family

In all of his personal biographical notes, Teddy rarely mentioned specific women. Indeed, the only people named were Joan Llewellyn, his tennis partner in Budleigh Salterton, and his cousin Catherine at Merrow. His wife is mentioned two years after their marriage on the occasion of the birth of their son, Anthony Edmund Hudleston, on 18 April 1938.

At this point it is important to clarify that there are two Nan(cy)s in this biography. The first is Nan(cy) Davis, who often called herself Nancy, but was known by most people as Nan. The other is her first cousin, Nancy Moss, who married Johnny Collingwood in 1935. In order to make the tale a little simpler to understand, Nan will always be the wife of Teddy Hudleston, and Nancy will be the wife of Johnny Collingwood.

Teddy's encounter with his future wife was a whirlwind romance. Nan Davis was a raven-haired beauty from Australia, aged 20. She was vibrant, intelligent, well-read, witty, extremely well-travelled, and utterly captivating. She had received her first proposal of marriage shortly after her eighteenth birthday in Sydney. Her cousin, Geoffrey Moss, was to be disappointed. Nan wrote in her diary, 'I am too restless for marriage.'

In 1935 an Army officer based in India sought her hand in marriage and she travelled from Sydney to Bombay, arriving in October 1935, to see him. To her surprise, she met a much more interesting Air Force officer. Teddy was smitten. So was she. Without embarrassment or regret, she abandoned her fiancé and accepted Teddy's invitation to marry. The army officer was less accommodating and Nan recounted in later life that he had tried to drown her.

She sailed to Sydney in January 1936 to consult her parents and arrived back in India with her father, Herbert (Boydie) Davis, at the beginning of July. The marriage took place on 24 July 1936 in All Saints Church, Srinagar, Kashmir. During the intervening months, Teddy received his first public commendation when he was Mentioned in Despatches on 8 May 1936.

Despite Vincent Orange's wise advice to mention my subject on every page, the Davis story is relevant and important. Without doubt it shaped the remainder of Teddy's life, so it takes up more space.

Herbert Davis was the fourth of eight children of Moss and Leah Davis of Nelson, New Zealand. Moss and Leah's marriage was a total triumph, a genuine love story which lasted for 63 years until Moss died in London in 1933. This was a very Jewish family, with Leah the powerful matriarch and Moss the entrepreneurial wealth creator. In his early twenties, Moss had received a letter from his sister in England in which she reported that the Kent hop harvest had failed. After a two-minute conversation with the bank manager, Moss enlisted a clerk and hired two horses to ride around the Nelson region, which was to become the hop centre of New Zealand, to buy forward on the crops. He made a complete killing. With the enormous profits from his calculated gamble, he bought an ailing brewing business called Hancocks and built it into the southern hemisphere's largest brewing concern. It is now known as Lion.

Herbert was quickly nicknamed 'Boy D' as the fourth child. This metamorphosed into Boydie, the name which stuck with him for the rest of his life. Born on 11 November 1879, he quickly realised that he was never going to be the top dog at Hancocks because he had two older brothers and they were active in the business long before he left school. He performed the bare minimum of work at the firm, where the staff adored him because he was a character and an immensely strong man who could move loaded beer barrels that older and more experienced men wouldn't touch alone. He had two other useful traits. He could crack a bullwhip around someone's waist without touching them, and he developed a resounding whistle, which never failed to attract a taxi when he needed it.

The Davis children all got on together, but Boydie was soon perceived as the wild card. His brother, Eliot Rypinsky Davis, better known as Ally, wrote an amusing book about the family and its contacts. It had to be removed from bookshops when someone threatened to sue Ally for an assault on their character. In the book, Ally recorded that his brother Boydie was a playboy who promoted the concept that 'it is a pretty poor sort of family that cannot afford at least one toff,' in which role he cast himself.

At the age of 22 Boydie decided to go against his father's wishes and left abruptly for South Africa, where he signed up as a trooper in the 7th New Zealand Regiment to fight in the Boer War. By his own report, not wholly believed by his grandson, but subsequently verified from military records held at Kew, he was promoted to Sergeant Major within weeks. Boydie always claimed it was because he had the loudest voice to issue commands on the barrack square. Two months later his commission as Lieutenant Herbert Davis was gazetted.

At the end of the War, Boydie realised that he really had to make his peace at home. Glumly he returned to the family business, keeping his nose to the grindstone to demonstrate to his parents that he had the capacity for hard work and endurance. But with considerable wealth, he and his siblings enjoyed travels around the world with regular visits to London, Paris, Deauville, Le Touquet, Monte Carlo and St Moritz. Gambling, both cards and horses, was a shared family passion.

During the early 1910s, Boydie started to visit Australia often on Hancock's business. On one such trip, he spotted, met, wooed and married the most lovely young Australian girl, Ida Mary (Molly) Beard. The Beard family were honest and relatively prosperous protestant folk, with Molly's father running a station in Queensland called Terri Hi Hi. In those days they would not talk about or acknowledge the family ancestry, which was littered with no fewer than seven convicts transported from England and Ireland between 1788 and 1830. In today's world, that makes the family minor Australian aristocrats.

In 1924 Boydie persuaded his father to underpin his ambition to train racehorses in England. The Davis family found and bought an estate at Ely Place, near Frant in Sussex, from John Quiller Rowett, patron of the late Sir Ernest Shackleton. He established a racing stable and set about his task with great enthusiasm and more than a little success. The bad news was that his years as an inveterate gambler led to disaster when he lost the whole lot in a single hand of cards at Deauville in 1935. In the same game Andre Citroen, a renowned gambler who seemed to take pleasure in spectacular losses, finally lost so much that his car empire went too. Boydie was forced to sell Ely Place and accepted his family's generous help for a move back to Australia.

Boydie and Molly had five children. Nan was the eldest,

born in April 1916. Billy followed in 1917, Jo in 1918, Pip in 1924 and Pam in 1926. Each of them, therefore, had experienced the life of the hugely wealthy, and the despair of relative penury.

Nan was a specifically gifted linguist. She spoke fluent French and German by the time she was sixteen and added total proficiency in Urdu and Turkish by the age of twenty-five. In the early 1950s she added Spanish. She was also bright, well read and highly articulate. This was extremely helpful for Teddy. On the other hand, Nan and her siblings were to cause him more than a little difficulty over the years.

Billy lacked the flair of his eldest sister but, despite many childhood squabbles, he was a dedicated and loving brother. His father decided that he must go to Harrow, which was a monumental shock to a young man for whom discipline and organised activity were always an alien tradition. Billy spent his whole life sailing close to the wind. Money was a powerful motivator, but he didn't much care how he earned it. It must be said that this lent him colour, because he was so different from the conventional folks most of us meet in life. Over time he managed to buy two flats in different buildings in Grosvenor Square; the first was where he entertained and lived, the second was where he kept his enormous collection of clothes - tailored suits and shirts, handmade shoes, and astonishing ties (he was colour blind, like all but one of the male descendants of Molly Beard, his mother). This unusual arrangement derived from his failure to secure his first job in Sydney simply because he did not own a suit.

Billy's business activity was wide-ranging and increasingly shady. He fell into business dealing in gaming machines in

Nigeria. With the exceptional profits, which never appeared in any tax schedule, he bought a building in Shepherd's Market, London, where a half-caste Jamaican female manager ran a 'club'. Ostensibly the focus of the club was its intimate bar; the bedrooms were far more discreet.

He had a wife, a Jewish lady called Lee, with whom he was unable to produce children. In fairness, it is far from clear whether the pair ever wanted them. He also had a long-term mistress who was physically the Scandinavian opposite of his wife. She was lovely, both in body and character, and for years she harboured the ambition that Billy would eventually marry her. But when Lee died, he swiftly found another lover and, without dropping or avoiding the original arrangements, he simply failed to ask for her hand in marriage. Sadly this changed her attitude to the Davis family and any sense of friendship or common purpose evaporated.

There is no fool like an old fool. Billy wanted to expand his gaming machine business into Jamaica, where it was important to have local knowledge and influence, quite apart from formal business partners with their own shareholding. The girl who ran his Shepherd's Market club had a brother and cousins in Jamaica so, thinking he had an elegant solution, Billy married the club manager.

None of the family was able to define precisely how Billy's business progressed thereafter, but the day came when he was arrested by the Bureau of Tobacco and Firearms while sitting on an aircraft waiting to return to England from New York. He had in his possession a suitcase stuffed full of money. The money was confiscated, although he was released on bail and allowed to return to England to prepare his defence. The stress was far too much for a man with high blood pressure and within a week of his return, his sister Jo found him dead on the bathroom floor of his residential flat in Grosvenor Square.

Jo lived a purer and more solitary life than her siblings. During the course of the War, she met an American sailor called Dick Vogt in Sydney and moved to America to marry him. They produced the bright spark, probably the brightest of the cousins of this generation, Susan Harriet, better known to her family as Suzie or Snooze, and to her professional colleagues as Harriet. The marriage did not prosper and the Vogts divorced. Then, much to the amazement of the family, Jo decided to give it another try and moved back to Washington. Experience provides hard lessons. The second marriage to the same man led to a second divorce and a return to England, where Jo lived in a small flat for the rest of her life. A devoted mother and grandmother, she was little interested in communicating with the wider world, although she was extremely well read. But she did maintain a good relationship with Teddy, her brother-in-law, until he died.

Pip, also known as Betty, always lived life to the full. She was energetic, able and opinionated. Towards the end of the War she enlisted as a VAD (volunteer nurse), but in peacetime she steered a calculated course as a highly competent PA. She did not marry until her 50th birthday, when she became the second wife of Captain Robert Mackenzie, MBE, LVO, RN. Her role in Teddy's life is described more fully in a later chapter.

The bad girl of the family was Pamela, whose thirst for money and excitement far outstripped the capacity of family and lovers to provide. She too met and married an American sailor, Ted Grounds, whose first wife, Lorraine, had just absconded with his best friend from Stamford University. He was susceptible because Pam was a near clone of the previous model. With the rueful consent of her parents, Pam set off for Missouri and twelve months later gave birth to her first son, Eric. Over the next four years Pam created a minor legend of booze and infidelity which ultimately had to lead to divorce. Travelling via her husband's family in Hawaii, she progressed to stay with her uncle Ernest in New Zealand (he was the Mayor of Auckland at the time), then on to Sydney to live with her parents at Point Piper. This proved to be a very stressful period for her parents, who reported in letters to Nan that Pam was increasingly difficult to deal with.

Pam and her son made their way by freighter from Australia through the Suez Canal to Marseilles, thence by train to Paris to stay with Teddy and Nan outside Paris. In due course they moved on to London. Eleven years after Eric's birth, she produced another son from a liaison with a man who claimed much but could substantiate little. He duly disappeared and the child was adopted within forty-eight hours of his birth. Happily he was sufficiently interested as an adult to find out about his natural family and spotted the notice of his mother's death in the British newspapers while he was waiting for a flight from Frankfurt. This allowed him to attend her funeral at the Knightsbridge Russian Orthodox church. The first and only time he saw his natural mother, therefore, was in her open coffin.

But it was drink and drugs that ruled Pam's behaviour. Despite being naturally able and amusing, her immediate response to pressure was chemical oblivion. She was casual about whose money she spent, so it cost her relatives a fortune.

Of course you do not normally live with the whole of your wife's family, but the Davises were Jewish in nature, if not in religion. Each one would defend the rest with their life, but the internal arguments and squabbles were intense and often long-lasting. The emotions swirled in and out of the Hudleston household, affecting all within range. Curiously, Nan and Pip were never more united than when they looked after Pam.

CHAPTER 3

KASHMIR AND THE STAFF COLLEGE

Teddy was a diligent correspondent with his uncle and aunt, Arthur and Clare Martindale. In December 1936 he wrote a long report of a two-week trek that he and Nan had undertaken in September from Srinagar to Kargil. The trip was managed by a splendid character called Izza Doono, which they translated to James, who greeted them in black and white check plus fours, yellow and red stockings and a pink shirt. He brought a lorry, stores, tents, live fowls and an amusing dog called Bisal. The mechanised part of the journey lasted no more than an hour and from the Sind River onwards, the party marched over wild, undulating country which took them from 3,000 to 10,000 feet on a 125-mile roller-coaster. Once they reached Kargil they had to make the difficult decision whether to press on for Leh, a popular destination, or turn back for Srinagar. James advised that it would take another five marches of 15-20 miles to reach Leh so there was nothing for it but to turn back. Once the decision was made, they forced the pace, covering the first sixty miles in three days. By the time they reached Srinagar, they had walked 250 miles, were extremely fit, and rather pleased with themselves for having avoided the conventional 'Cook's Tour.'

Just before Christmas 1936, Nan discovered she had mumps, which meant that the Hudlestons missed out on the gaiety of Christmas, spending the time together in enforced isolation. For Teddy, this was a useful opportunity to complete his reading in preparation for his Staff College exam.

Posted in October 1936, Teddy spent the next year on the staff as the Armaments Officer at No 1 Indian Group Headquarters under Group Captain Norman Bottomley. This was to be the foundation for his future success, because his methodical approach to problem solving, combined with his quick intelligence and ability to express thoughts fluently, were recognised immediately. On the other hand, Teddy was mildly frustrated that he had no operational role in the campaign against the Faqir of Ipi, whose insurrection gained pace when the British response to his activity made them look weak. Wazirs, Mahsuds, Bhittanis, and even Afghans from across the border rallied to support the Faqir's cause. By April 1937, four extra brigades had been brought in to reinforce the garrisons at Razmak, Bannu and Wana and at the height of the campaign in 1937, some 60,000 regular and irregular troops were employed by the British in an effort to bring to battle an estimated 4,000 hostile tribesmen. Six squadrons of aircraft took part in the campaign and towards the end of the year, the Faqir of Ipi's support began to drain away. He himself remained at large. Indeed, he was never caught.

On 3 November 1937 Teddy handed his job over to Flight Lieutenant Donald Macdonald and was granted almost ten weeks' leave to cover his return to England, settle his family in quarters and prepare for the Staff College. In the middle of his leave, his promotion to Squadron Leader was published and he was taken on the strength of the Station Flight at Andover.

On 24 January 1938, at the ripe old age of 29, he reported with 44 others for No. 16 Staff Course. This proved to be a high-powered team: four went on to become Air Chief Marshals. Harry Broadhurst became AOC Desert Air Force in 1943, then AOC No 83 Group with 2nd Tactical Air Force advancing on Germany in 1944. Teddy would be his opposite number in the adjacent No. 84 Group. His final job was Commander Allied Air Forces Central Europe. The Earl of Bandon, who was famously unstuffy, was generally known as Paddy and would become AOC-in-C Far East in the late Fifties. He too finished as Commander Allied Air Forces Central Europe, handing over to Teddy in December 1963. The fourth one to become an Air Chief Marshal was Walter Cheshire, who ended up as Air Member for Personnel. The directing staff were even more distinguished, with one becoming a Marshal of the Royal Air Force: Wing Commander William Dickson, OBE, DSO, AFC, was Chief of the Air Staff (CAS) in 1953 and the first ever Chief of the Defence Staff (CDS) in 1959. Two, Arthur Barrett and Arthur Sanders, would become Air Chief Marshals, Aubrey

Ellwood an Air Marshal, and Ronald Graham, Robert Whitham and William Yool became Air Vice-Marshals.

Teddy had managed to borrow a house from a brother officer in India. It was an old mill house on the banks of the River Test at Wherwell, just south of Andover, with the stream running under the house. He swiftly employed a married couple from the village to help in and around the house, all in good time for Nan to produce No. 1 son, Tony, on 18 April 1938.

Staff College students then and now enjoy a wide range of visits to learn about the wider world of defence. Every activity had an extra zing because of the Anschluss, Germany's annexation of Austria, in March 1938. Teddy greatly enjoyed his first time out with the Navy in August 1938 when he joined HMS *Forrester* for a large-scale manoeuvre in the Irish Sea. He also had a fascinating insight to the world of international collaboration when, as part of the Staff course, he was sent to the newly established Advanced Air Striking Force (AASF) at Harwell as a member of the air staff. AASF was to consist of eight Fairey Battle bomber squadrons, and their first task was to consult with the French to determine where they would be based in France. As a result of the talks, AASF was allocated the use of four or five airfields in France. The French produced comprehensive dossiers on each airfield itemising what was available and where. Something wasn't right. Nobody could put a finger on it, but there was a clear feeling that the dossiers were too good to be true. Teddy and another officer secured permission from the AOC, Air Vice-Marshal Patrick Playfair, to fly over to France to inspect the airfields. This they did and to their astonishment, the dossiers proved to be complete fakes. The alleged airfields were all virgin farmland with no sign of a landing ground or buildings. They promptly returned to Harwell to brief an incredulous AOC. Nobody could quite believe that an ally could deliberately and creatively mislead them. Chamberlain's visit to Berchtesgaden in September gained a little more time to develop more candid relationships with the French Air Force.

As the staff course drew to a close, the students were asked to indicate what they would like to do next. Almost all said that they would like to have a command appointment with a fighter squadron. When the postings finally appeared, Teddy was deeply disappointed to discover that he was to take up an Armaments post at the Air Armament School at Eastchurch on the Isle of Sheppey. He remonstrated but was told that his services at the school were indispensable. With the benefit of hindsight, the lack of experience as a squadron commander, for he never did command an operational squadron or wing, was to prove one of the defining reasons for his failure to achieve his ultimate goal.

Teddy was inclined to do what he was told, so he decided to drive over to Eastchurch with Nan to have a good look around. She, of course, was made of sterner stuff. She made it abundantly clear that she would never live there and if Teddy wanted to keep his wife, he had better find another job. Back to Andover they went and Teddy studied a notice board which advertised requests for volunteers to go to Egypt, the Sudan and Turkey. He applied for the whole lot and was duly called for by the Adjutant, who said that the Air Ministry wanted to know which of these jobs he really wanted. Privately, he admitted to a sense of shock because it was only a matter of weeks since he

had been told that he was indispensable to the Armaments
School. He considered Egypt, and recalled that a relation of his
had enjoyed a distinguished career in the Sudan. So in a contrary
way, he thought the best plan was to opt for Turkey and was
given the job as an instructor in air tactics at the Turkish Flying
School, Hava Okulu at Eskisehir. He promptly telephoned Nan,
who was staying with army friends in Camberley. She borrowed
an encyclopaedia from the friends and looked it up. Eskisehir
was in the centre of Anatolia, hot and dusty in the summer and
bitterly cold in the winter. She gave the plan her assent.

Turkey

The appointment was a two-year loan to the Turkish
Government, who would be the paymasters too. The job was to
begin in January 1939 and somehow Teddy and Nan had to
move their entire possessions, plus a nanny by rail to Turkey.
Their own journey began at Victoria Station, where they
boarded the Toros Express, which had at one time been the
Orient Express. On arrival in Venice, they transferred to an
Italian ship of the Adriatica Line and set sail for Istanbul via
Athens. As Australians, both were fascinated to see Gallipoli from
the sea and they truly enjoyed the transit through the straits into
the Sea of Marmara.

Leaving Nan and Tony at the Park Oteli, Teddy first reported
to the British Embassy, who knew nothing about him, then
arranged his trip to Eskisehir. Nan immediately started to learn
Turkish, while her husband travelled by train to his new base,
where he was met by his interpreter, Najif Bey, who became a

good friend. In very little time Najif Bey introduced Teddy to the Parsuk Palar Oteli, where he took two adjacent bedrooms and sent for his wife. By the time she arrived, he learned that he had been allocated a flat located on the edge of the town opposite the Officers' Club. The flat had four rooms and a bathroom with a normal western loo, which was infinitely superior to the local, traditional and rather malodorous arrangements. In fact it was the only one of its kind in Eskisehir and became 'the place' to visit when being entertained by the Hudlestons.

Ataturk had died the month before the Hudlestons arrived in Turkey. He had ensured that his successor as President would be his former chief of staff, Mustafa Ismet Inonu, who selected Şükrü Saracoğlu as his Foreign Minister. Both were able politicians, and they kept Turkey stable. On the military side, General Fevzi Çakmak headed the armed forces (from 1921 to 1944) and there were four generals of equal rank who rotated as head of the Air Force and the three Air Force regiments based at Eskisehir, Izmir and Diarbakir. The commander at Eskisehir was Ya Ya Pasha, who was not a pilot himself and wisely left air force matters to his staff. The regiment had two squadrons of Heinkel 111 bombers, a couple of squadrons of P.Z.Ls (Polish high wing, all metal aircraft), and a squadron of Curtiss SB2C Helldivers, an American diver bomber. While Teddy was still there a squadron of Fairey Battles was brought in from the United Kingdom.

Hava Okulu was the Turkish equivalent of Cranwell and delivered a two-year course for young pilot officers. The Commandant was a Lieutenant Colonel Ihsan Orgun, who was a qualified pilot but never seemed to fly. The most erudite officer on his staff was Captain Hussein Turgut, who had been born in Georgia and was extremely intelligent, intellectual and articulate. He and his wife became close friends of the young Hudlestons. There was also an aircraft and engine repair depot run by a major who had been captured by the British at Gallipoli and interned in Egypt. He was at pains to be nice to the Hudlestons because the British had treated him so well as a prisoner of war. The hangars at Eskisehir had been built by the Germans in 1915-1916 with wooden framework of geodetic construction. This amused Teddy, who had visited an aircraft factory in Weybridge in 1938 where they were shown aircraft which were also of geodetic design. This was regarded as a brand new method of design and apparently no one knew that the Germans had deployed it more than 20 years earlier. The Wellington bomber was built using the geodetic principle.

The language of communication was often based on age, dependant largely upon the political alignment of Turkey over the previous half-century. At the turn of the century and up to the end of the Great War, Turkey was an ally of Germany. The country then became more closely aligned with France and then in the 1930s allegiance veered towards Britain and America. As a generality therefore, the older officers tended to speak German, 30-35-year-olds spoke French and young officers spoke English. But the Hudlestons correctly appreciated that their success would hinge to some extent upon their ability to communicate in Turkish. They engaged a teacher who ensured that Nan became fluent within three months, while Teddy was sufficiently proficient to make himself understood.

The young couple decided that they could now communicate sufficiently well, and knew enough people, to throw a party. Invitations went to 20 officers and their wives and all were accepted. But from about 4 pm on the appointed day, messages began to arrive at the flat with various excuses for not being able to attend. By 6 pm, the scheduled starting time, it was clear that no guests were going to appear, leaving Teddy and Nan to eat and drink alone. They later learned that they had not been cleared by the police as being acceptable hosts. This was a big embarrassment for the Turks because they had no wish to offend their British visitors. It never happened again and they were fully and warmly accepted in the community.

During his time in Turkey, Teddy flew to visit Turkish air force outposts at Diyarbakır, near the Syrian and Iraq borders, where there was an air regiment, Merzifon near the Black Sea, Kutahya, south west of Eskisehir and Izmir on the south coast. He was pleased to discover two RAF officers in Izmir, helping with the advanced training of pilots and navigators. One of them, Jack Davis, was to become Air Chief Marshal Sir John Davis, serving on the Air Council almost a quarter of a century later as Air Member for Supply and Organisation. The other, Edward Howell, was shot down in the desert, captured and sent to Greece, where he effected a Boys' Own escape by seizing a small caique and sailing single handed to Turkey with almost no food or water.

Both Teddy and Nan enjoyed time exploring Istanbul and the Dardanelles, which the Turks allowed despite it being a restricted military zone, so that they could see where Australians had fought and died at Gallipoli. Reflecting in later years, they admitted that one of the abiding and astonishing memories of their visit was to see Tate & Lyle Golden Syrup tins with labels intact in some of the trenches.

Soon after war was declared a small biplane with RAF roundels landed at Eskisehir, where it was surrounded immediately by an armed guard. Teddy had not been warned from Ankara that it was due, so he swiftly made his way to the airfield, where he discovered that the pilot was the Assistant Air Attaché, Lord Arthur Forbes, who was based in Bucharest. The aircraft belonged to Forbes and Teddy had never seen its style before, so he pressed Forbes to allow him to look over it. When he looked inside, he was very surprised to see a man lashed to the floor. It turned out that it was a German spy whom Forbes had managed to capture in Bucharest and was now flying to Egypt for interrogation: it was a major coup which never hit the airwaves.

As the situation in western Europe continued to deteriorate, it was far from clear how Turkey would play her cards. Both Britain and Germany viewed Turkey as a most valuable ally and even after war had been declared, the Turkish position remained unclear. There came a moment in November 1939 when it was announced that a Romanian trade delegation would visit Ankara. This did not feel like good news to the Allies, but the Turkish government continued to play an ambivalent game. They announced a full-scale reception for the Romanians and invitations were sent to all of the diplomatic missions in Ankara, including the British and Germans. Teddy and Nan were invited to attend by the Air Attaché in Ankara, Wing Commander Bobby George, whose career culminated in his appointment as Governor of South Australia from 1953 to 1960.

The reception at the Ankara Palas, the only good hotel in the capital, was studded with diplomats. The Allied contingent was headed by Hughe Knatchbull-Hugessen, the ambassador, who had been severely wounded in 1937 when a Japanese aircraft had fired on his ambassadorial car in China. Also present was Franz von Papen, the German ambassador. With a deft nod to protocol, the Turks had established two large bars at opposite ends of the ballroom and after an hour, when the party was at its noisiest, the band struck up. The roar of conversation died immediately and everyone waited to see who the Foreign Minister would ask to dance first. Time stood still until Saracoğlu, the Foreign Minister, turned to the wife of the British Ambassador. It was an overt declaration of intent from which Turkey never deviated and they remained a friendly neutral throughout the war. This stance was to play a decisive role as hostilities intensified in the Middle East.

As the months of 1940 ticked away, Teddy began to fear that Germany might launch an attack against European Turkey and possibly into Anatolia itself. This would present enormous difficulties for the evacuation of Nan and Tony. After careful family discussion, Teddy and Nan agreed that she should take Tony to live with her parents in Sydney. On 5 July, Nan set off with Tony and his nanny, Violet Hooper, by road via Damascus to Baghdad, then by train to Basra and boat to Bombay, where they arrived in the middle of August. Their ship was not due to sail to Australia for more than a fortnight, so Nan parted company with her much-valued nanny and took Tony to Poona to stay with friends. Later she boarded the SS *Stratheden* for Fremantle, where they arrived on 9 October 1940, three months after leaving their home in Eskisehir.

Teddy was fortunate to be promoted to Temporary Wing Commander on 1 June 1940. He was 31 years old and his latent ambition was moving into a higher gear. With the family safely out of immediate harm's way, he sought permission to go to the Middle East over Christmas 1940. He travelled by train to Adana on the south east coast of Turkey, then by plane to Cairo. Old mentors were surprised and delighted to see him, chief amongst them being Air Vice-Marshal Peter Drummond, the man who had guided him into the RAF, and Air Chief Marshal Sir Arthur Longmore, who had been the Commandant at Cranwell when Teddy was an instructor there and was now AOC-in-C Middle East.

The headquarters was frantic because they were planning and about to implement a major attack on the Italians, who were sitting on the border between Cyrenaica and Egypt. Pleased as they were to see Teddy, nobody knew what to do with him. He was, after all, still on loan to the Turkish Government. Almost to get him out of the way, he was sent to join Air Commodore Raymond (Collie) Collishaw, a highly decorated World War I Canadian fighter pilot at No 202 Group near Sidi Barrani. The intelligence reports indicated that the Italians outnumbered Collishaw's force by 400 aircraft to 200.

For several days Teddy was able to enjoy a novel form of wartime tourism. First he was attached to No. 113 Squadron commanded by Squadron Leader Bob Bateson, with whom he went on a couple of reconnaissance missions in a Blenheim bomber. He then spent time with No. 28 Squadron, which was run by a Squadron Leader Wilson, who was equipped with Atlas, and undertook two more reconnaissance flights, one in a Proctor aircraft to fly over the Italian garrison at Badia.

His education went further when he managed to attach himself to a medium Field Artillery Battery which was shelling Badia. Within days the Italians surrendered and Teddy, with another man, decided to set off on foot to look at their positions. Within a short time they were greatly surprised to discover that they were walking on a collision course with a large group of some 1,500 Italians. They pressed on and realised that the whole group was being marshalled by two British soldiers who were so much in command of their prisoners that two Italians were carrying the British soldiers' weapons.

Teddy was due to remain in Turkey until May 1941 and one of his last tasks was to undertake a reconnaissance for HQ Middle East Air Force of the Anatalya area, roughly midway between Izmir and Adana on the south coast. He travelled by train in the company of Flight Lieutenant Aidan Crawley, the second of three great games-playing brothers and later to become a Labour MP from 1945 to 1951, then a Conservative MP from 1962 to 1967. He was a journalist and senior mover in commercial television, becoming Chairman of London Weekend Television. They got on famously for, despite the wide gap in their ranks, Crawley was only eight months older than Teddy. Together they surveyed a number of sites, one of which had a disused mosque which they earmarked as an ammunition store. Both airmen were wearing shorts with long socks and as he left the mosque, Teddy noticed that his socks had turned black. He bent down to dust them and discovered that it was not dust but an army of small, black and very ferocious fleas. It took at least two days to clean themselves up fully.

Middle East

Finally orders came through for Teddy to join HQ Middle East in May 1941. He was still a substantive Squadron Leader but managed to hold on to his temporary rank as a Wing Commander. He left Turkey with some sadness, for they had treated him and his wife with great kindness. But there was a war on, and he needed to be involved.

Up until this point, nobody in the services rated Teddy specifically highly. Yes, he was a top class pilot and flying instructor. He was well versed in armament. Clearly he could do international work, because the Turks had liked him. But he was not a renowned fighter ace, nor did he have experience of operational command. What he did have was a first-class brain which analysed problems and found solutions. One retired Air Chief Marshal who contributed to this account of Teddy's life said 'he had a brain like a bacon slicer.'

But at this stage, nobody was overly interested in Teddy's arrival, so he dug around until he found Peter Drummond again. Drummond said he was to join the Air Plans section of the Headquarters, working under Group Captain Claude Pelly MC. His opposite number was an old friend from the Armament course and Staff College, Montague Philpott, now a Wing Commander too.

For the first time in his career, Teddy was now regularly in front of the senior officers running the war in the Middle East. He started to record his often trenchant views on colleagues and senior commanders. He felt sympathy and respect for Wavell, Cunningham, Tedder, Longmore and Coningham, but judged the

Army Chief of Staff, Major General Arthur Smith, to be one of the most incompetent soldiers he ever met. Teddy was evidently not alone. Adrian Fort in his excellent biography of Wavell wrote in relation to Smith: '...*not without his critics - who suggested that he ran his office inefficiently, (he) gave Wavell bad advice and was partly responsible for allowing GHQ to turn into an unwieldy octopus.*'

These sentiments did nothing to hinder Smith's progress. He went on to become Lieutenant General Sir Arthur Smith, Chief of the General Staff in India in 1946 and Commander of British Forces in India and Pakistan in 1947.

Other individuals, like Colonel Freddie de Guingand, Colonel Terence Airey and Brigadier Jack Whiteley, were praised for their charm, common sense and effectiveness.

Appraisal is a two-way business, which worked very favourably for Teddy, who quickly found himself an acting Group Captain at the relatively youthful age of 33. Wartime breeds the opportunity for bright young individuals to prosper and there are many examples of very young men rising to high rank. The Australian Don Bennett, for example, was an Air Vice-Marshal at the age of 33. Fred Rosier was a Group Captain at 27 and both Gus Walker and Kenneth Cross achieved that rank at 29; indeed, Walker and Cross were Air Commodores at the ages of 30 and 31 respectively. In the Army, Michael Carver, who ended up as a Field Marshal and Chief of the Defence Staff, became a Brigadier at 29. Enoch Powell, who was only a wartime soldier, was 30 when he was made a Brigadier. So at this stage, Teddy was clearly near the top of the field, but not exceptional. He prospered not just because of his razor-sharp professional brain, but also because he was an amusing, well informed and articulate conversationalist who could spar effectively over the dinner table.

The entertaining memoires of Hermione Ranfurly, who became the private secretary to 'Jumbo' Wilson in Cairo, revealed the growing sense of confidence about the Allies' success in the desert war during 1942. Many wives found their way to Egypt and sought work in the headquarters. Thus encouraged, Teddy persuaded Nan to leave Australia to join him in Cairo, where she duly acquired a post with the intelligence team. She left Tony, then aged only four, with her parents in Sydney. Truthfully, life was tremendous for the young Hudlestons, both of them gainfully employed on interesting tasks and living in a vibrant social environment to which the war added colour.

The Caucasus Initiative

The Soviet Union had been pressing the US and Britain to start operations in Europe by opening a second front to reduce the pressure of German forces on Soviet troops. American commanders favoured Operation Sledgehammer, which involved a landing in occupied Europe as soon as possible. British commanders believed that such a course would end in disaster. An attack on French North Africa was proposed instead, which would clear the Axis Powers from North Africa, improve naval control of the Mediterranean and prepare for an invasion of Southern Europe in 1943. The US President Franklin D. Roosevelt suspected the African operation would rule out an invasion of Europe in 1943 but agreed to support Winston Churchill.

Anxious to offset the announcement of the change in their plans for a second front in 1942, the President and Prime Minister were eager to do something to show that they were still determined to defeat Germany as quickly as possible, and were convinced that it would require the combined efforts of all three nations to do so. One means of doing so would be to establish direct military relations with the Soviet Union in the field, in an area in which the Soviet forces were adjacent – the Middle East – by committing a small British and American force to the direct support of Soviet forces in the Caucasus.

A proposal to send a British-American air force to the Caucasus was introduced by Churchill into his conversations with Stalin in mid-August 1942. He suggested transferring air forces from Egypt to the Baku-Batumi area. His offer was contingent on the success of operations in the Libyan Desert. Stalin did not reject the idea, but nothing was settled at the time, beyond an agreement in principle that once a definite offer had been made and accepted, British air representatives should go to Moscow and thence to the Caucasus to make plans and preparations.

During the following weeks there was a great deal of political and military scheming about the composition of any force and its command. Matters started to crystallise in early October, when Stalin told General Bradley that the Allies could undertake a survey in the Caucasus as well as in Siberia, stating that he considered the Caucasus project to have priority. According to Bradley, Stalin and Molotov regarded the situation in the Caucasus as most serious. Bradley was determined that any force should be entirely American. The US War Department demurred because they felt that they didn't have sufficient manpower to spare.

On 13 October, in response to questions from the Joint Chiefs of Staff, the British made definite recommendations on the composition and authority of a mission to Moscow to work out details, as soon as the Soviet Government accepted the offer of the President and Prime Minister. They proposed that the mission would resolve problems like the operational role, the facilities required for airfields and road reconnaissance and the tonnage needed to maintain the British-American force. The mission would be sent by the British Middle Fast Command, with American representatives to come from USAFIME. Clearly they needed a very senior airman in charge, so Air Marshal Sir Peter Drummond was to lead the team and he chose as his right hand man Group Captain Teddy Hudleston. The senior American representative was to be the 50-year-old commanding general of the IX Air Force Service Command, Brigadier General Elmer E. Adler.

The mission was instructed to leave Cairo by air for Baghdad on 13 November. There they caught a train to Tehran. Their visa for entry to Russia was issued on 16 November 1942, which allowed them to continue by train to Moscow. At the Russian border they were joined by a determined cohort of NKVD whose mission was to keep the British delegation firmly in their sights throughout their stay. It was a journey of more than 3,000 km and the weather was bitterly, unbearably cold. When they reached Moscow on 21 November, they were accommodated in a single hotel, which was a relief, but also an obvious hint about their conversations being monitored. Their first task was to take their rooms apart to uncover the bugs, and then they played the BBC World Service as loudly as possible to hinder any unfound devices.

It quickly became clear that the Russians wanted to complain but didn't really want a solution. Three weeks passed while the mission and the British and American Governments waited for Stalin to make a formal proposal. Eventually discussions developed about the composition of any allied force, although the Russians were keener to have the aircraft without the crews.

Part way through the five-week stay Messrs Drummond and Hudleston, who both enjoyed skiing, decided to form the Lubyanka Ski Club. They had established rather good relations with officers at the Air Ministry, who enjoyed the opportunity to pull a sly trick on the NKVD by lending the British a car so that they could reach hilly country outside the city for their skiing. Their followers invariably had difficulty securing a car for themselves, thereby adding to the sense of fun and gratification. The mission also enjoyed the ballet, which was ludicrously cheap – a matter of a few kopecks for the finest performances. They met Stalin and Molotov briefly; indeed, Teddy was able to present his wife with a magnificent fur hat which was a gift from Stalin. But it was transparent that the Russians did not intend to discuss business seriously. On 13 December Molotov informed Air Marshal Drummond that since the United States and Great Britain were apparently not going to accept the Soviet views as a basis for discussions, the Soviet Government was unwilling to proceed. The Soviets immediately asked when the mission was planning to leave, explaining that flying conditions would soon become very bad.

But this was not quite the end. The US President remained unwilling to drop the project until he knew for certain that Stalin would not accept it. On 16 December the President formally asked for Stalin's views. He offered the concession that the force need not operate as a whole under a single British or American commander, but only under British and American commanders by units. On 20 December Stalin answered, stating that the crisis had passed in the Caucasus and that he expected the main fighting to be on the central front. Stalin said that he would be very happy to get planes for use there, especially fighter planes, but he had enough pilots and crews. The President replied that he was glad to know there was no longer any need of British and American help in the Caucasus and that he meant to do everything within his power to keep deliveries of planes up to schedule. He finished by pointing out that the United States, like the Soviet Union, lacked planes, not men to fly them. On this note the negotiations ended.

On 25 December 1942 the mission left Moscow for the Middle East by train and reached Cairo on 30 December 1942. Two days later he learned that he had been mentioned in despatches for the second time and a little under nine months after that, Teddy and Nan were the proud parents of their second child, Sally, whom they dubbed 'the Russian Bogey'.

During the War, all the neighbours of Turkey were either a part of the Axis powers or the Allies. Turkey itself was resolutely neutral. At the Casablanca Conference from 14 to 24 January 1943, Churchill proposed to force Turkey to join the Allies in the war. General Marshall and other senior American military figures showed extreme reluctance for fear that the extension of the war to a new Turkish front would 'burn the Allied logistics down the line'. Nevertheless, President Roosevelt gave Churchill the green light on 18 January to 'play the Turkish hand'. On 25 January, Churchill asked for an appointment with the Turkish President, İnönü, and this led to the Adana Meeting, which was held between 30 January and 1 February 1943. The teams were headed by Ismet İnönü and Winston Churchill. The other members of the Turkish side were Prime minister Şükrü Saracoğlu, Foreign minister Numan Menemencioğlu, Field Marshal Fevzi Çakmak, and a group of advisers. The British team included General Sir Harold Alexander, General Sir Henry Maitland Wilson ('Jumbo'), General Sir Alan Brooke, Sir Alexander Cadogan, the Permanent Under Secretary for Foreign Affairs, and Air Marshal Peter Drummond. The group was enlarged by four of Churchill's personal team: Lord Moran (doctor), Ian Jacob (Military Assistant Secretary), John Martin (Principal Private Secretary) and Tommy Thompson (ADC). In his diary, Brooke also mentioned the presence of two unnamed detectives and a valet, but overlooked Commodore John Dundas and the 33-year-old acting Group Captain Teddy Hudleston, who was there because of his recent experience with the Turkish Air Force.

At the meeting, which was conducted on two trains parked in a siding in the wilderness, the British tried to persuade the Turkish side to join the Allies. İnönü was not even remotely tempted to join the war. Churchill made lavish promises of military help (code-named operation 'Hardihood') and a list of military equipment was drawn up. In return, Churchill wanted access to Turkish air bases for the RAF so the British could bomb the oil fields of Ploieşti in Romania, the principal source of oil for Germany and the Italian positions in the Dodecanese. Although Churchill did not extract any binding commitment from İnönü, he was assured that Turkey would do all it could to aid the Allies without violating its neutrality.

By now the desert war was going the way of the Allies. Indeed, it ended on 13 May 1943. Commanders were keen to get on with the next phase, which had to be the invasion of Italy via Sicily and/or Sardinia. Resources were too scarce to conduct a combined attack on both islands and after much debate the choice was made to go for Sicily. Operation Husky was under way.

When Eisenhower was appointed commander of the European Theatre of Operations in June 1942, he specifically requested that Walter Bedell Smith be sent from Washington as his chief of staff. His record as a staff officer and his proven ability to work harmoniously with the British made him a natural choice for the post. Reluctantly, Marshall acceded to this request and Bedell Smith took over as chief of staff at Allied Forces Headquarters (AFHQ) on 15 September 1942. Reporting to him were two deputy chiefs of staff, Brigadier General Alfred Gruenther and Brigadier John Whiteley; the Chief Administrative Officer (CAO) was Major General Humphrey Gale. AFHQ was a balanced bi-national organisation, in which the chief of each section was paired with a deputy of the other nationality. As Chief of Staff, Bedell Smith zealously guarded access to Eisenhower. He acquired a reputation as a tough and brusque manager, and was often referred to as Eisenhower's 'hatchet man'.

Changes in the North African High Command were announced by Churchill in the House of Commons on 10 February 1943. Allied Force Headquarters was established in Algiers with Eisenhower in overall command and Tedder as his deputy. Admiral Cunningham remained as C-in-C Mediterranean. General Harold Alexander would move from Cairo to Algiers to become Deputy Commander-in-Chief of the Allied Force and head of 18 Army Group.

Planning for the invasion of Sicily was impeded by the existing focus of commanders on the successful completion of the North African campaign. Despite the optimistic Allied mood, military setbacks continued to unsettle progress. US forces experienced a severe blow at Kasserine Pass in the second half of February 1943.

On 1 March 1943 Teddy was transferred from Cairo to Algiers to work in the joint Anglo-American planning centre in a former nunnery at Bouzareah on the outskirts of the city. Nan was left in Cairo but started to lay plans for her return to Sydney, because it was far from clear where the next stage of the war would take Teddy. Moreover, she now realised that she was pregnant and it was important to the Hudlestons that their next child should be an Australian like them.

The planning centre was fully integrated, with all arms and nationalities neatly woven into a single design. Named after the hotel room in Algiers in which the organisers first met, Force 141 would later metamorphose into 15th Army Group. In 2010, Lieutenant Colonel Stephen Cote of the US Marine Corps published a paper 'Operation Husky: A Critical Analysis', which rightly observed that the Husky planning staff faced many huge challenges, not least of which was that they were littered around four different centres in Cairo, Algiers, Malta and the United Kingdom. This was no small handicap for what was to be the biggest and most ambitious combined operation ever attempted by the British and American forces.

Underlying all of the joint planning there was a battle of wills between the separate force commanders about the organisation and handling of air forces. Most land commanders wanted their own private air resource. The air force commanders fought for control of their own specific weapons systems, arguing for the concentrated but flexible delivery of air power. Airmen also believed firmly that no land commander truly understood how to use their air force colleagues.

Teddy's notes defined the challenges:

'The most difficult phase of the operation was clearly the naval one, with troops coming from England, North America, North Africa, Egypt and Malta. All had to be in position on D Day and married up with their landing ships. It was a very significant planning challenge. None of the planning staff could claim to have huge experience of amphibious operations, apart from minor attacks made on Greek islands and Operation Torch.

'We had to try first to prevent the detection of the Allied convoys from both sides of the Mediterranean by enemy reconnaissance aircraft. Secondly, we had to provide air cover and support for the assault forces before and after landing, and thirdly we had to prevent the movement of enemy ground forces on the north and north east side of the island of Sicily. As a supplementary task, we had to establish landing grounds ashore as soon as possible after the troops had landed safely.'

The close proximity of Malta to Sicily – less than 100 miles

- made it the obvious place for Allied fighters and fighter bombers. The existing airfields had to be improved and added to, with Gozo providing additional landing ground. This was achieved after brief negotiations with the Bishop of Gozo and by the time the landing took place, the airfield complex on Malta itself was so comprehensive that it was possible to taxi from one end of the island to the other. As Husky was launched, Malta was home to some 600 fighters and fighter bombers.

The nunnery-based planning team in Algiers was commanded by a British Major General with an American Brigadier as his deputy. Teddy's immediate boss was Air Commodore RM (Paddy) Foster, of whom he became extremely fond. A year after starting work with Foster, Teddy's diary for 12 March 1944 reported, 'Dear Paddy goes to Malta as AOC and I am delighted.'

Foster was ten years older, a Wykehamist and, ultimately, an Air Chief Marshal who finished his career as C-in-C British Air Forces of Occupation, 2 Tactical Air Force in Germany. An American Colonel, Charles Pollinger, was Teddy's opposite number on the air force side, while the naval planners included Captain Tom Brownrigg, who Teddy described as slight and volatile, and Commander Manley Power, who had a huge frame and was completely unflappable.

Following his retirement from the navy, Brownrigg became General Manager of the Bracknell New Town Development Corporation. With his experience in planning for Operation Husky and Operation Overlord, he was considered the ideal choice for implementing the development of a New Town. Then in 1954 the Television Act created the framework for commercial broadcasting in the United Kingdom. British Electric Traction's Broadcast Relay Services subsidiary and Associated Newspapers formed Associated-Rediffusion to bid for a commercial television contract and Brownrigg was swiftly recruited to manage the process. He established his imprint across the entire structure and output of the company. Contemporaries reported that he commanded Associated Rediffusion as though it were a battleship and he became a legend throughout ITV. Under his leadership, the company went from having one employee (himself) to becoming Europe's first and largest commercial television broadcaster in under a year

Power ultimately became Allied Commander-in-Chief, Channel in 1959. He is chiefly remembered for leading the 26th Destroyer flotilla that sank the Japanese cruiser *Haguro* in the Malacca Strait during Operation Dukedom in 1945.

Husky progressed well, despite the development of seven separate plans before a final one was agreed. One source commented 'beset by rivalry and conflict, the planning for Husky quickly bogged down, and for some time there was a real possibility that there would be no invasion of Sicily. The crisis was not resolved until 3 May, when Eisenhower intervened decisively, enabling the project to proceed.'

Launched on 10 July 1943, Husky achieved the goals set by the planners in less than eight weeks. The Allies drove Axis air, land and naval forces from the island, the Mediterranean's sea lanes were opened and Italian dictator Benito Mussolini was toppled from power. It opened the way for the Allied invasion of Italy. The planners, of course, were thinking about the next phase long before that happened.

CHAPTER 4

ITALY

The completion of the North African campaign led to a flurry of changes in the command structures and appointments of the Allies. The newly-formed Mediterranean Allied Tactical Air Force was to be commanded by Major General John Cannon, an American infantryman turned airman who was born in Salt Lake City, Utah, on 2 March 1892. During Operation Torch in November 1942, Cannon was the commanding general of the XII Air Support Command for the Western Task Force during the invasion of French Morocco. He moved to Algeria as commanding general of the XII Bomber Command. During March and April 1943, Cannon organised and commanded the Northwest African Training Command in the Northwest African Air Forces of the Mediterranean Air Command (MAC), the official Allied air force command organisation in the

Mediterranean Theatre. In May 1943, he became deputy commanding general of the Northwest African Tactical Air Force under Air Marshal Sir Arthur Coningham for the Sicilian campaign and the invasion of Italy. He was promoted to Major General in June and after Mediterranean Air Command (MAC) was disbanded in December, became commanding general of both the Twelfth Air Force and the Mediterranean Allied Tactical Air Force (MATAF) in the newly-organised Mediterranean Allied Air Forces (MAAF) under the initial command of Air Chief Marshal Sir Arthur Tedder. In January 1944, when Tedder was chosen by Eisenhower as his Deputy Supreme Allied Commander for the invasion of Normandy, the American Lieutenant General Ira Eaker took over as AOC-in-C MAAF.

September 1943 brought an agreeable harvest. Not only was Husky successfully finished but on 18 September Sarah Jane Hudleston was born in Sydney. Communication was considerably slower, so Teddy only learned of this excellent news a matter of days before he was posted on 26 September to be Senior Air Staff Officer (SASO) of the Mediterranean Allied Tactical Air Force in the rank of Air Commodore. But war always brings pestilence and on the day of his promotion, Teddy heard that his best man, Harry Wheeler, had been killed in a road accident on 21[st.]

Any airman reading this will know all about the role of SASO; civilian readers will not. A Group is a formation, normally commanded by an Air Vice-Marshal, containing a number of Wings and/or Stations. Operational matters are dealt with by the SASO and all other administrative affairs are dealt with by the Air or Senior Officer i/c Administration

(AOA/SOA). These two officers, normally of one star (Air Commodore) rank, are crucial to the successful management of the Group.

Teddy's appointment was clearly managed by 'Mary' Coningham. His previous SASO, George Beamish, and AOA, Tommy Elmhirst, were returning to England to grapple with 2nd Allied Tactical Air Force (2ATAF). Although Coningham's own appointment for Overlord was not confirmed until December, most seasoned commentators would have found it difficult to imagine any other air commander at the sharp end for the final push. In anticipation of events, he wanted to ensure that his successor in the newly-established formation (MATAF) was supported by someone who was utterly reliable and with fire in his belly. The new AOC might have been Keith Park; certainly that is what Portal wanted, but Tedder, doubtless nudged by Mary Coningham, argued that the Americans should take their turn with this command and Joe Cannon was both ready and able. With the established system of integrating US and UK commands, the new US commander would need a British SASO. Fortuitously, the ideal candidate was Coningham's protégé, who had amply distinguished himself as a planner, administrator and senior manager in the lead up to the invasion of Italy. Teddy Hudleston had to be the best candidate and, if there were any doubt, Coningham had almost three months to 'smooth' him into the job in much the same way as he had settled young trainee pilots at Cranwell and the Central Flying School. Teddy was amply ready for the challenge.

His appointment neatly coincided with the arrival of Coningham's headquarters at San Spirito in Bari on 26

September. The boss declared: 'the organisation of the building is to be based on the importance of the machine working'. This meant that Teddy acquired the most imposing office because it would be the busiest place. Coningham and his deputy, Joe Cannon, were relegated to more intimate surroundings.

Bari boasted a major port on the Adriatic coast and this was quickly put to good effect for the landing of materiel to support the war effort. Unfortunately, it proved to be the only European city to experience chemical warfare in the course of the war.

On the night of 2 December 1943, German bombers attacked the port. Oddly there was no effective port defence in place. There were no fighter squadrons close by and the resident US heavy bombers were completely unhelpful for any defensive role. Ground defences were inadequate and there was an underlying conviction that the Germans lacked the capacity or will to make an attack. Indeed, on the afternoon of 2 December, Mary Coningham held a press conference in Bari to reassure everyone that the Germans had been defeated in the air.

A few hours later 23 Allied ships were sunk or severely damaged in the overcrowded harbour, including the US Liberty ship *John Harvey*, which was carrying mustard gas; further gas supplies were reported to have been stacked on the quayside awaiting transport. The agent was intended for use if German forces initiated chemical warfare. The presence of the gas was highly classified, and the authorities ashore had no knowledge of it. This increased the number of fatalities, since physicians, who had no idea that they were dealing with the effects of mustard gas, prescribed treatment appropriate for those suffering from exposure and immersion, and it proved fatal in many cases.

Many additional casualties were caused among the rescuers through contact with the contaminated skin and clothing of those more directly exposed to the gas. On the orders of Allied leaders Franklin D. Roosevelt, Winston Churchill and Dwight D. Eisenhower, records were destroyed and the whole affair was kept secret for many years after the war. The US records of the attack were declassified in 1959, but the episode remained obscure until 1967.

Coningham's departure on 8 January 1944 offered Teddy a brief opportunity for a break. His diary for 9 January recorded:

Left Bari for Cairo 0700hrs. My first break for nearly two years - the last one being with N(an) at Alex. Amazing feeling of relief at being able to drop everything, and a rather guilty one for doing so. Found my conscience became less sensitive as we neared the African coast. Landed Benina (Benghazi, Libya) about midday and shed overcoats, sweaters and scarves ... felt better and freer. Arrived Heliopolis (Cairo) 1715 hrs almost expecting N to be there and eventually fetched up at Norman Allinson's flat.

For much of the next four days he was able to pretend that there was no war, hugely enjoying lazy visits to old friends and dining out in Cairo's newest haunts. Reality was reasserted when he was tracked down to give a briefing to the new AOC-in-C Middle East Command, the freshly promoted Air Marshal Sir Keith Park, on Thursday 13 January. At dawn the next morning, he was back at Heliopolis and after a nine-hour journey via Benghazi he was in his office in Bari wondering why he had gone on leave because the backlog of work was so heavy.

The diary for the weekend reveals much about Teddy's thinking and links:

Sat 15 Jan 1944

A hectic day working full out on 'Shingle'. The Army still has no idea of air power and its employment or conception or limitations. 15AG (Army Group, commanded by General Sir Harold Alexander) beginning to flap. They follow a very normal pattern - hysterically optimistic or unduly depressed. HQ very uncomfortable owing to process of moving and removal of most of our gear. It has been a good site and a happy halting ground but time to move on - all of us becoming groove bound.

Sunday 16 Jan 44

Ronnie Lees to conference at MAAF result of which more detail required in plan. Decided to issue supplementary op instruction. Broadhurst to lunch - somewhat concerned as to D/AOC and his own position and Harcourt Smith who is worried about getting command. Airborne plan still unsettled.

Harry Broadhurst was at this point AOC Desert Air Force. 'Broady', as he was generally known, was a natural leader of great charm and ability. He is often credited with being the youngest Air Vice-Marshal and it is true that on the date of his appointment at the age of 37 (31 January 1943) he was. But the honour of being the youngest ever Air Vice-Marshal actually belongs to the Australian Don Bennett, who was promoted on 6 December 1943 at the age of 33. For the record, Teddy was promoted Air Vice-Marshal on 10 November 1944 at the age of 35, thereby establishing the interesting record that Australia has provided two of the three youngest Air Vice-Marshals in the history of the RAF.

Gilbert Harcourt Smith was Broadhurst's SASO and had been a flight commander with 25 Squadron when Teddy arrived at

Hawkinge as a newly–commissioned pilot. His worries about securing a command were unfounded, because five weeks later he became AOC 242 Group, which he led for the invasion of Greece.

On Tuesday 18 January 1944 Teddy reported that his new office in Naples was in the Palace at Caserta: *'Every room like St Pancras and filling up fast with high powered HQ - with the usual resultant flap. Too many people with too little to do.'*

His testiness was faithfully recorded every day, with a growing disenchantment with the Army. On 21 January he wrote: *'Jumbo Wilson expressed view air must concentrate on communications - what the hell else have and are we doing? Also asked Alex if he had enough tactical air - felt like telling him he had everything in Mediterranean'*.

On the other hand, he was immensely proud of the Air Force productivity: *'The eve of 'Shingle' and the air has done a marvellous job - the bombers have been magnificent. Three lines of cuts across communications in Florence area, north of Rome and across line through Sulmona'* (East of Rome in the centre of the country).

His jottings for Sunday 23 January help to bring the strategic situation to life but also betray his conviction that the Army was underperforming:

The air yesterday continued magnificent job; it will probably go down as classic example of air power. Army still wavering and uncertain where and what to do. 2 US Corps taken very bad knock and tomorrow 10 Corps going. Effort being expended piecemeal. No co-ordination or initiative. 6 Corps on 'Shingle' beaches has achieved such astonishing initial success now have no idea how to exploit it. A more incompetent performance I have never seen. Intelligence information taken as it comes and not correlated with general situation.

As the days flow by, the diary is littered with the conduct of daily business with individuals who would bounce into his life frequently over the next twenty years. Important contacts for the future included Lauris Norstad and Lyman Lemnitzer, who would both become SACEUR, and Harold Macmillan, the future Prime Minister. Indeed, Teddy often dined in the senior officers' mess with Macmillan and other luminaries. At the end of January, Macmillan noted in his own diary:

I got back to Caserta around seven and dined very pleasantly with General Alex. General Wilson was a guest and a most jolly and even uproarious meeting - General Cannon (US) and General Lemnitzer (US) were there and lots of good talk and good stories.

Teddy's diary for the same evening records:

Amusing supper with Macmillan, Jumbo and CGS India. First named in tremendous form - carried on political argument with him for best part of an hour and thoroughly enjoyed it. And then Macmillan gave us amusing stories of the Great War. Become more and more infuriated with Army.

(Macmillan served with distinction as a captain in the Grenadier Guards during the First World War, and was wounded on three occasions. During the Battle of the Somme, he spent an entire day wounded and lying in a slit trench with a bullet in his pelvis, reading Aeschylus in the original Greek).

Terrible weather hindered operations throughout February. On the 10th Teddy recorded that gales, snow and thunderstorms were causing severe difficulties:

Air support planned for bridgehead on greatest scale in history. Some 800 heavy bombers (B17, B24) and 200 medium (B25, 26). Unfortunately serious interference by weather and project never materialised. Most disappointing as experience would have been invaluable for rehearsal for West Europe.

The following Monday, he noted the current main problem: the destruction of Cassino Benedictine Abbey:

Gen Clarke against - Air against - Freyburg for. Decided to attack. Army plan still vague. Much destruction on road to Cassino and front. We shall see much more. Not an encouraging outlook. ACM Brooke-Popham to dinner. Difficult to realise he was Governor of Singapore. An old man now.

And the following day:

Completely demolished Benedictine Abbey at Cassino. Never has a target been more reluctantly attacked. Very sad and exemplifies futility of this business.

On the 16th he recorded that Geoffrey Tuttle, Bruce Bennett, Tom Pike and Leonard Pankhurst, all men older than himself, had been promoted to Air Commodore. Five days later Tom Pike took over as SASO of the Desert Air Force and on 27th he arrived at Caserta in good time to attend a conference the following morning convened for Generals Alexander, Clarke, Leese and Cannon to discuss future plans. Teddy noted that the meeting led to an 'interminable argument with Saville (Major General Gordon Saville, commander XII Air Support Command), and Pike regarding air responsibility'.

Cassino remained a major focus of interest and there was a sense of things just not flowing smoothly. On 14 March Teddy wrote:

Decided to go nap on weather for 15th and agree to all out air attack on Cassino. Means Army must withdraw from town outskirts after two months of fighting on promise by air to open way for occupation by bombing. Weather at 1am 15th shaky but decided to go ahead.

He spent the whole of the next day on the Cassino front, where the weather turned out to be excellent. The New Zealand Corps withdrew from the town and heavy air started at 8.30 am. 5 Medium Bomber and 9 Heavy Bomber Groups attacked. In summing up, Teddy wrote: *Very impressive despite two loose bombs which came unpleasantly close. Number of casualties caused.*

On the 16th March he wrote: *Army advanced at Cassino but in half-baked way. Socially the more I see of individual soldiers, the better I like them. Militarily we should sack the lot if they belonged to the Air Force. No intelligence or initiative and ingrained inferiority complex.*

As if the weather were not enough of a problem, on 18 March 1944 Mount Vesuvius, which had not produced a major eruption since 1872, although there were intermittent lava flows over the years, went into full operational mode. Teddy noted 'great flames shooting out and hot lava running in two red-hot streams down the mountainside'. On Wednesday 22 March he wrote:

Spent most of day on Pompeii airfield - a scene of utter desolation. Vesuvius very active. 15 inches of ash since 2am, eruption at 1100. Stones size of bricks raining down in most disconcerting way. All aircraft damaged some badly with metal skin smashed in. All have glass broken. Wings deep in ash. Ordered clearing to avoid the collapse of wings. Impossible to fly aircraft out. Will try and drag away but flying bricks not healthy. Saw lava stream at close quarters pushing structures over, advancing two feet per minute. About 90 feet thick. A fearful sight.

A fortnight later he described the arrival of Air Vice-Marshal William Dickson, who was taking over as AOC Desert Air Force. His diary note observes, '*Dickson arrived from UK. Well briefed but sad.*'

This is an interesting and, perhaps, unfortunate glimpse of Teddy's intellectual arrogance. Sitting with his diary, it is all too easy to see that Teddy had less than the highest regard for Dickson. On 18 June, for example, he wrote:

Dickson visited here today. Am becoming intolerant - they will not give one intelligence for seeing their point of view, which they labour until you are sick of it, especially when you agree with them and have seen it for some time past.

From time to time, he expressed similar irritation about Tom Pike, Dickson's SASO. It must be said that Dickson was not a fool. After all, he went on to become CAS, then Chairman of the Chiefs of Staff Committee, which led to him being appointed as the first-ever Chief of the Defence Staff. Tom Pike also became CAS, so they were both men with the ability to make decisions and lead. There is just a hint that Dickson, who was ten years older, considered that Teddy was too young, abrasive and ambitious, quite apart from lacking experience in the operational command of a fighting unit. The body language, and maybe the nature of the business conversations would have revealed Teddy's attitude and it is reasonably fair to guess that this was one reason why Teddy's career languished in the doldrums in the early 1950s when Dickson was the Chief (Teddy was an Air Vice-Marshal from 1944 to 1957, apart from a period of 29 days in March 1946, when he started work at the Air Ministry and four months as an Air Marshal at SHAPE).

General Joe Cannon will have seen the signs of stress in his SASO and on 17 April 1944 he insisted that Teddy take leave in England. Teddy was not wildly excited about the prospect, although he did see it as an opportunity to sort out accommodation for his wife and children, who were planning to travel from Australia and were due to arrive a month after his own visit. (In fact they didn't arrive until October because of constraints on shipping). He also realised the opportunity to see what action was developing for Operation Overlord. So on 19 April he handed over to Ronnie Lees, another Australian, and prepared for an early flight the following morning. Hard as it is for modern travellers to appreciate it, this journey took two days, with a full overnight stop outside Tunis and a few hours on the ground in Casablanca. He landed at St Mawgan in Cornwall on 22 April and made his way to London, where he spent 48 hours making his mark with contacts and family, including a trip to see his Martindale aunt at Merrow. But his real objective appeared in his notes for Tuesday 25 April:

Went Uxbridge to see Mary Coningham. Met Saunders and Groom. Mary talked vaguely about getting me a command and must try and keep him to it.

Twenty-four hours later Coningham confirmed that Teddy '*might get 84 Group later*'.

On Saturday 29 April the 'young bloods' of the Desert Air Force and 2ATAF – Teddy, Harry Broadhurst, Claude Pelly, Alexander Montgomery and John Whitford (actually John Whitford was substantially older, having been born in 1892) enjoyed a long lunch at the Bagatelle Restaurant, which was one of the 'in' places in London in 1944.

With no hint of the complex relationships that would develop six years later, Teddy spent time with Nan's relatives: first with Blanche, a Davis maiden aunt who lived in grand style in the Dorchester for thirty years, although she maintained a flat in Park Street during the War. Then:

Johnny and Nancy (Collingwood) all well and little changed and delighted to hear Nan coming home. Walked in Park after lunch and tea with Nancy and Johnny, who are living at 17 Albion Gate. Blanche in Fountain House. Both have very nice flats. Johnny looking rather seedy after a bad go of lung trouble but hoping to get back to work in a few weeks. Dinner at Club with Peter Drummond and brief visit to Aunt Mary and Florence Dunlop in evening, both as charming as ever. Walked back to Club from Baker Street. Spoke to Muriel (Mackenzie-Wood - another Davis aunt) on the phone.

The following day he had lunch with Johnny Collingwood at the United Hunts Club, 17 Upper Grosvenor Street, which he described as a very pleasant little club which might suit him and Nan because couples could stay there.

And that was the end of the holiday. He left London seconds after midnight and set off for St Mawgan for the prolonged flight back to Italy, where he arrived at midday on Saturday 6 May, having endured a forced break in a lovely villa in Casablanca while the aircraft underwent urgent repairs to one of its four engines.

As always, the return from leave felt like a penance, although Teddy did acknowledge that he felt sharper because of the break. Over the next six weeks the pace of action with the advance on Rome was more frenetic but also much more successful. Day after day he recorded the large numbers of enemy vehicles and aircraft destroyed or damaged, while his opinion of Army performance became increasingly mellow. 8th Army did not receive the same praise:

'8 Army slow and lacking initiative'; '8 Army not being hand-held too well'; 'Battle going well at 5 Army but 8 Army still showing no great initiative'; '8 Army still floundering.'

And with scant regard for reputations:

'Afraid Oliver Leese has not shown any great qualities of generalship and is lacking imagination.'

The evenings seem to have been completely divorced from the battlefields a few miles away. Dinner in the mess produced an array of interesting and amusing visitors, including the composer Irving Berlin; Mlle Eve Curie, the daughter of Marie Curie; Lady Maude Bailey, who was the C-in-C of the ATS; General Lyman Lemnitzer, who produced a bottle of Benedictine liqueur to celebrate the success at Cassino; Paul Vellacott, the former head of Harrow (and them Master of Peterhouse, Cambridge). And frequent guests included Harold Macmillan and Field Marshal Jan Smuts, with whom Teddy regularly enjoyed sparring over biblical quotations and interpretation.

On Tuesday 6 June he noted:

'Overlord launched. Interesting to be the spectator for once. But cannot help feeling a little sad at not being in on it more closely. Attended a dance at the Villa Roaberry in Naples. Well done and an excellent band. Couldn't help wishing Nan were there. Dancing out of doors overlooking the Bay of Naples was too good to be wasted on one's own.'

A third mention in despatches was published on 8 June 1944. The mailbag the next day produced three notes from Nan. In one she reported that she had taken Tony to see the news reel on Cassino, in which Teddy played a starring role. Both parents agreed that it was an unusual way for a son to see and learn about his father. For the next fortnight Teddy's diary reads like a travel article; he reports upon visits to Capri in company with Air Vice Marshal d'Albiac, General Alexander and Air

Commodore Falconer to see the Blue Grotto, to Sardinia and to Rome where, on 23 June 1944 he was photographed at the dinner table with Air Marshal D'Albiac, General Venter, General Cannon, Field Marshal Smuts, General Alexander, General Van Ryneveld, General Harding, General Theron, General Lemnitzer, General Robertson, and one Captain Grimsley.

The following day General Alexander held a conference for his Army commanders to discuss plans following Operation Anvil. Teddy noted in his diary:

Highlight of the day and in some ways of my life was that Gen Smuts had dinner in mess. I have never heard such a brilliant exposé of world affairs and Germany in particular in my life. Theme built from Hannibal, 1st, 2nd and 3rd Punic Wars, through Napoleon, Mussolini to Hitler, for whom Smuts has no time. Thinks he is mad and has imparted the same phobias to the whole German race. Quoted freely from Latin classics, bible and modern authors. Finally quoted Churchill 'we cannot expect to settle all problems for posterity'. Captive conference.

Life around the dinner table provided him with many opportunities to learn about his masters and he greatly enjoyed discussing painting and architecture with Alexander, but frequently argued with Brian Robertson, of whom he wrote:

He makes such outrageous statements with such a sanctimonious expression it simply infuriates me.

Brian Robertson at the time was a 48-year-old substantive major, temporary Major General and Acting Lieutenant General, a baronet, Sapper and Chief Administration Officer of Alexander's Amy Group. When he retired from the Army in 1953 he was General The Rt. Hon. The Lord Robertson of Oakridge, Bt., GCB, GBE, KCMG, KCVO, DSO, MC.

Interestingly he became the Chairman of the British Transport Commission in 1953 and was succeeded by Dr Richard Beeching in 1961.

At the beginning of July, Teddy noted a conference at XII TAC with Saville and Dickson, writing in particular:

Latter completely overshadowed by Saville.

In fact Teddy's opinion of Dickson was almost an obsession. On 18 July he wrote:

Conference with Dickson and Pike. Afraid they lack grip. DAF not what it was. Too much 'can't' about everything.

The next day his office moved to Corsica at Bevenico, just south of Bastia. He flew himself there in a Spitfire, which he described as a lovely aeroplane. He was very sorry to leave Alex and Lake Bolsano but, of course, he continued to range far and wide. During the following week he flew to Caserta and Naples:

Saw Eaker who is beginning to ape the little Napoleon, which he is on paper but in no other sense. Becomes less impressive daily. Jack Slessor becoming restive as his deputy. In fact whole afternoon at MAAF not good.

At the end of July the King paid a flying visit to the Desert Air Force and Teddy sat next to him over lunch, finding him very approachable and amusing. At this stage, though, Teddy was beginning to feel rather isolated in a headquarters that was almost entirely American. He clearly had itchy feet and wanted to 're-join the RAF'. In a detached way, he described the launch of Anvil at 0415 on Tuesday 15 August 1944 and the battle proceeded well, although Generals Alexander and Harding expressed concern that they were not engaged in the real action any more.

On 24 August his diary notes:

Paris recaptured. Marseilles taken. Toulon almost.

Curiously Teddy exercised more power than he expected. General Joe Cannon was frequently absent, leaving Teddy to run the show as he thought fit.

Sunday 3 September

Gen Cannon left for SHAEF and left me with a beautiful collection of headaches - including formation of US Tactical Air Command. Supply situation of forward troops and air in S France becoming critical. Decided to move C47 groups over.

Monday 4 September 1944

Long meeting on formation of new TAC. All American officers with myself in the chair. They are very tolerant.

Tuesday 5 September 1944

Visited Saville at Valence in S France. Main problem at present one of supply and we are having great difficulty keeping aircraft far enough forward to hit the Hun.

Evidently he was acquitting himself well and the decision makers in the RAF were aware of it. This led to welcome news on Wednesday 27 September:

Letter from Jack Slessor to AVM D'Albiac telling him I am more or less certain to get a command. A wonderful opportunity and hope I can make the grade and don't let my backers down. There will be some heartburning in many places. Would be happier if I had opportunity of doing some fighting.

A fortnight later, on 12 October, he left Sienna and flew to Hendon. The following morning he reported to the Air Ministry and was told that he would take over 84 Group from Leslie 'Bingo' Brown in the next few weeks. Air Vice-Marshal Bingo

Brown, a South African, was a relatively old man of 51 and was not entirely thrilled to be moved after precisely one year in the job, particularly because he was posted to become Commandant of the School of Land/Air Warfare. Mary Coningham, his boss, and Fred Rosier, his Group Captain (Ops), recorded their views that Brown was not the ideal leader for a tactical fighter group. In Rosier's words 'Bingo, a First World War ace, was too old and out of touch to understand such things' (as operational fatigue).

Flushed with the excellent news, Teddy spent time that day with Johnny and Nancy Collingwood and sought their guidance on accommodation for his family, who would arrive in England in about a fortnight. Finally, after a separation of nineteen months, he was able to record in his diary for Saturday 4 November 1944:

Nan and family arrive. All looking tired but well. Tony a fine lad and Sally adorable. Betty most helpful. Moved into Euston Hotel. Handy but not very comfortable. It is great to have them back and it makes me regret having to go abroad again. We have been separated more than enough.

CHAPTER 5

84 GROUP

On 10 November 1944, Teddy, a 35-year-old substantive Wing Commander with the wartime acting rank of Air Commodore, was promoted to Air Vice-Marshal and nominally took command of his Group, although it took him two days to do so in person because of a short stay with Mary Coningham in Belgium, where he felt that the atmosphere in the Headquarters was 'odd'. Air Chief Marshal Tedder and Lady (Nan) Coningham were present for dinner that night and the assembled company was distinctly uncomfortable when the Coninghams engaged in a public argument. The next night was spent with Harry Broadhurst at 83 Group, which he described as 'a happy setup'. Dermot Boyle was the SASO at 83 Group and, although he must have been nettled by Teddy's preferment for command, he was the model of amicable, courteous and professional behaviour.

On his arrival in Antwerp on 12 November, Teddy was greeted warmly by Bingo Brown, who went out of his way to make the handover easy. They dined that night in the Army mess and it was clear that Teddy had formed a swift opinion of his new colleagues:

Too formal and mess too big. Crerar friendly but not impressive. Staff very young and restrained.

For the next two days Teddy was shepherded around the Group by his SASO, Theodore (Mac) McEvoy, meeting as many of his team as he could. McEvoy was four years older than his new boss and was highly experienced in the role, having been the person in charge of the Group from its formation in July 1943 until Bingo Brown's arrival on 10 November. He had been SASO at 11 Group in 1942 and the Desert Air Force in 1943, so the arrival of a young thruster whom he barely knew must have been galling. Let it be said that McEvoy was entirely professional, ultimately becoming a friend of the Hudlestons when Teddy became Vice Chief of the Air Staff.

McEvoy moved on to become Director of Staff Duties in the Air Ministry on 20 January 1945 and was replaced by Group Captain Douglas (Zulu) Morris. Zulu Morris would become Air Marshal Sir Douglas Morris, KCB, CBE, DSO, DFC. Born in Margam, South Wales, on 8 Dec 1908, he was three weeks older than Teddy. He was educated at St John's College, Johannesburg, where he gained his nickname 'Zulu'. From 2 Sep 1957 to 9 Feb 1960 he was Assistant Chief of the Air Staff, Air Defence (thereby working for Teddy again). His last post was AOC-in-C Fighter Command from 8 May 1962 to 1966, when Fred Rosier took over from him.

Teddy noted in his diary that he was impressed with his Wing Commanders, but he was very anxious to move units out of Antwerp, which was under a regular barrage of flying bombs. His own headquarters was making a planned move to Breda, where he feared that the set up was not what he wished it to be. Not surprisingly, he immediately changed things on his arrival on 16th. On Wednesday 15 November he wrote:

Said goodbye to Bingo and am now in sole charge. Am not thrilled and can only think of home. Attended dinner given by Canadian Admin staff. Extremely well done. But quite clear AOC not properly rated by Army. Am going to have an uphill struggle. RAF is not in proper perspective. Bingo would seem to have placed himself on too low a level.

The timing could not have been worse, for Geoffrey Spencer, the AOA, moved during the week after Teddy's arrival. This, together with the news that the house he had arranged for his family in England had fallen through, provided unwanted challenges to his new role. When he rang Tommy Elmhirst and Mary Coningham to discuss a new AOA, it dawned on him that his colleagues were patiently waiting for him to scream for help. At least this was a source of amusement: in spite of his thoughts of home, he was enjoying his job and had no thought of asking for additional support.

On 25 November 1944 Bill MacDonald (later Air Chief Marshal Sir William MacDonald, GCB, CBE, DFC, ADC) arrived to fill the gap left by Spencer's departure. Teddy had not met him before but instantly rated him 'a good type' and recorded that he had been strongly recommended by Basil Embry. The fourth crucial member of the headquarters was the youthful Group Captain Fred Rosier (just 29 years old), who would also become an Air Chief Marshal and remained a close friend of Teddy's for the remainder of his life. Indeed, Rosier gave the address at Teddy's memorial service at St Clement Danes.

Teddy had much to do. His predecessor had never persuaded the Canadians that aircraft were a support, not a substitute for ground action. It is no surprise that Teddy's thinking was wholly in line with that of his boss, Mary Coningham. Both had very firm opinions of the use of 'air' and they remained in close contact throughout 1944 after Coningham's move from Italy to England. All lessons learned from the Italian campaign were summarised for Coningham by Teddy for implementation in the plans for Overlord.

Both men also shared a degree of reserve and cynicism about relations with the Army. Vincent Orange, in his book *Coningham* reports the detail of a note from Coningham to Teddy: '*As you know, the Army cannot be blamed, so in all reports over here the Air Force bombing of Cassino was quoted as the reason for the Army's failure - in other words, the attack was used as a weapon to beat us.*'

The role of the AOC was wide ranging. Teddy had operational command of 176 units, which included seven Wings, more than 30 fighter squadrons manned by at least eight different nations (Argentina, Belgium, Britain, France, Holland, New Zealand, Norway, and Poland) and equipped with many variations of aircraft in the 720 or so in the Group (Spitfire, Tempest, Typhoon, Mosquito, Mustang and Auster). Clearly the first priority was to deliver the air support needed by the Army, but this could be accomplished only by the acquisition of serviceable airfields, the efficient delivery of stores and equipment ranging from bombs, bullets, rockets and fuel to accommodation, clothing, rations and pay for the troops. A huge amount of time had to be devoted to matters of discipline, honours and awards, letters of condolence or congratulation, promotions, postings and dismissals, visits to units, daily meetings with senior and junior colleagues, conferences and the planning of future operations, quite apart from regular scheduled meetings with his boss, Mary Coningham, and other Group commanders. During January, for example, Teddy was responsible also for the planning and execution of 2TAF's air support for Operation Veritable – one part of the advance to the Rhine (the other part being Operation Grenade, which was planned by Brigadier General Richard Nugent, AOC 29 Tactical Air Command).

Visitors flowed through in a constant stream: Montgomery came to lunch on 20 November, then CAS, who was Portal, and Coningham the following day when they all went to talk to the pilots of 145 and 35 Wings. He himself dropped in to see Toby Pearson (Air Commodore Herbert MacDonald Pearson), who had been a direct contemporary at Cranwell and who was SASO of 85 Group but was holding the reins until a new AOC arrived. It was Teddy's sad duty to break the news to Pearson ten days later that his brother had been killed. One night he enjoyed dinner in the Canadian mess with the Canadian ambassador, the Bishop of Dover and a Canadian Senator. But on 27 November he wrote:

General Webster (Quarter-Master General) to dinner. Dead from the neck up. God knows why the Army keep him on. As in Italy, I had to shoot him down. The man is, by virtue of his position, a dangerous fool.

The following day he hosted the head of the Polish Air

Force and wrote in glowing terms about a Dutch irregular who had volunteered to stand on the roof of a building which housed a German headquarters which the Group intended to attack, in order to ensure that they hit the correct place.

He was pleased to meet the New Zealand High Commissioner, William Jordan, on a visit to 135 Wing at Maldegen, not least because he knew the Davis family well. But his private appraisal was '*A very pleasant sincere old boy* (he was 65) *but as a high government official not very impressive*'.

He attended his first commanders' conference in Versailles on 4 and 5 December. All of the great and good were on parade and, although the conference was a little dull, Teddy was gratified to share lunch and dinner with Tedder (Air C-in-C and Deputy Supreme Allied Commander, SHAEF}, Harris (AOC-in-C Bomber Command), Robb (Deputy Chief of Staff (Air), SHAEF) and Hill (AOC-in-C Fighter Command).

Teddy had the time to join the Army Commander, the newly-promoted and first-ever Canadian operational four-star General, Henry Crerar, and Fred Rosier to see *Blithe Spirit* on 9 Dec 44; he had last seen it in June outside Rome. This 'work hard, play hard' culture was part of Coningham's very strong leadership profile. As Vincent Orange quoted, Coningham's determination was to "feed, clothe, house and entertain' those under his command better than they expected'.

One unusual incident merited two entries in the diary. On 7 December he wrote:

Freddie de Guingand to lunch. Long day in the office culminating in telephone call from Willie (Merton) to say Boydie had died on the first. Only wish I could be with Nan to whom it will be a great blow.

All the more of a shock as he was apparently so well when she left a few weeks ago. It will also be a great blow to Mollie D and a further worry to Nan. When one remembers his amazing vitality it is difficult to realise he is dead.

This was confirmed by Nan, whose letter breaking the news arrived on 12 December. Although there is no evidence to prove it, Teddy was such a punctilious person that he will have written immediately to his mother-in-law to commiserate. This must have caused great hilarity in Point Piper when it arrived, because Boydie was very much alive and did not die until he was 89 in 1969.

In a bold move, Teddy opened his own mess on 14 December. It was a risk splitting the RAF from the Army, but he believed that the atmosphere in the Army mess was actively hindering the free exchange of ideas. Canadian officers seemed to be frightened of their seniors (noticeably so in Guy Simonds' mess)' whereas Teddy's view was that he could only learn about his team if they felt free to debate openly. The move was greeted with enthusiasm by the officers of 84 Group and in no time at all visitors from other Groups were beating a path to Teddy's mess.

Jeffery Williams' book *The Long Left Flank* provides a very clear picture of land operations for the Canadian Army. The Battle of the Scheldt, which finally secured Antwerp, a vital port for the Allies, was a Canadian Army triumph. Although the British had captured Antwerp on 4 September, it was barely usable until the strong German presence was cleared from the north side of the Scheldt. The Canadians had been totally responsible for land operations in the coastal area at a cost of 17,000 casualties, of whom 3,000 were killed in action or died of wounds. Now, from 8 November 1944 to 8 February 1945, there were no major operations on their front. The Army was able to enjoy a brief respite which allowed them to ensure that they were at full strength and properly trained before the next offensive.

Every history of the War spends time on the competing personalities of the commanders. Montgomery, a prickly man by nature, was constantly at odds with Eisenhower, Patton, Coningham and others. The Air Force griped about the Army and vice versa. But there were some real difficulties in the Canadian Army, brought on in part by 'the Normandy Glide' – severe dysentery – which laid Crerar low and from which he did not seem to be able to recover. Eventually he conceded the need for extensive treatment and handed over his command on 27 September to Lieutenant General Guy Simonds. Charles Foulkes took command of 2 Corps and Brigadier Holley Keefler took over 2nd Division.

Simonds, born an Englishman in Bury St Edmunds in 1903, was a brilliant soldier but something of a prima donna. Crerar, who sincerely believed that Simonds was an outstanding Divisional Commander with all the potential to be equally successful as a Corps Commander, became increasingly concerned by Simonds' state of mind. No matter what Crerar did, nor how carefully he phrased his thoughts and actions, Simonds was determined to take offence. Despite his concerns, however, he continued to support Simonds, confirming his promotion to Lieutenant General and appointing him as his temporary replacement while he was recuperating in England. Simonds chose to misinterpret even this overt sign of confidence and was profoundly irritated when he had to hand command of the Army back to Crerar, who not only had missed the entire Battle of the Scheldt but had received promotion to full General on his return. It did not add to Simonds' reputation that he always thereafter found opportunities to run down Crerar.

So Teddy had diplomatic challenges to handle in his dealing with the Army. It happens that his style and ability made him a good working colleague, and there were no national or professional jealousies to undermine relationships. He was not a competitor for senior appointments that the vying Army officers craved. But he was eternally conscious of the potential for internal strife, which extended throughout the most senior ranks of the Canadian Army.

1945 started with a bang on New Year's Day:

A lively day. The Hun attempted blitz on airfields and just missed causing heavy damage. Brussels, Eindhoven, St Denis Westram all took a knock. Half a dozen 109s slid past my office about 60 yards away. He is getting uppish. 131 Wing shot down 21 over their own airfield while Hun shooting it up to tune of 18. Broady also lost some in couple of squadrons caught taking off. Brussels also hit hard. But the excitement has done us some good. Everyone keyed up. Signal from Archibald Sinclair to say I have been given CB. Basil and Tommy also listed.

Bing Cross arrived in the evening in great form and thoroughly enjoyed his visit. Also had first-hand news of Nan, which was a pleasant surprise.

Operation Veritable began on 8 February 1945. The battle had to be fought on the flood plain between the Maas and the Rhine and the water table was high after the excessive rainfall of that winter. The cold weather of January had frozen the ground, but February brought a thaw and the area quickly became a mud bath. Moreover, although there was high ground near the Maas, the Germans might decide to blow up the winter dykes of the Rhine, thereby flooding more than half the battlefield. It was clear that this was to be an infantry battle. The concern turned into reality when the Germans opened a sluice gate on the Roer, releasing more than one hundred million gallons of water. Within hours the Roer rose by five feet, overflowing its banks across the whole front and causing the Maas to flood for eleven days.

The Long Left Flank provides a graphic description of the start of the operation:

Then, precisely at five o'clock in the morning (of 8 February), the artillery opened fire. The whole sky to the west was lit by a flashing wall of light, and overhead came the rushing sigh of a thousand shells. Moments later, on the enemy positions opposite, orange flashes marked their explosion followed by a mounting, echoing roar of sound as the crump of their bursts merged into a continuous monstrous bellow.'

…At ten o'clock, half an hour before H Hour, the full force of the artillery and the Pepper Pot groups fell upon the German forward defences. To the almost unimaginable noise now was added the sound of aircraft overhead and of tanks grinding forward to their attack position.

From the German perspective, this was an introduction to Dante's Inferno. From the Allies' point of view, it was a gratifying demonstration of commitment. Prisoners admitted to the devastating effect. They were completely shattered, their communications destroyed and soldiers thoroughly demoralised by overwhelming force.

But this early success was quickly neutralised by God's right hand. The rain continued and low cloud effectively prevented the ground attack efforts of the air forces. This allowed the Germans to raise their strength opposite the First Canadian Army to nine divisions. There was a real danger of a stalemate developing. For ten days both sides fought ferociously – and valiantly – with grave losses.

At last, on 21 February, 84 Group was able to take to the air. They attacked at ground level, using rockets on entrenched enemy positions, and the Canadians were ready to follow up with concentrated infantry attacks. The ten-mile journey to the banks of the Rhine now seemed to be possible. In the event, the weather remained so appalling that 2TAF was able to give major support on just one day, 28 February, in the last two weeks of the battle.

On the German side, General Alfred Schlemm was struggling to deal with a military position that grew worse by the hour. To compound the difficult realities, he started to receive orders from an hysterical Führer. He was to be held personally responsible for the defence of the west bank of the Rhine and was to ensure that not one of the nine bridge should be ceded to the enemy. Nor, indeed, were they to be destroyed until the threat was immediate and direct. Hitler ordered that no man could cross the Rhine without his personal permission. Failure to obey would lead to execution.

The fighting was fierce and now entirely on German soil. On 6 March, the Guards Armoured Division under Major General Sir Allan Adair attained a key objective, the village of Bonninghardt, which was some 65 feet higher than the surrounding countryside. This gave the Allies a clear view of the entire German bridgehead around Wesel. Observed artillery fire and forward air controlled attacks could now be delivered with spectacular accuracy.

Despite many setbacks, there was a real sense of impetus to the Allied advance. On 10 March 1945 in the early morning, two loud explosions heralded the destruction of the last two bridges over the Rhine. The battle for the Rhineland was over. First Canadian Army had 15,634 casualties, of whom 10,330 were British and 5,655 were Canadian. Overall the Allies lost 23,000 men and the Germans 90,000.

Fred Rosier, who was Group Captain (Operations), had anxieties about the management of the Group Control Centre (GCC). He still didn't know his boss well enough to be sure what the reaction would be to his forensic criticism, but he screwed up his courage and told the AOC about his concerns. Teddy approved and promptly transferred Rosier to run it on 12 Mar 1945. Group Captain Denys Gillam took over Rosier's role and proved himself a worthy selection. Teddy was desperately sad that Gillam decided to go back into civilian life in mid-October. 'A great loss to the service', he wrote.

On 22 March bridgeheads were established over the river and the first crossing took place the next day. The Germans still resisted, but the advance of the Allies had become a charge. Over the next six weeks the Allies moved north and east, clearing the whole of the coast of northern Holland and Germany, and racing eastwards to take Bielefeld, Osnabruck, and Bremen.

By mid-April the fighter wings were operating from permanent airfields in the Rhine area. Fred Rosier's GCC moved to Brogbern, close to Lingen, which proved to be its last location of the War. From 17 Apr to 6 May, 84 Group flew 4672 sorties, 1674 close support and army targets. But Teddy noted with deep regret the early fragmentation of his Group before the end of hostilities with the Germans. On 24 April he wrote:

C-in-C arrived to say goodbye to the Norwegian 331 and 332 Squadrons who are returning to England, and tell 66 and 127 Squadrons that they are to be disbanded.

2TAF had covered itself in glory. Coningham's three key British commanders were totally on top of their jobs and had earned the respect of soldiers and airmen alike. Tommy Elmhirst, AOA 2TAF, noted in April 1945 'Harry Broadhurst, Basil Embry and Teddy Hudleston don't want teaching their jobs.' That mood persisted and Teddy noted in his diary on 23 August 1945:

84 Gp seemingly very much in the good books. We shall have to watch for any reaction - we are almost too popular to be true.

And then, suddenly, it was all over. On 25 April Teddy noted that the 1st US Army and Russians had joined up south of Berlin. Senior Commanders from the battlefield were recalled to Old Sarum for a conference to discuss the future. On 28 April Teddy flew back to England and went to see his family at Merrow but spent the night at the Savoy in London, having seen Johnny and Nancy Collingwood for a drink. He drove to Old Sarum on Sunday afternoon, meeting up with George Beamish, Basil Embry, James Scarlett-Streatfeild, who would die in an air crash in Norway ten days later, Bing Cross, Douglas Evill, who was then VCAS, and many others. Interestingly Teddy had to give two lectures and chastised himself for being in less than perfect form. '*Still too damn self-conscious,*' he wrote of himself.

Back at his Group, he noted on 4 May that TAF had

announced that the Germans had accepted 21 Army Groups terms and the ceasefire would be implemented at 0800 the next morning. Curiously this was repeated on Monday 7 May – and this time the notice was right. Tuesday 8 May was christened VE Day. In his diary for that day he recorded:

No very great emotion shown. Some jubilation in village in evening, but all very restrained. An anti-climax and end of an era.

In the following days, a sort of holiday atmosphere developed. Group Captain Peter Hamley, an acquaintance from Kohat in 1933/34, appeared, but at TAF HQ everyone disappeared. The C-in-C and AOA went to Copenhagen and SASO to England. '*God knows when we will get on with the job. Maybe I don't relax enough*', wrote Teddy.

As May drew to a close, a stream of visitors visited 84 Group: Tedder, Coningham, the Chief of the Canadian General Staff, the Canadian Army Commander, and Major General Ivor Thomas, who was commanding 43 (Wessex) Division. He wanted to haggle over accommodation in Celle where Teddy's Group was due to go at the end of the week. There were farewell dinners, medal presentations, fly pasts and parades. But service life had to go on and Teddy's diary for Saturday 26 May reads:

Left for Celle 0700 hrs by road. Drove via the Rhur (sic) and Essen. The destruction in the Rhur has to be seen to be believed. I did not see a single habitable building and many streets still blocked by rubble. It will take 50-100 years to put this straight. In meantime the housing problem in England seems small compared with that in Germany. Many refugees, mainly women, on roads heading West towards Rhur I wondered if they knew what they were going back to. Two striking features: their cheerfulness and good physical appearance.

Secondly their cleanliness and good condition of their clothes. Spotless and perfectly pressed. Majority would appear to desire to be friendly to us, some indifferent, a few openly hostile.

Autobahn in Germany quite superlative and the best laid roads I have ever been on. Other roads poor.

84 Group's headquarters was based in a well-built German Army camp, which they promptly renamed Trenchard Barracks, a name it retains still. Initially the Mess was in a tent, but it didn't take long for Teddy to identify a suitable house in the town with a garden which stretched down to the bank of the River Aller.

Constantly on the move, Teddy visited every unit under his command regularly. He flew himself to Hildesheim on 16 June to see 146 Wing, 148 Wing in Enschede on 18th Broady's 85 Group HQ at Schleswig on 19th and Mary Coningham's HQ at Bad Eilsen on 20th. He enjoyed two visits to England during the month of June. The first was to attend the Jubilee celebrations at Cranwell on 13 June when the King visited, along with many of the Air Force's greatest celebrities. And then on Friday 22 June he was accompanied by his wife and son to his investiture with the order of a Commander of the Bath (CB) at Buckingham Palace. After the ceremony the family had lunch with the Collingwoods and then took Tony to the Zoo, which the Air Vice-Marshal enjoyed as much as his son.

With the advent of peace, the focus of his life as AOC shifted noticeably towards administrative and welfare issues. Many airmen wanted to leave the service, or return home, having been separated from their families for several years. More worryingly, he had to spend a great deal of time with legal 'wallahs', as he called them, reviewing criminal cases which included looting on a grand scale. In the middle of July he recorded that he harangued the OCs of his Wings on looting and discipline.

Another lightning visit to England from 23 to 26 July allowed him to celebrate his wedding anniversary with Nan for the first time in six years. They booked themselves into the Savoy and left Sally with the Collingwoods overnight. Three days later he was with the Americans in Frankfurt for his investiture as an Officer of the Legion of Merit.

In July, Fred Rosier moved back to Group Headquarters as Group Captain (Ops). Teddy already held him in high regard and noted in his diary after the surrender of Japan that on the night of 16 August:

Rosier held forth at length on the atomic bomb, and gave the most lucid dissertation on organic and inorganic chemistry I have ever heard. An extraordinarily versatile chap.

Not everyone was viewed in the same light. Two of his oldest and most staunch supporters came in for private criticism in Teddy's diary during June 1945. After his visit to 85 Group he wrote:

Broady has very comfortable house. Still do not like the atmosphere of his command.

And on 29 June:

Mary behaving like spoilt child; mixture of ballerina and emperor. Don't like it and felt rather sick. Maybe am too intolerant of genius but hate to see a man I like making a damn fool of himself.

One by one, the luminaries of 2TAF slipped away to different appointments. Mary Coningham was replaced by Sholto Douglas; Broady handed over to Tommy Traill; Denys Gillam retired from service life. Teddy was lucky to be kept on as AOC 84 Group because he continued to enjoy the rank and draw the pay of an Air Vice-Marshal although his substantive rank as a Group Captain had been gazetted only on 1 January 1946. On the same day he was mentioned in despatches for the fourth time.

At last he handed over the Group to Air Vice-Marshal Percy Maitland on 18 March 1946 and reverted to his Wartime rank as an Air Commodore. He and Fred Rosier travelled contentedly back to England together on the military train drinking some of the former Air Vice-Marshal's champagne.

1946-1950: The Imperial Defence College/Review of British Strategy/WEU

The original mission of the IDC when it was established in 1927 was to groom officers for senior appointments for the defence of the Kingdom. That metamorphosed over the years and the contemporary mission of the Royal College of Defence Studies (RCDS), which is the modern version of the IDC is:

'To prepare senior officers and officials of the United Kingdom and other countries and future leaders from the private and public sectors for high responsibilities in their respective organisations, by developing their analytical powers, knowledge of defence and international security, and strategic vision.'

Even in 1946, the IDC was a superb, tight-knit club in which British, Commonwealth and US soldiers and civil servants met on common territory. One ingredient of the course was the opportunity to develop high-level networks which would hold both students and staff in good stead for the remainder of their careers. The Commandant was General Sir William (Bill) Slim, recently the successful commander of the 14th Army in South East Asia. Teddy described him as 'a blunt and taciturn man with a nice sense of humour. He had the gift of being able to sum up a situation in fewer words than any man I met before or since.'

Senior directing staff included Guy Russell, who would be Commandant when Teddy returned to the IDC as one of the staff in 1956, and Jack Whiteley, who had impressed Teddy in the Middle East in 1942. Fellow students included Dermot Boyle; William Stratton, who was Teddy's opposite number as VCIGS when Teddy became VCAS; Guy Simonds, who had commanded II Canadian Corps during the advance on the Rhine; Frederick Scherger, who would become the RAAF CAS (1957-1961) and then Chairman of the Australian Chiefs of Staff (1961-1966); and the unusually colourful Don Zimmerman, an American from Oregon who had survived a disastrous dive bombing training mission in July 1931 (the bomb release gear stuck and while attempting an abrupt pull out, the airplane grazed the ground, did three complete rolls and stopped, right side up, minus the landing gear and with the upper wing sagging down on the lower wings of the biplane. The engine was located a quarter of a mile down the beach). Paul Caraway, another American (from Arkansas), ultimately reached three-star rank but never saw combat. The American Eric Bols, who had commanded an Airborne Division in the Normandy landings, raised every penny he could lay his hands on to back Tom Walls' horse 'Airborne' in the Derby. The horse won at long odds, which may have been a factor in Bols' decision to leave the Army a short time later.

The course was far shorter than the modern version, with only 29 students. The routine was relaxed, with a morning lecture by an individual drawn from the Services, industry, the universities or Trades Unions. This would be followed by discussions or syndicate meetings in the afternoon, focusing on problems of the day. Most students welcomed the time they had to study in the excellent library, which was a luxury most had not enjoyed for the past five or six years.

But towards the end of August Teddy's comfortable life was interrupted by the CAS, Lord Tedder. His new role was to be the RAF member of a team established by the Chiefs of Staff to undertake a review of British strategy. His official title was Assistant Chief of the Air Staff (Policy). The team was planted in an office in the present Ministry of Defence, known as Strange Gate. The Navy was represented by Admiral Charles Lambe, a gifted man who could have made a living as an artist or musician and was an excellent all-round sportsman. He went on to become the First Sea Lord in 1959 but was forced to retire early in May 1960 after a massive heart attack. He died on 29 August 1960. The Army was represented by a Sapper Brigadier called Charles Richardson, who later became Quartermaster General, and the Foreign Office sent William Hayter, who was to become Ambassador to Moscow and, after retirement, Master of New College, Oxford. This was a high powered team and much was expected of them.

The four men got along rather well together and it did not take them long to apply some structure to their plans. They were very conscious that the political strategy of the Empire was increasingly fragile and this was brought home to them quite forcibly by the sudden appearance in the office one day of Lord Mountbatten, who was an old friend of Charles Lambe. He announced that he had just left a meeting with the Prime Minister, who wanted him to go to India as Viceroy to preside over the dissolution of the Indian Empire. Mountbatten claimed that he had no wish to go, although the listeners quietly judged that he was absolutely determined to do it.

Up until this moment, Teddy and Mountbatten had not crossed paths often. As he was inclined to do, Teddy made a critical judgement about Mountbatten which he candidly admitted changing in later years when they worked together much more closely.

The strategy team was guided by a range of transparent issues. There was the significance of the Hiroshima bomb, which not only ended the Pacific War and killed a lot of Japanese citizens, but was also instrumental in saving the lives of many, many Allies. The new, overt threat was Russia, which would be fully armed with nuclear weapons in the near future, although they had not exploded a device thus far.

Interestingly Teddy went to see Portal, the former CAS, who was the Head of the Atomic Energy Commission. Portal predicted that the Russians would test a nuclear device in a few months. He went so far as to give a date, which proved to be just ten days out. Lurking in the background was the threat of chemical and biological warfare and there were many factors affecting maritime and land warfare, with technological developments on the drawing board which would transform capability. At the end of autumn the team felt that their ideas were crystallising, so they agreed that they should visit the

Pentagon in Washington to discuss their views on the future. Although the trip was useful, it did not achieve all that they expected because they found the Americans much more interested in China than they were in Europe.

They returned home on the Queen Elizabeth, which had been used as a troopship during the War and had been converted back into its original role as a luxury liner only in March 1946. The crossing proved to be ghastly. In fact the Captain said that it was the worst he had ever experienced. To compound the difficulties for passengers, all the carpets in the public areas had stretched, so it was impossible to attach the standard check lines on the furniture. In Teddy's words 'the main lounge, which was the size of a small aircraft hangar, quickly looked like the site of a western rodeo, with grand pianos, enormous settees and heavy armchairs charging about on their own kamikaze missions.' Non-sailors genuinely thought the vessel would never recover from some of the extravagant rolls in enormous seas. But they did, and shortly before Christmas the team reached dry land and set about completing their task.

They considered the final printed document to be impressive. To their dismay, the Chiefs of Staff did not agree. The First Sea Lord, Admiral Cunningham, and CIGS, Field Marshal Montgomery, definitely disliked it. Tedder was more muted, but he clearly wasn't enthusiastic. In the formal language of the ministries, the Chiefs of Staff 'took note' and ruled that no reference of the report was to be made in any official correspondence. The curious outcome, however, was that the document did become the textbook for military thinking in Whitehall for almost a generation.

Teddy was dying to get out of Whitehall, but CAS wasn't having any of that. His next appointment was as ACAS (Technical Requirements) working on the Defence Research Policy Committee, chaired by Sir Henry Tizard, the Chief Scientific Adviser.

Tizard was an interesting character who as a boy had harboured ambitions to join the Navy but was rejected because his eyesight was too poor. This seemed to be no impediment to him joining the Royal Flying Corps instead. But he was a scientist through and through. 'The secret of science,' he once said, 'is to ask the right question, and it is the choice of problem more than anything else that marks the man of genius in the scientific world.' He chose aeronautics as his special problem.

Scientists, particularly research scientists, never know where their research will take them. After all, that is the purpose of research. So it was not entirely absurd that Sir Henry insisted in 1950 that UFO sightings should not be dismissed without some form of proper scientific study. The Department set up the Flying Saucer Working Party (FSWP), still held to be one of the most exotic titles for the British civil service.

Teddy's opposite numbers were a Rear Admiral Engineer, John Langley, whose big claim to fame was that he lived with a mongoose, and Brigadier Hugo de Charleroi, a charming and intelligent Sapper. Teddy's office was supplemented by the arrival of a promising young Squadron Leader, Neil Wheeler, who would become an Air Chief Marshal 25 years later.

It was during the three years of work on a national defence strategy and the Defence Research Policy Committee that Teddy started to reflect upon the deterrent factor of nuclear weapons to offset the overwhelming conventional strength of the Soviet Union. The problem was how to develop an effective method of delivering the weapons. The ageing Lancasters and Flying Fortress B17s were clearly not capable of penetrating the opposition's improving air defence systems.

On the drawing board were two more sophisticated bombers: the delta wing Vulcan and the crescent wing Victor. Both had a potentially high sub-sonic performance, but the fear was that they might be found wanting. Teddy expressed his concerns to Air Vice-Marshal John Boothman, who was ACAS (Operational Requirements), arguing that there was an evident need for a highly sophisticated conventional bomber. In due course Vickers won the contract to provide the Valiant, designed by George Edwards.

This contract was two years behind the Vulcan and the Victor but it still was the first into service in 1954/55. Teddy later admitted that all three aircraft proved to be successful, leading to the creation of the so-called V Bomber Force, which comprised the three new arrivals.

On 29 April 1948 the Chief of the Air Staff, Lord Tedder, wrote to Sir Henry Tizard:

You may have heard that the Western Union governments are setting up a Military Staff committee to coordinate staff talks and plans. Our government has decided that we should be represented by one Air Officer who will have an adviser from each of the other services. This is naturally an extremely important appointment and the nominee must have the confidence of the other services. The person appointment must be the 'man for the job'. I can think of no one possessing the necessary qualifications who approaches Hudleston in suitability. CIGS and First

Sea Lord welcome him. I do hope you will agree to our taking Hudleston for this appointment. I would be very glad to discuss the question of his replacement with you.

Sir Henry responded immediately, acknowledging Teddy's special skills and welcoming the opportunity on his behalf. Just six months earlier his post had been upgraded to Air Commodore. Now, in the interests of international stature, he was to become an Air Vice-Marshal again. He was still only 39.

Under the Brussels treaty, five powers, the United Kingdom, France, Belgium, Netherlands and Luxembourg, agreed to collaborate in the defence field as well as in the political, economic and cultural fields. The object of the defence organisation was to provide for the co-ordination of defence between the five powers in the military and supply fields and for the study of tactical problems of the defence of Western Europe. In addition it was to provide a framework on which a command organisation could be established.

The very first meeting of the Western Union Defence Ministers took place on Friday 30 April 1948 at No 1 Carlton Gardens, London. Those attending included:

UNITED KINGDOM
Mr AV Alexander, Minister of Defence
Admiral Cunningham, First Sea Lord
Field Marshal Lord Montgomery, CIGS
Marshal of the RAF Lord Tedder, CAS
Sir Harold Parker, Permanent Secretary
General Hollis, Chief Staff Officer

BELGIUM

His Excellency Colonel de Fraiteur,
Minister of National Defence

Lt Gen Baele, Chief of Staff of the Army

Colonel Leboutte, Chief of Staff of the Air Force

General de Leval, Engineers

Monsieur Walravens. Counsellor, Belgian Embassy.

FRANCE

His Excellency Monsieur Teitgen,
Minister of the Armed Forces

General Lechères, Chairman of the Combined General
Staff Committee of the French

Armed Forces

General Ely

General Revers, Chief of Armed Forces Staff Committee

Admiral Lemonnier, Chief of Naval Staff

Monsieur P. Baudet, Minister, French Embassy,

LUXEMBOURG

His Excellency M. Lambert Schaus,
Minister of the Armed Forces

Colonel A Jacoby, Commander in Chief

NETHERLANDS

His Excellency Col A Fievez, Minister of War and Navy

Lieutenant General HJ Kruls, Chief of Staff, Army

Vice Admiral van Holthe, Chief of the Naval Staff

Major General Giebel, Chief of Staff, Air Force

Baron Bentinck, Counsellor in the Embassy

The conference issued a directive stating that the Defence Ministers of the five powers required the Military Committee to undertake the necessary examination in order to be able to provide answers to the questions:

- Would the resources and equipment of the five Powers be pooled?
- Were the types of equipment of the five Powers to be standardized?
- What forces could the five Powers assemble on the ground, in the air and at sea?
- What would be the plan of action of the five Powers until American help is available?
- What were the sources of supply of the five Powers?
  But first the committee had to:
- Prepare an inventory of the total military forces and resources of the five Powers at the time.
- Prepare an inventory of the potential military forces and resources of the five Powers.

- Assess what resources and assistance would be required from other sources

There were specific questions from the Americans:

- Was a combined staff contemplated in Europe?
- Would equipment be pooled?
- Would types of equipment be standardised?
- What ground and air forces could the Allies assemble?

Five days later, Air Vice-Marshal Teddy Hudleston started his new job as the Head of the Military Delegation to the Western Union. The Military Committee had its first meeting on the same day and unanimously elected Teddy as its chairman. In his notes to CAS at the end of that day, he observed that the French, despite their apparent ardour for his leadership, left him in little doubt that they would not be content with this arrangement forever. All of his experience in working with the French had taught him that their priority at all times was to serve their own national interest. He did not perceive them as international team players, so one way to weld them to the common purpose was to give them a sense of ownership. He had taken the canny decision, therefore, to suggest that they rotate the chairmanship and this had been received with evident relief by the French, if no one else.

The committee agreed to provide draft replies for the Americans by 10 May. They resolved to undertake an immediate stocktake (up to 12 months) and a long-term stocktake to define the position in 1950, 1952, and 1955.

Teddy's initial worry was security. He confided to the Assistant Chief of the Air Staff (Policy) (ACAS(P)), his old friend Paddy Foster, that his main preoccupation was the application of existing security measures within his own military committee. They militated against the development of mutual confidence.

Although it was a five-power committee, in practice only four would participate because Belgium represented Luxembourg. It was hard enough to secure agreement on the agenda for joint allied meetings and the whole issue of Western Union collaboration was undermined by financial concerns. Each nation had its own specific agenda, often without concern for their allies.

The French were worried about common control and the responsibilities of the Commander in Chief of the Western Union Air Forces. They were also exercised about the establishment of a French Fighter Command and how it was coordinated with WU Air Defence.

There were many big issues for all, which included aircraft specifications, airfields, a common training syllabus and radar. How were the Allies to deal with the pooling of resources and the co-ordination of mobilisation? Was it going to be practical to standardise operational and administrative procedures? Was there a rationale for common aircraft production and associated equipment? Was there the political will to agree a plan for taking over civilian airlines in the event of war?

Radar is a good example of the complexity of the challenge. The original target date for the supply of all ground radar equipment was December 1949. It was then discovered that certain 'new' and 'serviceable' equipment had deteriorated to such an extent during storage that extensive reconditioning was necessary. Each country had to organise its own shipping and installation of equipment. The United Kingdom, which was to supply the products, would inform allies of the dates on which goods would be ready for collection. Many months might elapse between notification and collection, which was an issue which had not previously been recognised. The Dutch needed five radar sets and these were supplied or were ready for collection on time, except for one Type 15 which would be ready in January 1951. But the Dutch were slow to collect because of financial constraints. The Belgians were supplied with Type 15s, although they were of all of an earlier mark. Typically the French were designing a 10 cm GCI somewhat similar to the British Type 70, rather than opting for the agreed common equipment. To add a degree of confusion, trials of the French model were not complete, so no one could assess their suitability.

There were deep concerns about standardising airfields capable of dealing with the different types and nationalities of aircraft. Of course each nation tended to make calculations in its own measuring units, which added a dimension for incremental cock up. For example, the British were told that their future airfields need not be more than 1800 yards long, and certainly not more than 2000 yards for either fighters or bombers. The Americans required 8000 feet for their fighters and 9000 feet for their bombers. One paper on the subject observed 'As it is more than probable that the continental Air Forces would be equipped with British types, the committee felt that they should be advised to concentrate on 1650 metre runways'. Clearly this would deny the Americans the ability to use the airfields (1650 metres equals 5,362 feet) and it would provide only just enough for British equipment because 1650 metres equals 1,787 yards.

The Air Advisory Committee asked the Chiefs of Staff to approve a target force of 1600 fighter/ground attack aircraft, 160 reconnaissance aircraft and 32 light bombers, amounting to 1792 overall by 1954. They agreed that a force of 4,200 aircraft was necessary but did not consider it feasible to build up a greater force than recommended within the timescale. The Cs-in-C advocated the inclusion of 200 bombers in the force and were prepared to sacrifice some 600 fighters in order to secure the bombers. They based their argument on the necessity to include an offensive element in the defence. Amusingly, the Western Union committee expressed the desire that the Air Force should be equipped with nothing less than the most modern and efficient aircraft available. This flew in the face of the Cs-in-C argument against the Advisory Committees view that obsolescent fighter aircraft would be useful for some years to come.

The UK perspective was not wholly supportive of unswerving collaboration. Bomber forces as they were then constituted would almost certainly be directed against tactical targets anyway, so it would probably be better to concentrate on the build-up of Bomber Command with new type aircraft as they became available, rather than building up a new Bomber Force on the Continent.

Political in-service fighting was manifest in questions about service manpower. In March 1949 the Military Supply Board assessed the relative cost of the services in terms of dollars, industrial manpower and steel, both for initial equipment and one year of maintenance. It seems that the initial equipment of the Armies was seven times that of the air forces and their annual maintenance roughly twice. This was a powerful argument for adjusting the ratio to the advantage of air forces.

Manpower was the elephant in the room, and it must be said that the issue was never properly addressed. The committee was well aware of the difficulty of maximising individual national potential and the ability, or inability, of one to support the other. There were deep concerns about facilities at home and abroad and the training of reserves. Beneath the surface of the big questions, there were concerns also about the movement of personnel between countries, quite apart from problems to do with national financing and foreign resources. No one addressed it in these formal meetings, but it was very doubtful that any nation would be able to fulfil its obligations. The one matter that was agreed without debate was that the common language would be English.

It was a solid grind for two years. Nevertheless, it was the catalyst for further negotiations with the US and Canada during 1948. Denmark, Italy, Iceland, Norway and Portugal were invited to join in the process and this led to the signing of the Washington Treaty in April 1949, when NATO was born.

In the weeks before Teddy moved to become AOC No. 1 Group, he organised a conference in Fontainebleau on 20 June 1950 for the Chiefs of Staff to conduct a formal review of the position. The Chairman was Field Marshal Montgomery. 'Monty' was robust with his introduction to the meeting:

The plain truth is that there is no reality whatever in the general defensive structure of Western Europe. We have plans, committees, paper and talk. We have practically nothing that would be of real value if battle in the West should develop. If we don't change our plans and build up organisations that will produce the forces required within the agreed time limits, those forces being battle worthy, we shall never be able to hold the West. As things stand today and in the foreseeable future, there would be scenes of appalling and indescribable confusion in Western Europe if we were ever attacked by the Russians.

Montgomery had discussed this with General de Lattre, who agreed that it was a complete façade and 'une tromperie'. But regardless of this unpalatable assessment, Teddy and his colleagues had contributed massively towards the foundation of NATO, and SHAPE (Supreme Headquarters Allied Powers Europe), which was established on 2 April 1951 in Rocquencourt, France.

The United Kingdom remains a full member of the WEU, which has continued to promote European co-operation in security and defence ever since the original committee was formed. The WEU is able to request the use of NATO assets and capabilities to undertake operations under European control when North American allies do not wish to take part, and also provides the EU with access to military capabilities.

No 1 Group, 8 Aug 1950

The handover between Teddy and his predecessor, George Mills, was slightly unusual because Mills moved in the reverse direction to take Teddy's recent role as Head of the UK Military Delegation to the Western Union Military Staff Committee. Mills was almost seven years older than Teddy and spent only months in his new role before becoming AOC Air HQ Malaya, then AOC-in-C Bomber Command. He spent three years as Commander Allied Air Forces Central Europe and his final job was Chairman of the NATO Standing Group in Washington from 1959 to 1962.

Wartime statistics show that the Group flew a total of approximately 57,900 operational bombing sorties during the war, dropping 238,356 tons of bombs and laying 8,147 sea mines. In these operations 8,577 aircrew lost their lives. It was a battle-scarred and experienced bomber force. By contrast, the monthly record of operations for No 1 Group in August 1950 shows that they flew just 2,419 sorties and 2,976 flying hours. There were two accidents, both of them involving equipment failures but no casualties.

The statistical evidence of Group activity accumulated over the years was incredibly detailed. The AOC could review the hours of daylight and night-time flying for every squadron, their level of efficiency, which was measured every month, the amount of ammunition used and the accuracy of their bombing, the nature and success of navigation and signals training or the list of those who reported sick. The troops were motivated by inter-squadron competitions and interesting exercises. Escape and evasion were always popular. In August 1950, for example, RAF Hemswell conducted an exercise designed to replicate conditions for aircrew forced to bail out over enemy territory. Issued with khaki denims, each evader was allowed to carry an escape compass, one shilling and ten pence, a penknife and some rations. No maps or other aids were allowed, although it was part of the game to try to secrete such things provided they were not discovered during the full body search at the start of the exercise. Crews were dropped in pairs at four in the morning at points at least 28 miles from base. They were not told where they were and had to make their way home avoiding a determined force of fully briefed Army and Police units. When captured, which many were, they were interrogated before being released to carry on with the exercise. One of the biggest lessons learned was that most aircrew were ingenious and cunning: most managed to conceal helpful material which was not detected. Indeed, one officer took apart one of his shoes, filled it with money and re-stitched the leather. Some purists thought that this was taking the exercise 'a step too far.'

No 1 Group was proud of its record on accidents, which at one point amounted to one avoidable flying accident for 6,830 flying hours. This was 4,747 hours better than the target set by Bomber Command. Sadly it didn't take much to destroy this magnificent record, because there were three avoidable accidents in one month in 1951.

By 1950 No 1 Group comprised three Stations. At Binbrook, there were four Squadrons, (9, 12, 101 and 617), equipped with Avro Lincolns, a British made long range heavy bomber developed from the original Avro Lancaster. 101 Squadron had received the new English Electric Canberra B2 at the end of May 1950, thereby becoming the RAF's first jet bomber unit. Group Captain, Walter Sheen, whose awards of a DSO and DFC were gazetted on the same day, 13 September 1940, was the Station Commander. He was promoted Air Commodore in 1952 and Air Vice-Marshal on taking over as Director-General of Manning in 1955. His final appointment was as Air Attaché in Washington, which provided the opportunity for his son to serve in the United States Air Force. He retired as a Colonel.

Hemswell hosted four Squadrons (83/150, 97, 109/105 and 139), equipped with Lincolns and de Havilland Mosquitos. The Rhodesian Thomas Parselle, who had been in B Squadron at Cranwell in 1930 and 1931, where one of his flying instructors was none other than Teddy Hudleston, was the Station Commander. He was flying Lancaster W5001 (EM-J) to Dusseldorf on 25/26 May 1943 when he was shot down by a night fighter and captured, having been blown out of the aircraft. He became a prisoner at Stalag Luft III until the end of the War. On release he was repatriated to England and almost immediately attended the RAF Staff College. Ultimately he rose to become an Air Vice-Marshal and found himself working as Deputy Air Secretary close to his former boss, Teddy, in the Air Ministry.

Johnnie Warfield was the Station Commander at Waddington and finished his career as Commandant of the Royal Observer Corps, retiring as an Air Commodore. His Station had four squadrons, (50/103, 57/104, 61/144 and 100), equipped with Lincolns. The bad news for Warfield was that 100 Squadron was consistently rated below average in the monthly efficiency trophy with the contrived Efficiency Figure in January 1951 of 0.66 compared with 83 Squadron (1.25), 97 Squadron (1.23), 12 Squadron (1.11), 50 Squadron (1.05) and 9 Squadron (1.03). At the top end of the scale, 97 Squadron, based at Hemswell, was normally close to the top of the ladder and in September 1950 it led by a considerable margin with a rating of 1.42.

One very interesting Squadron Leader was Peter Brothers, who was in command of 57 Squadron. He had been a 25-year-old Wing Commander in charge of 602 Squadron equipped with Spitfire Vs in 1942. When he was not offered a permanent commission at the end of the War, he went off to join the Colonial Service in Kenya. There he flew his own aircraft, which proved to be invaluable for getting around his enormous area. His heart lay with the RAF, so two years after leaving, he managed to regain his commission and was given command of 57 Squadron, which he led on operations in Malaysia. He was to meet Teddy Hudleston again at No 3 Group, where he was serving in the Headquarters during 1953.

Herbert Pringle had graduated from Cranwell, where he was in A Squadron, five months before Teddy in July 1928. His command was Scampton, which hosted No 230 Operational Conversion Unit. Created on 15 Mar 1947 at RAF Lindholme by the redesignation of No.1653 Heavy Conversion Unit, the unit's role was to convert crews onto the Avro Lancaster, Avro Lincoln and de Havilland Mosquito bombers.

The headquarters of No. 1 Group was at Bawtry, near Doncaster in South Yorkshire with the AOC's residence some ten miles away to the North at Lindholme. Teddy inherited Group Captain R A T Stowell as his SASO, and Group Captain Robert Gandy as his SOA. The last occasion on which Gandy and Hudleston had worked together was as Flying Instructors at Cranwell in late 1931 and early 1932. At that point Gandy was a forty-year-old Flying Officer, having joined the RAF somewhat later than his contemporaries.

The AOC-in-C of Bomber Command was Air Marshal Sir Hugh Lloyd. Teddy and he had first met in Kohat in India, where they served together from 1933 to 1936. At the time, of course,

Teddy was a callow youth and Lloyd was a rather senior Squadron Leader, so their relationship was more professional than social. Their contact was extended by the war in North Africa, when Lloyd was AOC North-West African Coastal Air Force, then AOC Mediterranean Allied Coastal Air Force.

In many ways this was an unsatisfactory and unsatisfying appointment for Teddy. Still only 41 years old, he was very pleased to be able to spend time commanding people, rather than desks, but there was none of the zing which went with running a Group in wartime. This was an administrative appointment in all but name and Teddy hardly had time to get his feet under the desk before he was whisked away again. Indeed, his time as AOC was so brief that most references to the Group fail to include his name in the list of Commanders.

Perhaps the most memorable experience he had with No. 1 Group was sporting. Always keen to stay fit, Teddy was delighted that there were squash courts at Bawtry. He found that sport was a helpful, informal way to learn about the views of the troops on the ground, so he had no hesitation one day in offering a game to a young coloured man in a track suit, whom he took to be a junior airman. He was pretty confident that he would acquit himself properly because he had represented the RAF on and off for more than 20 years. To his dismay, he found he was being pushed around the court like a raw beginner. Indeed, he was roundly beaten and was most amused to discover that his opponent was Abdul Bari, the runner up to the Egyptian, Mahmoud el Karim, in the British Open Squash championship, which at the time was regarded as the World Championship.

Affairs of the heart

In September 1944 Nan, Tony and Sally left Sydney for San Francisco accompanied by Pip, whom Teddy generally called Betty. They took the train to New York, which they left in October, sailing to England via the Azores, finally docking at Southampton on 4 November 1944, just six days before Teddy became AOC No. 84 Group. The plan was that Pip, then aged 20, would live with the Hudlestons for the foreseeable future. Thanks to the Martindales, they set up house at Merrow, outside Guildford. Fortuitously Johnny and Nancy Collingwood were just down the road at St Martin's Priory, Guildford. The two Nancys were 1st cousins and had forged a great friendship in Sydney in 1934. Indeed, Nancy Collingwood was Tony's godmother. During the latter days of the war, Teddy had spent much of his leave in London with the Collingwoods and recorded the many meals that they enjoyed together during his brief visits. Nancy Collingwood gave Teddy his 1945 diary, which was the only mail to reach him in the week of 22-28 January 1945. It was entirely natural that the interaction between the Hudlestons and Collingwoods was close.

On 18 March 1946 Teddy had to relinquish command of 84 Group to Air Vice Marshal Percy Maitland. His new job as Assistant Chief of the Air Staff (Policy) meant a dramatic reduction in rank and pay to his substantive rank of Group Captain. It was the sort of galling officer management which affected a considerable number of airmen during the turbulent years after the end of the war. First, though, there was a three-month course at the Imperial Defence College (IDC).

Pip was not supposed to be a surrogate nanny, so she swiftly secured a job in London, which meant that she generally travelled with Teddy on the train. Superficially, the Hudleston household was well settled. Beneath the surface, things were increasingly complicated.

In the 1960s Nan told the author that she had never made love to her husband after the birth of Sally. Separately, and far earlier chronologically, she admitted this to Johnny Collingwood. For some reason, Teddy was no longer interested in her sexually, although he seemed to be content to have the trappings of an established family. Nan, on the other hand, was a passionate woman with a healthy appetite for sex. Pip may or may not have known the detail, but she was perfectly clear in her own mind that she fancied Teddy Hudleston and was determined to get him.

Through the hundreds of love letters written by Johnny Collingwood to Nan Hudleston it is possible to trace the development of their affair. Johnny's marriage to his Nancy was tense and, if his letters are an honest reflection, she was independently minded and somewhat selfish. Johnny's work for a pharmaceutical business between 1946 and 1953 took him to South America for months at a time and his wife would rarely join him. Most damagingly, Nancy Collingwood terminated a pregnancy without telling her husband about it until after the event. He was appalled and deeply hurt; he absolutely adored children and was very keen to become a father.

During 1949 and 1950 Johnny's letters gently moved from chatty gossip to affectionate suggestion. At the beginning of September 1950 Johnny wrote to ask if he could stay at

Lindholme for the St Leger. The Hudlestons were there because Teddy had been appointed as AOC No 1. Group in August 1950. Nan agreed readily and even kept him company on the day of the race. His thank you letter was warm and affectionate and was followed just over a week later by a cryptic short note asking Nan to meet him in London on one of two days. It is pretty clear from a loving letter of 4 October 1950 that their physical relationship started in earnest on Tuesday 26 September. The affair was to last for 25 years.

It is far less obvious when Teddy and Pip started their affair. Certainly Nan Hudleston never imagined that this might be one of the outcomes from Pip's regular association with her husband. After all, Pip was her sister. But one of Nan's oldest friends from Heathfield, a wonderful woman who was a Russian émigré and child piano prodigy, Nina Cernosvitov, recognised the signs and warned Nan on a visit to the Hudlestons at Lindholme in 1950.

But this affair did not develop as Pip desired. Johnny swiftly told his wife that he was in love with another woman, but he carefully avoided telling her that it was her much-loved cousin. The information persuaded Nancy Collingwood to become much more concerned about maintaining her marriage, and she made many efforts to draw Johnny closer to her. For a time they agreed to try to make it work, but the fact was that Johnny had completely lost his heart and eventually he told his wife the whole truth. This changed her stance, although she took a long time to make up her mind.

Any doubts which Nan may have harboured were fully expunged by Johnny's letter to Nan on 20 February 1953 in which he reports that Pip has soulfully confessed that she would go anywhere and do anything for Teddy Hudleston.

The outside world was not aware of this very complex theatre, and it is interesting in the modern age that there was a group sentiment that nobody wanted to undermine the career of Teddy Hudleston. In the early 1950s, divorce was still a scandal which would probably have impeded his rise to very senior rank. But at the end of 1954, Nancy Collingwood finally decided that she was going to injure her rival and humiliate her if she could. All of the affection and goodwill of previous years had shrivelled to bitterness and acrimony. She proposed to push ahead with the divorce, naming Nan Hudleston as the co-respondent. Her intent was to gain as much publicity as possible, so she also broadcast the affair to the aunts and uncles common to them both.

Blood is thicker than water. Despite widespread dismay, this was seen as a family matter. Johnny Collingwood and Nan Hudleston swiftly agreed to let the action go forward with Nan cited as the other woman; they would not contest the action. This, they judged, would reduce the likelihood of the newspapers spotting the story. After all, there were plenty of peers of the realm providing salacious evidence for the public in the divorce courts and an Air Vice-Marshal paled to insignificance next to them.

There was an opportunity for an additional action in which Nan could divorce Teddy for his affair with her sister. Johnny was cautiously attracted to this idea, but Nan definitely was not. Nor, it seems, was Teddy.

Very complex emotions were brewing. Despite her sincere love for Johnny Collingwood, Nan felt the loyalty of an RAF wife and appreciated that a divorce would surely destroy Teddy's chances of reaching the pinnacle of the RAF. They resolved to brazen it out, working together for the benefit of Teddy's career at an intense emotional cost for all of the parties involved. Johnny could never wholly understand it and deeply resented being the casual lover. He wanted Nan as his wife, and the failure to make that happen caused him to suffer terrible depression for the final 23 years of his life.

The affair between Pip and Teddy was sporadic for many years. It was almost casual in style and although Pip loved him dearly, Teddy's emotion was limited to affection. He was never going to divorce his wife. Johnny Collingwood and Nan Hudleston, on the other hand, enjoyed a genuine, enduring and sincere love affair. Hudleston and Collingwood hardly ever appeared in the same room together again, with both men resenting the continuing presence of the other in Nan's life. But the marriage between Teddy and Nan continued and Johnny Collingwood continued to see the love of his life, and most of her extended family, as whirlwind visitors to his sprawling Borders manor. When Johnny died in April 1975, Nan was distraught and, in a private scrawled note among her papers, she commented that she contemplated committing suicide 'but didn't have the guts'. The impact on her was dramatic. Johnny left the remains of the Cornhill Estate in trust for her and the death duties seemed to be overwhelming. The sad truth is that she cared so little about the future that she wanted no more than to be shot of the whole thing. She disregarded both family and professional advice, selling off the fishing for a mere £45,000 (it sold for several millions some years later), and the farms went in different directions. Ultimately there was nothing to sustain

Cornhill House, which she sold for £40,000. The woman who bought it, Mairi Packshaw, by curious coincidence the former wife of another officer in the Queen's Bays, then sold the lodge at the end of the drive for £27,000, thereby acquiring a substantial Borders manor with 18 acres and one of the best views in Britain for a mere £13,000.

Once Cornhill House had gone, Teddy was prepared to countenance giving up his grace and favour house in Hampstead to live with Nan at Tor Cottage, a substantial four-bedroom property in the village of Cornhill on Tweed. One way and another, they were reconciled in the end. But a long retirement in friendship was not on the schedule. Early in January 1980 Nan was staying with her old friend, Bunty Capel, in Sherborne when she fell into a coma. She was moved to the King Edward VII hospital in London, where she died without regaining consciousness on 17 February 1980.

The funeral service at a London crematorium was deeply moving, although it was attended by only a small congregation, most of them family. Left to choose the hymns, it seemed to the author that this was an opportunity to merge the Jewish and Christian traditions, for Nan was a strong and committed Christian, despite her father's Jewish ancestry. The first hymn, therefore, was *The God of Abraham Praise*, which is set to the deeply spiritual music of the Jewish Yigdal. Big mistake! Not only were people too moved to sing it, most didn't know the tune. The unexpected and genuinely moving moment was when Teddy placed a bouquet of flowers on the coffin at the end of the service. It was a simple gesture which spoke volumes.

After the cremation, the author was despatched to collect

the ashes, then pick up Teddy and drive him north to Cornhill. It was a quiet and companionable journey during which Teddy talked a little about his life and his late wife. On arrival in Cornhill, they went to the vicarage to deliver the ashes to the Revd Arthur Wiltshire, who thoughtfully provided the first glass of whisky for the day. Then there was the short trip to Tor Cottage. The headstone on Nan's grave in the churchyard at St Helen's Cornhill on Tweed reads: 'For 45 years dear wife of Air Chief Marshal Sir Edmund Hudleston.'

SHAPE

The development of a major Allied headquarters in Europe was one of the logical outcomes of the Western Union talks which Teddy chaired during 1948 and 1949. The Korean War increased concerns over the strength of Europe's defences against a Soviet attack. On 19 December 1950 the North Atlantic Council announced the appointment of General Eisenhower as the first Supreme Allied Commander (SACEUR). Before accepting Truman's invitation 'to become the embodiment of NATO, its constant and visible leader', Eisenhower visited every European capital. Finally arriving in Paris on 7 January 1951, he addressed the Alliance, saying 'I return with no miraculous plans, no display of military force. I return with an unshakable faith in Europe – the land of our ancestors'.

In January 1951 39 officers from the assorted Allied countries joined a US planning group in the hotel Astoria in Paris. There was no precedent to guide them. This was the first time an Allied HQ was to be established in peacetime. Ike's directives were austerity and integration. The staff would be limited to some 200 officers from all Allied nations and the interests of the Alliance outweighed all considerations of national prestige. Indeed, one of Eisenhower's major lasting influences on SHAPE (Supreme Headquarters Allied Powers Europe) was his exhortation that loyalty was not to one's nation, but to NATO and SHAPE. As he explained to Belgian leaders early in 1951 he considered himself 'one twelfth Belgian.' He boldly stated 'here we know ourselves as a single entity in carrying out the objectives of NATO and in building up a strong defence for the purpose of preserving the peace. Actually, for the purpose of this operation, we shall set aside our individual nationalities.'

Teddy's abrupt move to SHAPE at the beginning of April 1951, during the very week that the headquarters was formed, was at the personal request of General Eisenhower, who took a great personal interest in the early appointments to his staff. Teddy was appointed Deputy Chief of Staff (Plans) in the rank of Air Vice-Marshal. This was a very senior appointment because he reported to Lieutenant General Alfred Gruenther, the Chief of Staff, and had regular engagement with Eisenhower as SACEUR and Montgomery as DSACEUR. The other Deputy Chief of Staff (Logistics and Administration) was the French Lieutenant General J Valluy.

Gruenther, a native of Nebraska born in 1899, had been the principal American planner of the Allied invasions of North Africa in 1942 and Italy in 1943, so he and Teddy had common links and had worked together nine years earlier. There was a considerable degree of mutual respect and, as his own appointment eventually bestowed four-star rank on him,

Gruenther made sure that Teddy's appointment evolved into a three-star role as Deputy Chief of Staff (Plans & Policy). This meant that Teddy became an Air Marshal on 1 April 1953 as a youthful 44-year-old. Down the road in Fontainebleau, Tom Pike, serving as the Deputy Chief of Staff (Operations) for Allied Air Forces Central Europe as an Air Vice-Marshal, must have wondered how it was that Teddy had beaten him to one, two and three-star rank. At this stage in their separate careers, the odds were that Teddy was the better candidate to become CAS.

The headquarters comprised 183 officers from nine nations of the twelve NATO allies. Portugal and Luxembourg sent staff to SHAPE later and Iceland has no armed forces. The Planning Group continued to work in the Hotel Astoria in central Paris while construction of a permanent facility began at Rocquencourt, part of Versailles just west of the city. Buildings were quickly constructed and the new HQ was handed over to SHAPE on 23 July 1951. In 1952, Greece and Turkey, followed by West Germany in 1955 joined NATO and all three nations sent officers to SHAPE, bringing the number of nations represented in the mid-1950s to twelve.

The Hudleston's first home in France was at the Trianon Palace Hotel in Versailles, but they soon established themselves at 19 Rue de Vindé, in La Celle-St-Cloud, midway between the new headquarters and the Arc de Triomphe in the very heart of Paris. Rue de Vindé is a quiet residential street, lined with pretty houses and large gardens; number 19 also boasted a grass tennis court on raised land, which did not benefit hugely from Sally and friends using it as their platform to dig their way to Australia.

Paris in the 1950s was energetically social. The wounds of the war were still physically visible and emotionally tangible. The counter-measure was to live life at the fastest pace. Dinner was often followed by dancing at any one of a range of night clubs, with everything fuelled by copious amounts of booze. Not everyone behaved perfectly and discreet sexual liaisons were not uncommon.

One addition to the mixture was a man called Henry Bleeker, who affected to be a friend of all the key players, frequently visiting the Hudlestons and the Collingwoods wherever they might be from 1949 to 1956. A married man, he was a sexual predator who managed to seduce both Nan Hudleston and her sister Pip at one time or another. For a long time they all trusted him, but his actions and words eventually proved him to be a false friend.

Teddy was wholly focused on his job. This was an exciting time for any serviceman, and to be involved in the construction of the most important peacetime command in the world was profoundly satisfying for all professionals. SHAPE was unusual in one key respect: its function was entirely defensive, not offensive. Moreover, it was based in France with little or no control over its long-term viability as a guest. Thus when General de Gaulle decided that France would no longer participate in the military structure of NATO, all NATO forces were obliged to leave the country.

The new Deputy Chief of Staff (Plans and Operations) had no template to follow. This was virgin territory without a single plan, policy, method of operation or history. No one in headquarters had worked on anything similar in the past. There were no experienced staff to rely upon. The one asset that Teddy did have was his experience as the Head of the Military Delegation to the Western Union. All original thought was his to propose and develop.

During the 28 months of his appointment there were three SACEURs. Eisenhower served from 2 April 1951 to 30 May 1952. General Matthew Ridgeway was in post from 30 May 1952 to 11 June 1953 and was replaced by the man who had been Chief of Staff since the beginning, General Alfred Gruenther, who was in post from 11 July 1953 to 20 November 1956.

On his departure, he received very personal letters from his bosses. General MB Ridgway wrote on 11 July 1953:

On the eve of my relinquishment of command of Allied Command Europe, I would like to express something of my appreciation for your services as DCoS SHAPE during the 13 months of my service here.

Your service has been characterised uniformly by those qualities of high principled integrity, of professional competency of the highest order, of devotion to duty, and of cooperative spirit contributory to harmonious atmosphere which has happily prevailed in my headquarters.

Your forceful and fearlessly expressed principles and balanced judgement have provided me with invaluable guidance, and your personal support has been a source of deep satisfaction. You have served with distinction in a conspicuously superior manner.

And on 31 July his successor, General Alfred E Gruenther, wrote:

It is very, very difficult to say goodbye to you. You were one of the early members of SHAPE, and much of the success of our organisation is attributable to your tact and to your selfless devotion to the cause. Your service has been an inspiration to all of us.

As you know, I have constantly leaned heavily on you for advice, and you have never let me down. I have never had the slightest hesitation in referring any problem to you, no matter how sensitive it was... Your calm, quiet demeanour, your friendly personality, and your keen sense of humor are qualities which have endeared you to all of your associates at SHAPE... we think you are tops.

No. 3 Group

Teddy's appointment as AOC No. 3 Group on 1 September 1953 was a mixed blessing because he had to drop a rank from Acting Air Marshal to substantive Air Vice-Marshal. His six months as a three-star officer had made him the youngest in a generation and still the second youngest ever, following Sir John Salmond who had achieved the same exalted rank at the age of 41 in 1923. Teddy had to wait until 1957 to regain the third star when he became Vice Chief of the Air Staff (VCAS).

The headquarters of No. 3 Group were at Mildenhall and the AOC's residence was a rambling old rectory in the nearby village of Barton Mills with its garden backing onto the River Lark. From a work-life balance perspective, this was an agreeable arrangement in every way.

Teddy's predecessor was Air Vice-Marshal William Brook, who was due to be promoted to Air Marshal and become VCAS. Shortly before taking up his new appointment, he was killed while attending a jet conversion course at the Bomber Command Jet Conversion Flight, RAF Coningsby. He was conducting a solo exercise in a Meteor near Stafford when his aircraft was seen to suddenly turn and dive into a haystack. The aircraft disintegrated, the haystack was set alight and AVM Brook died instantly.

The coroner returned a verdict of death by misadventure as no technical fault could be found, but it seems likely that he was a victim of the Meteor's design fault, subsequently discovered to be the cause of a number of crashes throughout its service career. A total of 890 Meteors were lost in RAF service, of which 145 occurred in 1953 alone, resulting in the deaths of 450 pilots. Contributory factors in the number of crashes were the high fuel consumption, which severely limited flight time to as little as one hour, and difficult handling issues when one engine wasn't working. The casualty rate was exacerbated by the lack of ejection seats in early series Meteors; ejection seats would be fitted in the later F.8, FR.9, PR.10 and some experimental Meteors. The difficulty of bailing out of the Meteor was noted by pilots during development, who also worried about the limited size and relative position of the cockpit to the rest of the aircraft. There was difficulty also in using the two-lever jettisonable hood mechanism.

At Barton Mills life was about to take an unfortunate turn. Pulmonary tuberculosis (TB) is caused by the bacteria *Mycobacterium tuberculosis*. The disease can be transmitted by breathing in air droplets from a cough or sneeze from an infected person and it is said that most people who develop the symptoms were probably infected at some earlier point. Nobody can say for sure, but the family believe that Nan was first infected when she and Teddy were in Turkey between 1940 and 1942. The diagnosis was confirmed at the beginning of 1954: the solution was to be admitted to the King Edward VII TB sanatorium at Midhurst in Sussex.

Clearly Teddy was not able to drop everything to run family affairs. By common agreement, Nan's younger sister, Pip, undertook to fill the gap as much as she could, commensurate with holding down a job in London. Tony was at home only during his school holidays from Wellington College but Sal was still at home as a ten-year-old, and the Hudlestons had taken on Eric Grounds, Nan's five-year-old American nephew and the author of this biography, only months earlier. It provided ample opportunity for Pip to fulfil her ambition.

No 3 Group had seven RAF Stations and eight stations controlled by the USAF with RAF liaison parties. In terms of the British units, RAF Coningsby had 15, 44, 57 and 149 Squadrons, together with seven other units, of which two were unmanned. RAF Marham had 35, 90, 115 and 207 Squadrons, with five other units, including the Bomber Command Furniture Store and two bombing ranges. RAF Nuneham Park hosted the Joint Air Photographic Intelligence Centre and the Joint School of Photographic Interpretation. RAF Upwood had 7, 148 and 214 Squadrons, with three further unmanned stations, No. 230 Operational Conversion Unit, 388 Signals Unit and the inactive bombing range at Whittlesey. RAF Wittering 40, 61, 76 and 100 Squadrons, the Bomber Command Armament School and four other units which were either unmanned or belonged to other commands. RAF Wyton hosted 58, 82 and 540 Squadrons, the Radar Reconnaissance Flight and nine random units, some of which were also unmanned. Finally the Chesil Bank Range Unit was under command.

For a period several squadrons flew Boeing Washingtons, the British name for the Boeing B-29s lent to the Britain until the

English Electric Canberra could enter service. During his period as AOC, Teddy handled the introduction of the Valiant, the first of the 'V' bombers into the nuclear deterrent force.

The USAF stations included Brize Norton, Fairford, Greenham Common, Lakenheath, Sculthorpe, Mildenhall, Upper Heyford and Molesworth.

Unlike No. 1 Group, No. 3 Groups monthly operational report included a fairly extensive diary of the AOC's schedule. In the style of his command of 84 Group, he spent as much time as he could getting to know his men and their performance. During the four weeks after his appointment, he made 13 visits to units under command, took the Battle of Britain Day salute outside Ely Cathedral, visited the RAF Horticultural Show and hosted a visit of the CAS, Sir William Dickson, at RAF Wyton. As the weeks flowed by, he started to attend more sporting events and guest nights, but the constant round of visits to Stations and Squadrons endured remorselessly.

The monthly operational report also revealed the good and the bad of the British services in the early 1950s. Things often failed, be it undercarriages, engines, navigation or communications equipment. In December 1954, for example, No. 3 Group reported on a fairly chaotic monthly operation known as 'Exercise Bomex', which involved 11 Canberras from Marham, six from Wittering and eight from Cottesmore flying as a force and carrying out Gee-H (radio navigation) bombing attacks on two targets, Luce Bay off Dumfries and Galloway and Theddlethorpe in Lincolnshire. Two aircraft from Marham had to return home almost immediately because of undercarriage difficulties. At about 1500 a deterioration in the weather was predicted, so the force was instructed via Bomber Command to return to the Group Dispersal area. Ten aircraft successfully carried out their mission at Luce Bay, but eleven did not attack: six because they returned as instructed, and five had faulty Gee-H equipment. At Theddlethorpe, eleven aircraft failed to receive the recall instruction and proceeded with their mission. Three succeeded but the other eight failed because their Gee-H equipment was faulty. Overall this was not a glorious record and a fortnight later similar problems with Gee-H equipment undermined the success of Exercise 'Kingpin.' Indeed, throughout his time as AOC, Gee-H was a thorn in the flesh of the Group. The AOC was not amused.

Hugh Lloyd retired from the Air Force on 4 June 1953, having handed over Bomber Command to Sir George Mills on 9 April. Teddy and George Mills, who was almost seven years older, were old acquaintances and had served closely together on and off ever since 1933 in India. Their mutual handover of jobs between No.1 Group and the UK Military Delegation to Western Union Military Staff Committee in 1949 was later amplified by working relationships when Teddy was VCAS and Mills was Chairman of the NATO Standing Group in Washington. Teddy took over from Mills as Air ADC to the Queen in September 1962 and both men finished their RAF careers as Commander Allied Air Forces Central Europe. Their relationship was comfortable and mutually respectful. Mills went on to become Black Road from 1963 to 1970.

In May 1954 RAF Coningsby was closed and the whole station moved to RAF Cottesmore. Throughout the period Teddy continued to be a very active sportsman, almost losing an eye as a result. On 13 May 1954 he was wicketkeeper for the Group's cricket team when an awkward ball hit him full in the face. He was admitted to Ely Hospital and remained there until 22 May. The initial prognosis was discouraging and despite his desire to just get on with the job, he was firmly instructed to lie still and let the doctors try to save his sight. He returned home to convalesce until the end of the month, allowing Air Commodore Douglas Candy, an Australian who had been lent by the RAAF to become Teddy's SASO at the end of March to stand in as AOC.

On 11 November 1954, ten years and one day after his original promotion to Air Vice Marshal, Teddy took a 20-minute flight to RAF Wittering for the visit of CAS, Sir William Dickson, who had been promoted Marshal of the Royal Air Force on 1 June.

Teddy's two-and-a-half-year command as AOC No. 3 Group came to an end when he handed over to Air Vice-Marshal Kenneth Cross on 2 February 1956. Oddly, he was to hand over a further senior appointment as AOC-in-C Transport Command to 'Bing' Cross at the beginning of December 1963.

After three weeks leave, he started his new job as an Instructor at the Imperial Defence College (IDC) on 24 February. This new appointment persuaded him that he should buy a London property and within weeks Nan found a two-storey flat at the top of No. 3 Eaton Place, a two-minute walk from the IDC. Although Teddy's relationship with his parents-in-law was always amiable, he must have been a bit surprised when they bought the first floor flat in the same building a couple of years later.

Admiral the Honourable Sir Guy Russell had become the Commandant of the IDC in January after a two-year tour as Second Sea Lord. Russell was ten years older than his new recruit and was generally seen as a bluff, amiable and highly intelligent officer with extensive operational experience, which included service in the Dardanelles and Jutland during the Great War, and command of HMS *Duke of York* when it sank the *Scharnhorst* at the Battle of North Cape. Professional colleagues on the directing staff included Theodore McEvoy, who had been SASO at 84 Group when Teddy became AOC; William Crawford, a New Zealander by birth, who had been the successful gunnery officer on HMS Rodney whose excellent range judgement at 13½ miles ensured that they hit the *Bismarck* with their third salvo; Roddy McLeod, who had just finished commanding 6 Division; and Evelyn Shuckburgh, a diplomat who had just spent two years as Anthony Eden's PPS and who moved on the work in Paris with NATO from 1958.

This would have been a very congenial posting, but Teddy's career continued to experience abrupt changes of direction.

The Venerable Cuthbert Hudleston, Archdeacon of
Perth and Western Australia

Julia Phillips

(From left) Marjorie, Bill and Ted Hudleston, November 1915

(From left) Nan Davis, Boydie Davis and Nancy Moss, 1933

Ted and Nan Hudleston, December 1936

Nan Hudleston with her son, Anthony Edmund, 9 July 1938

Air Commodore Teddy Hudleston, July 1944

(From left) Air Commodore Teddy Hudleston, Major General Joe Cannon, Air
Marshal Sir Arthur Coningham, Air Commodore Colin Falconer, July 1944

Lieutenant Colonel Johnny Collingwood, 1970

(From left) Air Chief Marshal Sir Edmund Hudleston, Air Commodore
Denis Rixson, Group Captain Ricky Merrick, 1966

Handover to General Graf von Kielmansegg, March 1967

CHAPTER 6

SUEZ

1956 provided world leaders with three significant challenges. In chronological order, the first was President Nasser's decision of 26 July 1956 to nationalise the Suez Canal, after the withdrawal of an offer by Britain and the United States to fund the building of the Aswan Dam. The British and American offer was an attempt to undermine Egypt's new ties with the Soviet Union. Then in October, sparked by a student demonstration in Budapest, there was a popular revolution against the Hungarian Government, which fell abruptly. A new government was swiftly formed and declared its intention to withdraw from the Warsaw Pact, pledging to re-establish free elections. By the end of October, fighting had almost stopped and a sense of normality began to return. The Soviet Union, having declared a willingness to negotiate a withdrawal of Soviet forces, changed its mind and moved to crush the revolution. On 4 November, a large Soviet force invaded Hungary. And this happened in the final days of the four-yearly United States Presidential elections. It distracted President Eisenhower, who was fighting for a second term, which he duly won with a landslide (457 electoral college votes against Adlai Stevenson's 73).

On 9 May 1956, long before the invasion of Suez was publicly debated, Teddy was whisked out of the IDC and appointed as Chief of Staff (Air) for Operation Musketeer. His record in planning was extensive (Middle East 1942/1943, in the Air Ministry in 1946 and at SHAPE in 1950) which made him the safest pair of hands for the recently-appointed CAS, Dermot Boyle.

Good plans take time. On 31 July the Chiefs of Staff received an outline for a British operation with the probability of French collaboration. By this time the decision had been made to run the operation with three Allied task force commanders. Lieutenant General Sir Hugh Stockwell would command the land force, Vice Admiral Sir Maxwell Richmond the naval force and Dennis Barnett, a New Zealander who had only been in post as Commandant of the RAF Staff College for three months, was promoted acting Air Marshal to take on the Air Force element. This pleased his wife immensely; in-service gossip had it that she was infinitely more ambitious than her husband. His selection and the appointment of a planning staff divorced from the existing Middle East command structure was not a popular move with the resident Middle Eastern commanders (Air Marshal Sir Hubert Patch, C-in-C Middle East Air Force from 24 September 1956, and Air Vice-Marshal

William Crisham, who was AOC AHQ Levant). Arguably Teddy could have been Air Force commander himself, but Denis Barnett had very recent experience of operations in Egypt, far more than any other serving Air Officer, and this swung the decision in his favour.

The outline plan was discussed on 2 August. At that stage, the one thing that was clear was that nuclear weapons would not be used but no other impediments would be placed on attacks on military targets. Whitehall and the Allies were profoundly concerned about the potential for civilian casualties.

The objective of Op Musketeer was to restore the Suez Canal to international control by armed force. This plan visualised an Anglo-French action against Egypt and the positioning of forces within striking range of Egypt. When this was sufficiently far advanced, an ultimatum would be issued, failing the acceptance of which a maritime blockade and air action would be instituted and, if necessary, an assault would be made on Port Said and a threat posed to Alexandria. The assault force, which could be mounted quickly, was small and it would be necessary to mount and maintain an air offensive sufficiently heavy to ensure that the assault would not meet serious opposition. The initial aim of the air action would be the neutralisation of the Egyptian Air Force and for this purpose advance photographic reconnaissance would be essential.

Plans for Middle East operations were extraordinarily complicated over this period. On a global scale, there was a long-considered plan for dealing with war between Britain and Israel. Operation Cordage, which provided for the neutralisation of the Israeli Air Force, the imposition of a naval blockade and

associated land operations, was endorsed by the Chiefs of Staff
on 26 January 1956. Then there was the burgeoning and highly
secret plan which envisioned an Israeli attack on Egypt
supported by Britain and France. Here Britain's treaty with
Jordan added a further layer of confusion because Israel and
Jordan undertook a series of local assaults on each other in
August and September 1956. There were real fears that Israel
would take the opportunity to resolve Arab/Israeli relations by
force in the very near future. As late as 18 October 1956 the
Navy was warning commanders to be ready to implement
Cordage at 72 hours' notice. Fortunately naval dispositions in
the Mediterranean could be deployed as easily for Cordage
(against Israel) as they could for Musketeer (against Egypt), but
nobody in the theatre had any idea which would be
implemented.

Land Task Force HQ was established in the Montagu House
Annex of the War Office. It was later to be known as HQ 2
(BR) Corps with Brigadier KT Darling as Chief of Staff. At this
time, the Chiefs of Staff changed their thoughts on the
command structure and recommended that there should be an
Allied Commander-in-Chief. With little time to cast around for
candidates, the appointment went to the existing Commander-
in-Chief, General Sir Charles Keightley, on 11 August 1956.

A small French planning staff arrived on 9 August 1956. A
close friendship rapidly sprang up between the Allied staffs,
which developed and matured throughout the operation.
Nevertheless, there was a considerable security problem
connected with dealing with the French. Until certain measures
had been agreed by the Anglo-French governments, the Task

Force Commanders were forced to mislead the French commanders and planners as to what the actual current plan was. At one particular meeting, Hugh Stockwell spent over two hours explaining to General Beaufre, the French Land Task Force Commander, the merits of the plan aimed at landing at Port Said, while, in fact, the current plan and the one recommended by the Joint Task Force Commanders was the Alexandria operation.

The plan for Musketeer was described with careful attention to detail by General Stockwell in his post-operation report. It revealed the confusion which characterised the whole initiative. At first, the key was the dismissal of the concept of 10 (BR) Armoured Division concentrating on the Libyan/Egyptian border to menace Alexandria. It was ruled out as being slow, logistically very expensive and possibly politically unacceptable (as, indeed, proved to be the case). An assault on Port Said would secure the immediate control of one end of the Suez Canal but would have certain difficulties, for example, a limited choice of beaches which were shallow and flat with virtually no tidal range, slow discharge of stores and the potential for damage to Canal installations which would cause the Egyptians to block the south end of the Canal. Moreover, it had a 25-mile-long narrow causeway to the mainland, which was all too easy for the Egyptians to defend with mines. And finally, this causeway would impose time delays for linking up with airborne troops dropped further south. For these reasons, the Port Said plan was dropped and an assault on Alexandria preferred. Alexandria had a port of much greater capacity. The beaches were believed to be more suitable for assault landing. A suitable operational airfield was close to the port and the exits from Alexandria were not so canalised. An advance on Cairo from the desert road would menace the seat of government, forcing the Egyptians either to capitulate or stand and fight north-west of Cairo.

But Charles Keightley was increasingly nervous. To guarantee success, the landing would have to be preceded by a massive bombardment by sea and air. The Alexandria assault would almost certainly cause a very large number of civilian casualties and urban destruction. Contrary to the belief of many politicians, he did not wish to underestimate the will of Egyptian soldiers to fight for their own land. He believed that any plan 'must be capable of being held until our moral cause is unassailable.' And all of the planning to date had been based upon a range of imprecise factors to create a planned D-Day which had been delayed already on three occasions. At a meeting with the Prime Minister on 7 September, attended by the Chiefs of Staff, Keightley was robust, confronting Anthony Eden for the first time with the full consequences of Musketeer. The Prime Minister was not going to be easily swayed because he was convinced that the Egyptians would not fight. Mountbatten and his colleagues were not going to give in. After heated discussion, Eden cautiously assented to discuss the matter at a Cabinet meeting that afternoon. As a result the Cabinet ordered the Chiefs of Staff to draft a modified plan and on 10 September 1956, the Joint Task Force Commanders were instructed to prepare plans for Op Musketeer Revise – an assault on Port Said. At a stroke, the Alexandria plan was dead.

Muddled political thinking steadily created a climate of indecision and confusion. Anthony Eden, the Prime Minister, was physically unwell and flustered. Slowly but surely, Eden closed down the opportunity for close political scrutiny, drawing the strands of planning to an extremely limited constituency under his personal direction. This behaviour was mirrored further down the chain. Sir Gladwyn Jebb, British Ambassador in Paris, wrote in relation to a meeting between the Foreign Secretary, Selwyn Lloyd, and the French Prime Minister, Guy Mollet: 'It is, I believe, a novel arrangement for diplomatic business of the highest importance to be conducted by the principals without any official being present.'

Lloyd wrote down an account of the meeting two days later and there was no other official record. Sir Anthony Nutting, who read it thirty years afterwards, described it as 'a shocking attempt to mislead future historians'.

Eden was doing the same thing. Teddy's diary for Friday 26 October 1956 reads:

The end of a most intensive ten days - the history of which may never be written. Everything done on the basis of Prime Minister, Foreign Secretary, COS, Hobbs (Major General G (Pooh) Hobbs) and myself and all in manuscript.

None of the key players were aware that Eden had been secretly hospitalised from 5 to 8 October. He had been susceptible to infection ever since his bile duct was damaged during an operation for gallstones in 1953. His abdominal infection became so agonising that he was admitted to hospital with a temperature reaching 106°F. More importantly, he was prescribed a powerful combination of amphetamines and barbiturates called Drinamyl. Better known in post–war Britain as 'purple hearts', they can impair judgement, cause paranoia and even make the person taking them lose contact with reality. Drinamyl was banned in 1978. Most commentators accept that the drugs were a significant contributory factor in Eden's misjudgement of the Suez crisis.

Keith Kyle, in his excellent and detailed account of Suez, wrote :'It becomes extremely important to know who had access to how much information in the ensuing days (after 16 October). Even now one cannot be quite certain. But it seems unlikely, for example, that the Chiefs of Staff or General Sir Charles Keightley were told in a direct way that action against Egypt was being co-ordinated with the Israelis. It seems that they were given information in line with the Lloyd version of what happened in Paris on 16 October. Others below the rank of Chiefs of Staff or allied Commander-in-Chief were not in the know including, supposedly, the Vice Chiefs of Staff and the Task Force commanders'.

The CAS, Dermot Boyle, sympathised with the Commander-in-Chief Middle East Air Forces, who justifiably complained about his isolation from planned operations in his command area. He cabled Patch on 27 October 1956:

I appreciate the complexity of the present situation and the worry it must be causing you. When you have seen Hudleston, who is coming out tonight, situation will be much clearer.

Teddy arrived at Nicosia at 6.30 am on Sunday 28 October and was briefing Air Marshal Hubert ('Sam') Patch by 8 am. The clarity was that Cordage was to be abandoned in favour of Musketeer. Teddy's role was the sensitive selection of those targets which would defeat the Egyptians without too great a loss of life. His first task, though, was to authorise aerial reconnaissance over Cairo.

Shortly after his arrival on 30 October, the Land Force Commander found that the concept of operations had changed. Teddy's diary noted:

Utmost confusion throughout the day about start of operations. Much wavering and demands made regardless of military requirements or recognition of operating difficulties. Much delay on signals - up to two hours to flash [the fastest form of signal in 1956, which should have been immediate]. *Astonishing ignorance re Israeli activities. Complete breakdown of photographic reconnaissance processing facilities.*

Allied Force Headquarters announced that the psychological warfare campaign was not to take place, and that the Allied Air Forces were to concentrate their attacks solely on military targets. In broad outline, the concept of air operations was high-level bombing attacks at night by Valiant and Canberra aircraft from Malta and Cyprus against Egyptian airfields, and daylight attacks against airfields and other military targets by the carrier-based aircraft operating from the Allied carrier group stationed some 100 miles offshore from Egypt, and by land-based fighter/ground attack aircraft from Cyprus. Despite the extensive planning, there remained misunderstanding between commanders, and Teddy quietly recorded the difficult conversation between the C-in-C and Air Marshal Denis Barnett on the conduct of air operations and action in daylight.

The Allied Air Forces achieved mixed results. Some photographs purported to show the success of their bombing, but it is generally recognised that the high-level bombing by Canberras and Valiants was not at all accurate. Nevertheless, only on two occasions did any aircraft of the Egyptian Air Force take off and engage them. In the period of 48 hours, as visualised as far back as August, the Egyptian Air Force had been completely neutralised.

But people back in London were extremely edgy. This signal late on 1 November reveals the thinking:

Flash - Top Secret Terrapin. Originator's number DEF/4847. From MINDEF to AFHQ. Exclusive for General Keightley from Ministry of Defence. For urgent political reasons you should avoid heavy ARMY casualties which might result from attacking large occupied personnel camps and such targets during overnight November 2/3. Distribution to MA to C-in-C, CofS, CofS (Air), Political advisor.

Teddy was vastly amused by this, noting that it must be unique in military history to receive orders not to attack the enemy's Army during active operations. The continuing sense of muddle and political interference was not easy to cope with and the announcement of a ceasefire on 5 November, which was greeted with great jubilation and statements in Parliament, was followed by total consternation when the Egyptians rejected it at 9 pm the same day . Teddy observed:

More orders re no bombing. Must be the oddest war to happen outside South America.

Support from the Air Ministry was solid, however. Air Vice-Marshal Ronnie Lees, who was ACAS (Ops) and a fellow Australian, wrote to Teddy on 3 Nov 1956 a letter full of vitality and helpfulness. It ended:

I think you must have been near to despair on many occasions, I know I was, at the constant directions and changes of mind and heart which went on. The attack on Cairo International caused us a little flutter. So far it has apparently gone unnoticed, and we're not drawing attention to it. Not that it really matters of course but just at the time the anti-casualty brigade are pretty fussy.

In his diary, Teddy noted the lessons he had drawn from the operation:

National Policy: Clearly not a matter for the chiefs of Staff but the impact of national and world opinion over the conduct of Musketeer was so immediate and direct that it has to be scrutinised. In an age when the critical balance of world power lies outside the United Kingdom, it is evident that HMG can no longer initiate military action to achieve a political end.

Limited War. Even where action has full national support and US and Commonwealth opinion is at least not hostile, it is doubtful if the weight of non-hostile world opinion can be held in favourable balance for more than a few days.

This all led up to Propaganda and Psychological Warfare (PW). The national and world reaction to our action in Egypt was far quicker and more unanimous that anything envisaged. This emphasised the inadequacy of our PW, the shortcomings of which were never more apparent than after the fighting had ceased. Before the ceasefire, our efforts were confined to broadcasts and warnings. Leaflets were prepared daily but for tactical reasons, without exception, were never dropped. Radio was inadequate and was further handicapped by the defection of the British Manager of SHARQ and the unreliability of the Arabic speaking broadcasters. Despite these setbacks, it is doubtful if a more professional organisation would have made any more significant a contribution

The real weakness of the organisation showed itself after the ceasefire. Guidance from London was conspicuous by its absence, yet any local broadcasts had to be made within the concept of the long term policy of HMG. We lacked script writers. No film unit existed. No detail of Egyptian allegations was available, and no active counter propaganda existed. Indeed, our PW machinery was not only wholly inadequate but handling in London, as seen from Allied Force HQ, reflect inefficient amateurism at its worst. The harm which has resulted will take years to eradicate.

The lack of a clear strategic purpose and the swift resistance of the international community, particularly the Americans, meant that the Musketeer debacle irreparably damaged politicians, notably the Prime Minister, who resigned in January 1957. Relations with France and Israel were severely damaged because Eden called a ceasefire without notifying French or Israeli officials. But tactical performance on the ground was effective, so soldiers, sailors and airmen emerged with their reputations firmly intact. Teddy earned his fifth Mention in Despatches and a year later the French recognised him with a Croix de Guerre with Palms and he became an Officer of the Legion d'Honneur.

His role as the Chief of Staff (Air) for Operation Musketeer lasted well beyond the end of hostilities and he formally left the post in July 1957. Long before that, however, he was put in charge of a working party tasked with the review of the future organisation of the defence services. Two of his team of three civil servants and two airmen were colleagues from earlier postings: Air Vice-Marshal Herbert Kirkpatrick had been the Personal Assistant to the AOC RAF India in 1935, and Air Commodore Jack Davis had been in Turkey when Teddy was there in 1940/41.

With early notice that he would be the next VCAS, he attended his first meeting of the Air Council on Wednesday 22 May 1957, during which he presented the results of his working party's studies. The meeting was chaired by Rt Hon. George

Ward, MP, Secretary of State for Air. The CAS, Dermot Boyle, was present, as were Air Marshal Sir John Whitley, Air Member for Personnel, and Air Chief Marshal Sir Donald Hardman, who was Air Member for Supply and Organisation, along with a range of civil servants.

The thrust of Teddy's presentation was that there was a prima facie case for a unified defence department, although it was crucial that each service retain its own identity. The term 'prima facie' led to extended debate. R.H. Melville, the very experienced Assistant Undersecretary of State (Air Staff) (AUS(A)), disagreed with the term, although he did agree with the tenor of the working party's conclusions. As it turned out, he was a lone voice, because the remainder of the Air Council largely agreed with Teddy's thinking. Nevertheless, Sir Maurice Dean, the Permanent Under Secretary, suggested that the Council should take further time to consider the implications before coming to any firm decisions.

With time in hand to prepare himself thoroughly, Teddy conceived a plan to visit RAF commands in the Middle and Far East, taking an additional loop via Australia, which he had not visited since he left home as a seventeen-year-old in 1926. Accompanied by Wing Commander G.K. Birch and an ADC, Flight Lieutenant C. J. Petheram, as far as Singapore, the team left England on 15 July and returned at the end of August 1957. Petheram had often flown Teddy to visit outlying stations when he was in No 3. Group in 1954 and 1955, including several ten-minute flights from Mildenhall to Marham, which was a mere 29 miles by road.

On 16 September 1957 Teddy's nomination as the next Vice

Chief of the Air Staff (VCAS) was published formally and he was granted the acting rank of Air Marshal once again. At the age of 48, he was still below the average age for promotion (50 years and 10 months) and his career was back on track.

The announcement of Teddy's appointment as VCAS was greeted with widespread enthusiasm. Letters arrived from people as disparate as General Lauris Norstad (SACEUR), his old friend and mentor Air Chief Marshal Sir James Robb, himself a former VCAS, and Julian Amery, who was Under Secretary of State for War, and would become Secretary of State for Air in 1960. Amery had worked with Nan in the intelligence section of HQME and was to remain a lifelong friend.

Superficially, this was a marvellous appointment for Teddy. VCAS was the man who ran the internal affairs of the Air Force while the Chief of the Air Staff (CAS) did the political, outward looking work. He and Dermot Boyle rubbed along quite well and had known each other since the late 1920s, first when Teddy was a student at the Central Flying School where Boyle was a young instructor, then when they were both flying instructors at Cranwell. They overlapped for more than two years in India. From time to time Teddy held a more senior rank than Boyle, notably in late 1944 and early 1945 when Boyle was SASO to Harry Broadhurst at 83 Group and Teddy was AOC of 84 Group. They attended the same course at the Imperial Defence College (IDC) in 1946 and Boyle had taken over from Teddy as AOC No. 1 Group in April 1951 when Teddy was posted to a staff job at SHAPE after only eight months (Boyle was Director General of Manning for the same eight months). But Boyle was four years older and had the benefit of many operational commands, not least of which was AOC-in-C Fighter Command, which he held from 7 April 1953 until he became CAS on 1 January 1956. Whatever chances Teddy may have had of becoming CAS, Boyle was always going to get there before him.

Boyle clearly thought highly of Teddy's strategic and management skills, because he had personally selected him for the task of representing national and Air Force interests at the highest level in the lead up to Operation Musketeer and then supported his appointment as VCAS.

Teddy's predecessor had been in post for just over four years. Sir Ronald Ivelaw-Chapman had enlisted in the Army in 1917 while still a pupil at Cheltenham College. He became a 3rd Class Air Mechanic on his 18th birthday but swiftly went on to officer training and gained his wings on 11 January 1918. By chance he was on air patrol on the Western Front from 1030-11.15 am on 11 November 1918, which became one of the final operational flights of the First World War. He had two other unusual claims to fame, because twice in his career he became the prisoner of an enemy. During his two years in Iraq he was involved in the evacuation of personnel from the British Legation in Kabul to India as a result of the civil unrest in Afghanistan at the time. Whilst flying Victoria J7926, he suffered engine problems which resulted in him having to make a forced landing. He was captured by the rebels and held from 29 January to 18 February 1929 before being released, later being awarded the AFC for his work during this operation.

Granted permission to accompany one of his crews on operations on the night of 6th May 1944, his aircraft was hit by a night fighter and the crew ordered to bale out. Only two of the crew managed to leave the aircraft, one being the bomb aimer, ~~Sergeant Ford and the other being Air Commodore~~ Ivelaw-Chapman. Ivelaw-Chapman reached the ground safely and was able to get in touch with the local resistance. Plans were set in motion to recover him and fly him back to England. When Churchill heard that Ivelaw-Chapman had been shot down, he issued an order that he should be killed if there was any danger of him being captured because of his knowledge of the plans for the impending invasion. Fortunately for Ivelaw-Chapman, he managed to avoid capture and following the invasion on 6 June 1944, the information he held was no longer compromising. But rescue eluded him and he was eventually captured hiding in a French farm two days after D-Day. He was released by the Americans in April 1945 and made his way back to England.

Teddy's feet were firmly under the desk by the time he assumed his new appointment. This was the ideal job for a man of his experience and calibre; his knowledge of the Whitehall machine was invaluable. The vast majority of senior colleagues in all three services knew him, or knew of him. His intellect was highly respected and it was common knowledge that the current US President, Eisenhower, and SACEUR, Lauris Norstad, both held him in the highest esteem.

The workload for VCAS and his staff was enormous. The paper trail was studied formally in 1962. That revealed that in 1957 more than 10,000 documents passed through VCAS' office. This grew steadily and in 1961 the figure amounted to a little more than 19,000. Clearly Teddy did not see them all, but his staff had to manage the flow, ensuring that the boss saw what he had to see and was properly briefed.

But the paper merely preceded or followed interaction with colleagues in Whitehall and the wider RAF. Teddy sat on the Air Council, the Air Council Standing Committee, the Chiefs of Staff Committee, the British Nuclear Deterrent Study Group, the Joint Global War Committee, the Sea/Air Warfare Committee, and the Air/Land Warfare Committee. Frequently he deputised for Dermot Boyle by attending the Defence Committee. In order to assimilate the depth of their discussions, he occasionally attended meetings of the Joint Planning Staff. And as if this was not enough, he was co-opted onto the Air Traffic Control Committee, the Euro Control Committee and the Military Board of Control.

The frenetic activity in meeting rooms was often focused on specific subjects which Teddy, as VCAS, was responsible for driving. And although the chairmanship of committees tended to rotate, he seems to have chaired more often than his colleagues, evidently because he did it so well. There is impressive evidence in the minutes of meetings that reveals the breadth and depth of the preparatory work which the chairman completed in order to chair effectively.

Teddy was not present at the Chiefs of Staff Committee meeting on 1 November 1957, which had been convened to discuss aspects of the defence programme which individual service heads considered worthy of more detailed examination in order to avoid significant differences of opinion between them. CIGS, Sir Gerald Templer, tabled a paper which proposed a different approach. He asked that each service head should write a paper from his own perspective on the role of the armed forces as a whole. After a short discussion, they all agreed to deal with the matter urgently. The follow up meeting on 7 November was not what the members anticipated; the heat of the debate is still tangible 57 years later.

Within seconds CIGS said that there were aspects of CAS' paper with which he could never agree. He said that he had always subscribed to the principle of the nuclear deterrent, but he could not accept the idea that the nuclear force should remain inviolate in any future defence cuts. Nor could he accept the statement that 'the nuclear retaliatory force itself was the most powerful cold war military weapon'. Dermot Boyle adopted a calming stance, saying that he could understand CIGS concern but the paper he had prepared was a straightforward and honest expression of his views and those of the Air Ministry. This meant that he could not alter his view of the role of the armed forces in the current era of scientific development to suit varying financial and economic considerations.

Sir William Dickson was chairing the meeting and was less than robust. In the face of CIGS anger, his instinct was to retreat. There was no discussion at all about the papers written by CIGS and the First Sea Lord and the committee agreed not to attempt to coordinate the three separate documents. Instead Dickson proposed to write a paper which would try to compromise and balance the divergent views of the three services. Very abruptly, the most urgent item on the agenda for the Chiefs of Staff was further delayed. He agreed also to ask the Joint Intelligence Committee to write a paper on world trends.

The Committee discussed the Chairman's paper on 12 November. CIGS remained bullish and strongly resisted any notion that the Army might reduce to 120,000. He accepted that it might reduce to 135,000 in 1963, but it should be back at 165,000 by 1970. CAS was equally direct. He 'strongly deprecated' any further cuts in the main deterrent force, which had been reduced already from 240 to 144 V bombers'. Sir William Dickson observed that the basis of his paper was that the Chiefs of Staff most strongly advised against further cuts in their services but if the Government ordered that it would happen, they must be prepared to indicate where cuts could be made with the least damage to the defence programme.

The areas of national and international life studied by the Chiefs of Staff were astonishing. In December 1957 the British Ambassador to Washington, Sir Harold Caccia, attended a meeting of the Chiefs of Staff at which Teddy was representing CAS. The key matters for discussion were the difficulties of dealing with the American administration as a result of the President's recent stroke (on 25 November 1957), and the potential for persuading the USA to amend the terms of the McMahon Act (the Atomic Energy Act of 1946). Teddy pointed out that the British Joint Intelligence Committee (JIC) had proved to be far more accurate than the Americans in predicting Soviet nuclear ability. They had accurately forecasted the first Soviet nuclear explosion. It would be a good plan to share the JIC current estimates with the Americans. Britain was having difficulty in financing the research and development programme, so this collaboration might encourage a willingness to amend the Act.

In the same week, the Committee commissioned the Joint Planning Staff to prepare thoughts on joint US/UK action in Jordan and Lebanon. Most unusually the Planning Staff felt obliged to express strong reservations about drafting military plans without the benefit of a political concept.

Issues of the day in 1958 included the possible evacuation of Commonwealth nationals from Indonesia, Pakistani naval policy, the order of battle for Burma's armed forces, developments in the Arabian peninsula over the next five years, United Kingdom representation at SHAPE, the outline plan for German reunification and European security arrangements, Hong Kong, Oman, Libya, the Air Defence of Europe, IRBM and the likelihood of global war between the Sino-Soviet Bloc and the free world. These 'big picture' issues concealed the bread and butter of the defence of the realm, with constant struggles over budget management and inter-service competition for scarce resources.

Looking back down the tunnel of more than fifty years, few would imagine that the Chiefs of Staff were considering the outline plan for German reunification in 1958. The issue had been formally presented to the Western Powers at a conference in Geneva in October 1955. Reunification proved to be delayed for more than 35 years.

The discussion about United Kingdom representation at SHAPE was Teddy's special subject, having been one of the founding fathers of the organisation and having held the specific appointment under review. The concern of the Chiefs of Staff was that Hugh Constantine would be removed from the HQ by virtue of SACEUR's plan to disestablish the post of Deputy Chief of Staff Plans and Policy. Teddy told the meeting that apart from SACEUR and his Chief of Staff, the Deputy CoS (Plans & Policy) was the most influential post in SHAPE. He was virtually responsible for the organisation and control of the HQ, since SACEUR and his CoS were heavily committed in the political field. Moreover, the role involved access to intelligence material which could be shared only with US and UK officers. It would make life very complicated if a German had the post. He provided food for thought by suggesting that if the objective were to satisfy the Germans with high-profile appointments, SACEUR might consider placing a German as the Principal Staff Officer to General Gale in his capacity as Land Deputy, and it might also be possible to appoint a German deputy to the C-in-C Allied Air Forces Central Europe.

Good as he was, Teddy did not win every argument. In February 1958 the Chiefs of Staff discussed future areas of responsibility in the Middle East Theatre. He stated that the basic issue was whether responsibility for the Somaliland Protectorate should remain with the Arabian Peninsula Command, as proposed by the Joint Planning staff, or whether the GOC East Africa should assume responsibility for the area as proposed by the British Defence Coordination Committee. In his view, the Commander British Forces Arabian Peninsula was already somewhat overloaded since he had to serve two political authorities separated by about 1,000 miles. If he remained responsible for the Somaliland area in addition, he would have to devote some of his time to that area to the detriment of the rest. CIGS and CNS disagreed with him and felt it should stay with Commander Arabian Peninsula, although CNS felt that it merited a three-star appointment. CDS opted to go with the Army and Navy view, acknowledging that all air support for Somaliland would have to come from Aden anyway.

As is the way with senior officers and foreign honours, the rewards for the Suez campaign were bestowed on Teddy on 15 April 1958 when he received the French Croix de Guerre with Palms and became an Officer of the Legion d'Honneur. This added agreeably to a chest already densely decorated in medals.

Two more awards would follow in due course. On 18 September 1962 he became an Air ADC to the Queen, and on 1 January 1963 his KCB was elevated to Knight Grand Cross of the Order of the Bath (GCB).

In June 1958 the debate about the nuclear deterrent continued to simmer. CAS believed that it was sufficient to deter global war and limited war in any part of the world. The First Sea Lord and CIGS disagreed, because they thought the Soviet Union believed that the West would resist deploying nuclear weapons. This might cause limited wars to escalate. CAS stated that he did not see this disagreement as inter-service rivalry, but merely the intellectual debate needed for a very complex subject.

Two days later the Committee considered the co-ordination of Anglo/American nuclear strike plans. A policy paper of October 1957 had set the broad principles for Bomber Command's (BC) activity. More recent discussions with the US Strategic Air Command (SAC) had found, unsurprisingly, that SAC and BC targets were generally duplicated. Moreover, both commands had doubled up strikes in order to ensure success. This had now been rationalised with each command clear about its primary and secondary targets. The Chiefs of Staff believed that they had full coverage of all key Soviet targets.

In April 1958 the British Governor of Aden, Sir William

Luce, had learned from a secret source that the Sultan of Lahej was considering joining the United Arab Republic under pressure from the three Jifri brothers, who were notorious trouble makers. Thinking that he had ample time to secure an arrest and deportation, operations were put in hand but the Governor then discovered that Mohammed Ali Jifri was planning to leave Aden immediately after Ramadan, which would foil the Governor's scheme. Although he planned to use the Aden police for the arrest, he considered that he needed a battalion of infantry to support them. He preferred not to call upon a battalion in Kenya, but sought the permission of the Chiefs of Staff to have the Parachute Regiment fly out from England. The request was denied, but internal security at Lahej remained an issue and the Commander British Forces Arabian Peninsula, Air Vice-Marshal Maurice Heath, continued to ask for reinforcements. Happily Teddy, who was chairing the meeting in early June, and VCIGS were in agreement with the findings of the Joint Planning Committee, who did not perceive a need for reinforcements.

Admiral Sir Caspar John chaired the Chiefs of Staff meeting of 28 November 1958. Teddy and Sir William Stratton, VCIGS, completed the Committee. In attendance was Lieutenant General Sir Roddie McLeod, Deputy Chief of the Defence Staff (DCDS) and Sir Frederick Brundrett, the Chairman of the Defence Research Policy Committee. The main item on the agenda was the second generation of Intermediate Range Ballistic Missiles (IRBM). This was a most important discussion. Teddy led the debate by saying that it had become clear that the United States were not going to develop a second generation of IRBM and that the United Kingdom would therefore have to do so themselves. Blue Streak was the only development and it would obviously be of advantage to the United Kingdom if the weapon could be sold to other NATO countries. The range of Blue Streak would admittedly be more than essential for European countries, but it was worth noting that excess range could be traded for increased payload and warhead.

Curiously Sir Frederick Brundrett had proposed a rocket with a range of about 1250 miles, which would not be suitable as a deterrent based in the United Kingdom. If NATO accepted Sir Frederick's proposal, the UK would still be left with the need to develop their own, with no prospect of sharing it. The Chiefs of Staff had considered range before. 1500 miles meant that 98% of targets could be attacked from bases in NATO countries and 75% from within the United Kingdom.

The irony is that Blue Streak never entered full production. The project was intended to maintain an independent British nuclear deterrent, replacing the V bomber fleet which would become obsolete by 1965. The operational requirement for the missile was issued in 1955 and the design was complete by 1957, but it became clear that the missile system was too expensive and too vulnerable to a pre-emptive strike. The Chiefs of Staff focused on the cancellation of the missile in early February and agreed that it was not a viable strategic deterrent. Tom Pike objected to the impact that the cancellation might have on the nation's ability to enter into space research, where military dividends might be considerable. Guidance on the costs for developing Blue Streak as a space research vehicle were conflicting. The project was cancelled in 1960, with US-led Skybolt becoming the preferred replacement.

Satellites and the deterrent remained on the agenda. In a note to Hayne Constant, the Scientific Adviser to the Air Ministry, in August 1960, Teddy felt the need for further discussion about the development potential of Skybolt and Polaris in terms of range and warhead. He was also anxious to define the possibility of a scientific breakthrough with random search equipment on fixed-wing aircraft, which would make the submarine too vulnerable. He wanted to give serious thought to manned and unmanned satellite platforms carrying destructive weapons, and asked the Scientific Adviser to prepare a paper not later than 1 December 1960 which would assume that the satellite force would be required by 1970/75 and that it would have a multi-weapon capacity of 5 to 10 weapons. Launch options and costs were to be offered only in terms of magnitude.

Disagreement among the participants did not necessarily mean outright conflict. Sir William Stratton and Teddy probably rather enjoyed their differing stances at a meeting chaired by CDS on 4 December 1958. After discussing intelligence targets and the likelihood of global war between the Sino-Soviet Bloc and the free world, they moved on to the subject of responsibility for the air defence of forces in the field: VCIGS and VCAS disagreed with each other about how and when to provide air cover. Teddy judged that only a small military force could operate without air protection and he could not visualise the Army ever operating in strength beyond the cover of land or water-based aircraft. Sir William Stratton did not agree that the size of the land force was a criterion. Nor did he agree that the effective range of fighter defences was a major factor. He then contradicted himself by saying that in all operations there were certain points for which an effective air defence was essential, but he used this to bolster his argument that the Army should always have available weapons for anti-aircraft defence. The VCNS, Sir Caspar John, said that whatever their views on the ability of fighter defences to meet the needs of ground forces under all circumstances, there were distinct advantages in giving the Army its own mobile weapon, since this would contribute to the flexible employment of our forces.

Goodwill was restored on the subject of tactical transport aircraft. Here Teddy agreed with VCIGS that it was a military requirement to have the capacity to drop two battalions of soldiers at the same time.

Throughout 1959 Teddy's voice prevailed on most subjects before the Chiefs of Staff. The issues were diverse. At his instigation, CDS called for research into the impact of nuclear weapons on communications. He challenged the extent of the Army requirement for utility and light cargo aircraft. They wanted to be able to have enough VTOL and STOL aircraft to be able to lift simultaneously 10 infantry companies (two in each of five active theatres). The Army calculated that this would mean 154 VTOL and STOL aircraft by 1965. Teddy judged that it would take 250 aircraft to achieve the objective and he questioned the need to simultaneously lift two companies in England and two in BAOR (British Army Of the Rhine), because it would be possible to reinforce one theatre from the other for exercise purposes. Mr Richard Chilver, the Deputy Secretary at the Ministry of Defence, interjected that if the Army requirement were to be satisfied, it would entail cuts elsewhere. As was common at the time, CDS thought that this merited another detailed study and no decision was made.

Teddy noted that the plan was to remove all fighter squadrons from Germany in 1960/61 on the assumption that the German air force expansion took place as planned. At the moment it was behind schedule and the UK might be pressed to retain squadrons in Germany after the planned withdrawal date. Another thorny subject was the rundown of BAOR, which was to be reduced to five Brigade Groups. The process was due to start on 1 January 1960. It was possible to maintain seven Brigade Groups until the end of 1960 if it was accepted that the strategic reserve in the UK should consist of no more than one Parachute Brigade and three Infantry Brigade Groups.

He had a very close personal interest in the Directive for the C-in-C British Forces Arabian Peninsula, because he knew he was in line for the appointment. The directive defined the operational area as Aden Colony and Protectorate, the Somaliland Protectorate, the Sultanate of Muscat and Oman, the Trucial Sheikhdoms, the Sheikhdoms of Bahrein, Qatar, Kuwait and the Kuwait neutral zone, the Persian Gulf, the coastal waters of the Arabian Peninsula and the Somaliland Protectorate, the coastal waters of South Iran and West Pakistan for maritime air support of the Baghdad Pact. Areas of general interest included East Africa, The Seychelles and Mauritius, Saudi Arabia, Yemen, Ethiopia, French Somaliland, Somalia, The Sudan, Iraq, Iran, United Arab Republic, Jordan, Afghanistan and Pakistan.

The strategic aims of the command were the security of the oil-producing areas in the Persian Gulf, the security of bases and sea and air communications, security against both external attack and internal subversion, and support for the Baghdad Pact.

Teddy formulated the view of the committee on the issue

of authority for initiating warlike operations and SACEURs military alerts.. He noted that if the declaration of war was preceded by the orderly implementation of SACEUR's Alert System, the draft paper prepared by Sir Richard Powell covered most eventualities. But neither this, nor the papers originally circulated appeared to cover the more difficult situation of a sudden emergency with no warning, followed almost immediately by war. It was desirable to mention this in the instructions to be sent to British Commanders, who should never be put in the position of having to refuse to take action on an order from his NATO supreme commander.

He was the main speaker in July when the Committee studied a report on the next decade in Africa. He was concerned that there were many risks inherent in too much 'compartmentation' in the long-term studies on policy or strategy for particular areas. He had hoped that the Africa (Official) Committee would have expanded their paper to take account of events in other areas of the world which could have a profound effect on the policy of the west towards Africa south of the Sahara over the next ten years. He hoped that a study might be prepared relating to the three recent long-term studies on Arabia, the Levant and Africa south of the Sahara. Recent improvements in the speed of communication and of dissemination of news might mean, for example, that events in Kuwait could influence developments in West Africa.

Mr Wright of the MoD said that the Africa (Official) Committee had considered at some length possible ways of inter-relating the assorted long-term studies now in progress, but they had come to the conclusion that it was not practicable to weave them all together. They had decided to go into the individual detail of each area, then relate them to each other in the recently initiated UK review of policy.

The Chiefs of Staff deployed an attractive technique of inviting important figures to attend their meetings to discuss issues of the day. In October 1960 CDS, Lord Mountbatten, welcomed General Valluy, Commander in Chief Allied Forces Central Europe and Air Chief Marshal Sir Harry Broadhurst, C-in-C Allied Air Forces Central Europe.

Valluy was asked for his view of the world. He said he was concerned at three levels: thermonuclear war, limited war and cold war. He then sketched out his views on each. Of course thermonuclear war, while being the worst case scenario, was also the least likely, because there was a form of mutual deterrent. It is interesting that he did not talk about Mutual Assured Destruction (MAD). The term had been coined by the brilliant Hungarian-American John von Neumann (1903-1957), who had a taste for humorous acronyms. Valluy did not imagine that any limited war could be contained, but equally he did not see it on the central front. No, it was Cold War which the Soviets were focusing upon. It was very difficult to identify and counteract. The objective was to persuade Germany to leave NATO. This would seriously affect the West's ability to counteract global or limited war. General Valluy's opinion was that, notwithstanding the physical resources, the single most important factor in the strength of the Western position was attitude of mind.

He discussed certain key issues. Intelligence was fragmented, and what tended to happen was that individual nations deployed their intelligence effort, which was then forwarded in an evaluated form towards SHAPE, where a centralised slant was applied. The trouble was that each nation weighed its information differently, so the results were not only late but often inaccurate.

It was troubling too that air defence was so poor. Not only was SHAPE's force 200 aircraft short of the agreed level, but nations were clearly keeping aircraft in reserve for their own national defence. On the ground, he was still 10 Divisions short of the agreed level.

Teddy chaired almost every meeting of the Chiefs of Staff from January to June 1960 unless Mountbatten was attending. In March one interesting item was the Defence implications of the definition of where outer space began. The planning committee proposed some interesting zonal segmentation: up to 20 miles above the earth would be national sovereignty, 21 miles to 2000 miles would be a temporary buffer zone until someone could properly define outer space, and level three was 2001 miles and upwards, on the basis that an ICBM travelling 6,000 miles would reach a maximum altitude of 1500 miles. The extra 500 miles had been added on 'for good measure'! In a fascinating table of heights and measures, the report tabulated the height of various weapons and vehicles: Bloodhound 12.5 miles; Bluestreak 1200 miles; Sputnik 1 145-560 miles; Sputnik II 140-1017 miles; Explorer I 221-1578 miles; Vanguard I 403-2463 miles. A year later, Teddy revisited the question of outer space and stated firmly that they ought to be thinking 15 to 20 years in the future. In his view, outer space would become an extremely important highway and it was only because the Chiefs of Staff committee had pushed it that the US Joint Chiefs of Staff had taken any interest.

The variety of issues remained a constant enjoyment. At the meeting on 7 April 1960, the agenda included Defence and internal security in the British Cameroons; Psychological Warfare; the strategic importance of Malta; the situation in British Somaliland and the post of Deputy Chief of Staff at 2ATAF. The team was incredibly well briefed on every subject that might affect the defence and welfare of the United Kingdom and Commonwealth.

In October Sir Frank Roberts, who was completing his term of office as the UK permanent representative on the North Atlantic Council and was about to become the Ambassador to the USSR, reported to the Committee that the relationship between France and Germany in NATO was so bad that Dr Adenauer was not willing to meet General de Gaulle for discussions. The position had been aggravated by certain actions of General Challe, then C-in-C Allied Forces Central Europe. This included the manner in which he was handling his proposed alterations to the command structure in Fontainebleau, the views he expressed on strategy in Germany, notably his plan for the erection along the border of a wire fence backed by atomic mines for the withdrawal of all French troops to France. He also proposed the reorganisation of German troops into a guerrilla-role basis. All of this caused complete dismay in Germany. One of Challe's proposals was to abandon the roles of Comlandcent and Comaircent. It is small wonder that he did not last long in the job (May 1960 to February 1961).

The French and Germans continued to exercise the minds of the Chiefs in November when they discussed contingency planning for Berlin. The underlying tensions within NATO were all too clear, with British and American politicians and soldiers deeply worried about leakage from French and German allies. The Chiefs of Staff considered that it would be best to brief CINCCENT (Challe) and CinCLandCent (Speidel) orally and definitely not on paper.

The Committee noted also that there would come a point at which all NATO Allies would have to be engaged. It was certain that the Russians would then learn about the plans, although they acknowledged that this was not necessarily a bad thing.

Seven months later Sir Frank Roberts expressed genuine concern that there could be a grave miscalculation about action and reaction in Berlin. The US did not believe that the USSR would force the issue to the point of war. But the USSR did not believe the USA declaration that they were ready to go to nuclear war was any more than bluff. Sir Frank felt that the time had come to persuade Mr Krushchev of American determination. The Committee asked the Director of Forward Plans to prepare a paper on the issue.

The Committee studied the paper on 18 July and CDS (Mountbatten) said firmly that this was a political issue which should be passed to the Foreign Office. Sir Evelyn Shuckburgh of the Foreign Office said that they were studying the matter already and were pleased that the Chiefs of Staff acknowledged the political obligations.

The levels of candour and deceit in government and the

defence of the realm were revealed in a confidential annex to a top secret document which was also given specially restricted circulation in February 1961. Teddy led the discussion on the whole issue of the British attitude towards SEATO planning. In his view, British planning to date had been largely 'in the nature of a façade.' He judged that the Asian members would not be prepared to accept this for much longer. Their representatives in SEATO were high-grade, knowledgeable officers and officials. Sooner or later they would force a showdown on Britain and the USA's real intentions. The lack of effective security in SEATO could not be quoted as an argument against more realistic planning; in fact it was probably no worse than in NATO. Mr Warner of the Foreign Office, accepting that this was really a political problem, felt that the USA would never agree to divulge to SEATO anything of their real plans. He judged that from a political perspective there was much to be said for allowing SEATO planning to continue along the present lines and, in a phrase which was later excised from the minutes, the Foreign Office would not wish to hasten an approach to more realistic planning.

The problem was that Teddy remained as VCAS for a little under four and a half years. This was at least twice the time he should have been there. Few people knew that he had been offered the post of AOC-in-C British Forces Arabian Peninsula in 1960. It was an important strategic command, which would metamorphose in 1961 into Middle East Command. In career terms, the appointment would have given him the credibility to be considered as CAS after Boyle's immediate successor.

But this was, perhaps, the lowest point in the Hudleston

marriage. The flat at Eaton Place was constantly tense with squabbles and high-octane rows. When Nan heard about the proposal to move to Aden, she bluntly refused to go. 'Take Sally or Pip as your hostess,' she said, 'but I am not going.'

It didn't take Teddy long to act. He could not have failed to appreciate the significance of the decision, which would severely limit his future in the RAF. Nevertheless, he came home later in the week and announced that he had declined to take the job. He had recommended that Sam Elworthy be appointed instead. Sam Elworthy was a hugely worthy candidate in any event and it was he who went on to become CAS after Tom Pike. He also became CDS. But herein lies the evidence that Teddy would always promote the interests of the most able individuals, regardless of any personal cost to him. Elworthy almost certainly did not know the manoeuvring at the time. Indeed, he told his family that he detected the hand of Mountbatten in the choice. But when Teddy retired, Elworthy wrote a genuinely heartfelt letter of appreciation for the way in which Teddy had always supported his younger colleague.

...I think you are generally and very rightly regarded as the classic example of those of the younger generation who showed such brilliance during the War that they quickly rose to positions of great responsibility and then in them more than confirmed the promise.

But my second and main purpose in writing is very personally to thank you for having been such a valuable guide, philosopher and friend to me. I particularly remember becoming a member of the Air Council as DCAS - very junior, very raw and very unsure. Your help and advice were invaluable and I profited greatly from the example you set on how Whitehall business should be conducted. And then later, because I was not involved in the Whitehall battles and so did not incur the enmity of the prime contestants, but rather acquired favour as a pale promoter of a fashionable concept of command, I found myself appointed CAS. Though senior to me and possessed of greater qualifications and experience, you have never hinted to me that you thought this unjust. On the contrary, you have continued to serve the RAF wholly unselfishly and with your usual flair and skill. For this I am most grateful and I humbly acknowledge my indebtedness.

The Whitehall battles were grim. Indeed, Sir Tim Elworthy, Sam Elworthy's son, described them as 'vituperative'. Although the Chiefs of Staff maintained a patina of polite, professional engagement, their senior staff would go to extreme lengths to protect and enhance their own service. Writing to Fred Rosier, who delivered the tribute to Teddy at his memorial service, Cecil James said:

At the beginning, 1956/1957, the RAF was riding high. They were custodians of the nuclear deterrent, the key to its defence policy. Yet in a few short years, it all went horribly wrong to the point after Nassau in December 1962 that some of the more thoughtful people in the Air Ministry, which included Teddy, were worried about the continued independence of the RAF

Losing an empire is bound to be a painful process. The Army suffered from cutbacks, though nothing like the RAF with the traumatic reduction of Fighter Command to a few Squadrons: a mere UK airspace police force. The Navy came out much the best whereas if the logic of nuclear deterrence had been more rigorously followed, the Navy would have come out worse.

This leads me to the influence of Mountbatten, who was there as CNS and CDS for the whole period. He failed to shake Duncan

Sandys on the principle of the primacy of nuclear deterrence but he had a big influence over him and others over pretty well the full range of defence policy issues. What Teddy Hudleston had to contend with was, in effect, a continuous broad base review of policy. Or more precisely, there is a strong case for saying that it was a Broadlands based policy.

Teddy never cracked under what must have been insupportable pressure for more than four years: a strong man, physically, mentally, professionally. He could in more propitious circumstances have been a Portal. It is a pity that his time as VCAS was so bedevilled.

Teddy was strong and he clearly enjoyed the cut and thrust of Whitehall debate where he frequently found brains as agile as his own. Like many of the senior mandarins in the Service ministries, he did not trust Mountbatten who, he believed, would always promote the Navy's cause while protesting the need for a unified Ministry of Defence. Mountbatten opposed the Royal Air Force's development of the TSR2, believing that it would be less expensive and more effective for the navy and air force to concentrate on the same aeroplane, the Buccaneer. Teddy, on the other hand, was a strong advocate of TSR2 and fought his corner ferociously. Mountbatten also entered the nuclear debate, arguing against tactical nuclear weapons and the independent development of a British missile, and in favour of the American missile, Polaris.

The major preoccupation of these years, however, was a move to restructure completely the central organisation for defence. In October 1962, Mountbatten produced a paper recommending the abolition of the separate service ministries and the creation of a single, centralised Ministry of Defence, which would co-ordinate all three services. These controversial proposals were embodied in 1963 in a White Paper and the reorganisation took place shortly afterwards. In 1965, the three intelligence directorates also merged. Complete centralisation, however, was never achieved, as vestiges of the old service ministries remained within the new structure.

All of this internal conflict landed up on Teddy's desk precisely because he had the intellect to marshal counter arguments. He was dealing also with problems which his professional colleagues did not see. He accepted that he was the author of his own difficulties at home, where he felt isolated and unable to lighten the burden of his professional difficulties. Tim Elworthy recalled being at home in 1960 when Teddy dropped in for a drink with his father. After the visit, Sam Elworthy, who was then DCAS, commented that Teddy was extremely tired. It is tempting to believe that the visit was Teddy's discreet reconnaissance before declining the Middle East job. What the Elworthys perceived to be tiredness was indubitably the uncharacteristic loss of morale over ambition abandoned.

Family played a part in the background. Tony was commissioned into the Queen's Bays in 1957. Being colour-blind, he could not consider a career in the RAF and Johnny Collingwood was all too happy to recommend him for a commission in his old regiment. Subsequently the author, who was colour-blind too, followed his uncle and cousin into the same regiment, although by then it was known as 1st The Queen's Dragoon Guards after amalgamation with the King's Dragoon Guards in 1959.

Like any other young officer, Tony would occasionally go home for a few days. With Nan away at Cornhill, there was one splendid week during which father and son lived in the flat at 3 Eaton Place without either of them knowing that the other was there. Based in Wolfenbüttel, Tony swiftly acquired a German girlfriend, who he brought back to London for a week. Nobody was prepared to say with certainty that she was an East German spy, but she was discovered by Corporal Scott going through papers on Teddy's desk. Her holiday in London and her relationship with Tony came to an abrupt end.

More amusingly, the Hudleston's telephone number was Sloane 3443, while that of the Pakistani Youth Hostel was Sloane 3433. All too often young foreign visitors to London would dial the wrong number. As a result, when incoming calls were too frequent, members of the family would sometimes answer the phone saying 'Pakistani Youth Hostel, may I help you?' in a sing-song accent. Sal practised this one day when the caller turned out to be Tom Pike, who stiffly said that he was the Chief of the Air Staff and was hoping to speak to Sir Edmund Hudleston. By her own admission, she made an error in not continuing with the joke, and apologised. Sadly Tom Pike did not see the joke and his opinion of the Hudleston household must have plummeted.

The number of individuals who think they might make it to the top is far higher than those who actually do so. Entirely suitable candidates suddenly falter, while less obvious ones reach the top of the rostrum. There is more than a little evidence that much depends upon mentors and protégées from an early point in a service career – at least that was the case in the 1940s, 50s and 60s. Teddy's great mentor was 'Mary' Coningham, who was his instructor at Cranwell and then at the Central Flying School.

It was Coningham who picked Teddy out of the pack to be his SASO for the invasion of Italy, then who provided the significant leap to command 84 Group as a 35 year old Air Vice-Marshal. But Coningham was abruptly and some may say unjustly edged out of the Services at the end of the War and, although Teddy was known, respected and valued by Tedder, Slessor, Dickson and Boyle when they were CAS, none of them regarded him as their special protégée.

Tom Pike, on the other hand, was constantly close to the coat tails of William Dickson from 1926 when Dickson became his flight commander in 56 Squadron. Dickson was an instructor at the RAF Staff College when Pike went through as a student in 1937 (and when Teddy was there in 1938, for that matter). By good luck or hidden design, Pike had been SASO of the Desert Air Force for two months when Dickson arrived as AOC in April 1944 and they served together in the Air Ministry when Dickson was VCAS in 1946/1947, then again for a longer period after Dickson became CAS in January 1953. Writing on 26 March 1959 in response to Dickson's congratulatory letter about the announcement of Pike's appointment to be CAS from January 1960, Pike admitted:

I have served under you more than I have served with any other officer, and I owe much to your tutelage.

I even remember being instructed at Biggin Hill to read the leading article in The Times every day. I have generally done what you told me to do, but in this respect I have often lapsed - I still find The Times rather dull

I think you taught me more whilst I was DCAS than at any other time, and looking back I realise just how much I had to learn. I have always been grateful for your friendliness and I shall do my best to follow in your footsteps.

Dickson was still Chief of the Defence Staff at this time. His own mentor was Sir Geoffrey Salmond, for whom he served as PA in India in 1930/1931. Salmond went on to become CAS in 1933, but died within a month of taking office.

If there was any competition between Teddy and Tom Pike to become CAS, the latter was in a far stronger position, because he had someone in power to keep the door open. The killer blow for Teddy was his lack of operational experience as the commander of a fighter or bomber squadron, and a relative lack of flying experience (only three to four dedicated flying years in a forty-year career), whereas Tom Pike had commanded 219 Squadron in 1941 (for a mere seven months) and had ten years of flying experience before he rose to command or staff appointments. He had the additional advantage of being AOC-in-C Fighter Command from August 1956 until he was appointed CAS on 1 January 1960. Boyle's views on his successor as CAS would have clinched the deal: he believed most strongly that the top job should be held by someone with masses of flying experience. Valid as the conviction may be, the fact is that Boyle himself only ever commanded a Squadron for a total of nine months, although he did boast eleven years of active flying, mostly as an instructor. Curiously he commanded 83 Squadron on two separate occasions, first in 1937 for six months, then again from November 1940 for three months. He, too, was AOC-in-C Fighter Command before being appointed as CAS. Many airmen have said that it gave them comfort to have a boss who had run Fighter Command.

Teddy holds one record: he managed to achieve and hold Air rank for 24 years, with a break of just twenty-nine days in 1946 and without the hands-on operational experience expected for very senior commanders. Every time he had to relinquish acting rank, he was re-promoted immediately for specialist jobs. Very few people ever achieved anything near that length of service in Air Rank: Sir Edgar Ludlow-Hewitt, but for a four-year break from 1919 to 1923, would have done a straight 28 years; Sam Elworthy had a postwar break of seven years between 1946 and 1953 in the 27 between becoming an Air Commodore for the first time and retirement as Marshal of the Royal Air Force. Gus Walker experienced a break of eight years between 1946 and 1954 in the 27 from first appointment as an Air Commodore; and 'Bing' Cross had a six-year break in his 24 years. But all of these apart from Teddy had the invaluable track record of commanding operational squadrons.

External observers offered a good perspective of Teddy. Sir Frank Cooper wrote:

Ike's confidential report on Teddy was 'this is the best staff officer of any nation that has ever served under me at any time.

Dermot Boyle's image of Teddy was certainly that of a staff officer. He never thought Teddy flew enough himself or had enough of the fighting leadership which Dermot prized so highly. In fact they complemented each other.

It was Teddy who established the VCAS as the co-ordinator of the whole of Air Ministry planning...a process started under Jack Slessor and Ralph Cochrane. He was a hard but fair taskmaster.

Sir Michael Quinlan, who spent time as Tom Pike's Private Secretary, wrote:

Relations between Pike and Hudleston were amicable rather than cordial. Teddy was undoubtedly the brains and the imagination at the top of the Air Staff. He was in most respects an abler man that Tom. He himself must have known that and I am sure that Tom, in his very honest way, realised it too. In my observation they managed pretty well together, barring the occasional flicker of intellectual impatience on Teddy's side and of crossness on Tom's side when Teddy rubbed up against the proprieties, for good or ill, of their respective roles.

In his book *In The Midst of Things*, Marshal of the Royal Air Force Sir Neil Cameron wrote:

In Edmund Hudleston, CAS had an ideal Vice-Chief, a 'thinking airman' in the tradition of Lord Tedder. He occupied this post with great distinction and longer than any of his predecessors or successors, for four and a half years.

And this tribute came from an officer who served with Teddy on several occasions:

Teddy undoubtedly had the shrewdest and finest mind to serve in the RAF. His habit of discussing problems personally with the staff member concerned, however lowly, and leaving them convinced that they had made a useful contribution, endeared him to his staff.

Appointment as AOC-in-C Transport Command on 30 April 1962 was a humbling experience. The Command didn't have the same cachet as Fighter or Bomber Commands, although there were major issues to be resolved with the transport fleet and its performance. All of Teddy's predecessors were three star (apart from Sir Frederick Bowhill, who was acting unpaid Air Chief Marshal in 1943/44). Teddy was the first AOC-in-C to be a substantive Air Chief Marshal, taking over from Denis Barnett, who was promoted to Air Chief Marshal only when he assumed his next appointment as AOC-in-C Near East Air Force. He was followed by 'Bing' Cross, who was a three-star Air Marshal for his first twenty-two months in office, although he was promoted on 1 October 1965. From Teddy's perspective, this was a temporary placement for a man who was still too young to be forcibly retired, but for whom there was no other suitable appointment.

The AOC-in-C's house was in need of extensive refurbishment, so the Hudlestons moved into a relatively modest quarter in Netheravon. Here the core of his long-serving house staff first coalesced. The team was led by Sergeant Morris Scott, who had worked for Teddy since 1960. At that time Scott was a bachelor Corporal and, it must be said, the family quietly wondered if he was gay because from time to time he would be seen performing ballet-like manoeuvres as he moved around the flat at 3 Eaton Place. Time was to prove that he was emphatically heterosexual, for he married when he left the Air Force and produced a fine family in Arbroath. Morris Scott was to stay with the Hudlestons until Teddy retired in June 1967.

Corporal Bigmore joined the team on Teddy's arrival at Upavon. He was in charge of the enormous Austin Princess, which drove the boss to work each day and was then available to ferry Nan around if she needed the support (which she rarely did). From time to time, Corporal Bigmore performed Samaritan duties, notably when the ADC's, Tim Cripps, tired Vespa scooter failed him on the way to work. All too often the AOC-in-C and Bigmore passed the poor ADC in the morning and Bigmore would be sent back to help him recover the scooter to get to the office.

Corporal Vic Vella was the superlative chef. He was hungry to learn and responded with vigour to the ideas and experience of his most important client, Nan. Both he and Bigmore stayed with the Hudlestons until the end of Teddy's service in the RAF.

Teddy's primary concern was to make his command perform more professionally. The RAF transport system had become infamous for delay and late departure, which he considered was unacceptable. He was also determined to follow through the concern he had championed when he was VCAS, which was the maintenance of the 'all red route'. As Sir Frank Cooper later wrote:

One of Teddy's preoccupations as VCAS was the maintenance of the 'all red route'. The objective was to be able to get British aircraft wherever we needed them despite the threat of over-flying bans or the imposition of them. He wanted to be sure that we could get to the Far East and Australia.

He was able to test the route to Australia in July 1962, when he and Nan flew to Singapore and Australia.

Squadron Leader Tim Cripps, who served as Teddy's ADC from early 1963 until his move to Fontainebleau that December, remembered having to organise a whirlwind tour of Africa and the Far East in May 1963 for which the objective was to evaluate alternative routes to the Far East in the event that middle eastern countries refused overflying rights. Tim blotted his copybook by becoming engaged to be married a month after starting his job as the ADC, having been told that it was important to remain a bachelor in this particular role. But there was certainly no ill will from the boss and both Teddy and Nan attended the wedding at Woodbury in Devon on 29 June 1963; they were driven there by Sergeant Bigmore in the Austin Princess. The fact is that Tim played a most important role as Teddy's eyes and ears. Many senior officers were in some awe of the AOC-in-C, leaving him wondering whether he was being told the whole truth. Tim was required to listen to his own friends and fellow officers to learn what 'the men' really felt. It proved to be invaluable when visiting Transport Command stations and gave Tim a real sense of purpose, instead of being a mere door opener.

The professional team accompanying the AOC-in-C included four staff officers from the Command, together with Teddy's Personal Staff Officer (PSO), Squadron Leader (later Air Commodore) Michael Rayson, his ADC, and his steward, Sergeant Scott.

It was a working tour, but it included a huge amount of fun. The party stayed in Aden, Gan, the Cocos Islands, Mauritius, Salisbury in Southern Rhodesia, Pretoria, Ascension Island, Lagos, the Cape Verde Islands and Gibraltar. In Aden he was greeted by Fred Rosier, now an Air Vice-Marshal and serving as AOC Air Force Middle East, and he stayed with Sam Elworthy who was AOC-in-C. Tim Cripps appointed himself as the purveyor of local currencies and anti-malaria tablets, but particularly enjoyed fishing all night in the Cocos Islands.

Three months after moving into the Netheravon quarter, Littlecote House in Enford was completed and the whole team, plus two new members, moved to the official residence of the AOC-in-C. It proved to be an excellent venue for the extensive entertainment expected of the Hudlestons. Tim Cripps particularly enjoyed Nan's efforts on behalf of SSAFA and reported upon a dinner which was attended by Douglas Bader and his wife. Nan's mission was to persuade Bader to make a substantial commitment to the charity. As Tim wrote:

She was a particularly forthright person and I recall her saying to Bader 'you are a mean old bugger.' He responded in kind, but his heart wasn't in the argument and Lady H won the day.

While Teddy's core interest was his new Command, he still exerted important influence in the corridors of Whitehall power. In August 1962 the Chiefs of Staff were having exceptional difficulty with Mountbatten, who was still CDS. Teddy was called upon to fix the issue so, taking the 15-year-old author of this biography on a day trip, he flew from Upavon to Broadlands. Collected by Mountbatten's car, Teddy went off for a two-hour meeting, then returned to the Devon of the Queen's Flight and flew back to Upavon, having achieved the aim.

In July 1962 Teddy and Nan flew to Australia on a flag-waving trip which included visits to Sydney, Melbourne and Perth, where Teddy was delighted to be welcomed back to his old school, Guildford Grammar, for the first time since 1926.

September 1962 was a notable month in Teddy's diary. On a personal level, he was deeply gratified to be appointed Air ADC to the Queen on the 18th. On a professional level, he was little more than a spectator when the Soviet Union agreed to send arms to Cuba. This led formally to what is known as the Cuban missile crisis. On 14 October, an American U2 spy plane took photographs of Cuba which revealed the construction of a missile site on the western side of the island. The following day photographic interpreters realised that they had images of medium range ballistic missiles and briefed the Secretary of Defense late on the night of 15th. They decided to tell the President the following morning. A deadly game of brinkmanship followed. It was exacerbated by Krushchev's conviction that Kennedy and his advisors did not have the stomach for a full-scale confrontation. The debacle of the 'Bay of Pigs' invasion persuaded Soviet strategists that Kennedy was weak-willed, politically immature and unwilling to address a crisis head-on. Their view was reinforced by the ease with which the Soviet and East German regime had created the Berlin Wall. Using the same techniques they use today (witness the Crimea and Ukraine infiltrations in 2014), the Soviets deployed denial and deception as they shipped missiles to Cuba. But Krushchev was to learn that Kennedy was made of sterner stuff. The United States blended military and political determination with back-door diplomacy, ultimately persuading the Soviet Union that the cost of continuing with the provision of missiles would be too high. Krushchev 'blinked' and the crisis drew to an end on 28 October, although the US blockade remained until 20 November.

The British winter of 1962/63 was terrible. On 29 and 30 December 1962 snow swept across the south of England, with drifts of up to 20 feet created by gale force easterly winds. The 'deep freeze' covered much of the country throughout the whole of January and further misery was added when more snow storms in February created even more deep drifts. The thaw started at the beginning of March and temperatures soared to 17 degrees on the 6th, swiftly turning the countryside into an open bog.

The New Year's Honours list for 1963 published Teddy's elevation to Knight Grand Cross of the Most Honourable Order of the Bath (GCB). Membership of this exclusive club is limited to 120 Knights and Dames and in 2014 there were just 55 members, all of them male.

The transport capability of the RAF was as deeply affected as other branches of the RAF by financial constraints. In October 1962, the Prime Minister wrote the briefest note to the Secretary of State for Air:

I see that there are a lot of second hand Britannias for sale from BOAC. Why don't you buy some? You could get them very cheap.

In fact BOAC was trying to offload 102 aircraft as quickly as they could. Officials in the Air Ministry were immediately against the idea because the aircraft was already obsolescent, experienced several maintenance difficulties and did not have any freighting capability. Within a week of the Prime Minister's note, the Secretary of State responded with good reasons for not pursuing the idea. But someone at BOAC was determined. Mr L.A. Rabbitts, the Director of Aircraft Sales, continued to promote the idea, this time with CAS, who mentioned it in passing to Teddy at an evening engagement in November. In no time at all, Teddy and his Transport Command staff studied the proposals in great detail, swiftly resolving that there was absolutely no merit in buying the aircraft as a stop-gap before the arrival of VC10 and Belfast. They had reviewed the options on a five-year hiring contract, but ultimately judged that the problems would far exceed the benefits. The case was closed.

Teddy's commitment to keeping airways open and effective was enshrined in the AOC-in-C's report on island strategy on 31 May 1963. El Adam (in Libya) became a beneficiary of the report, which resolved that the RAF base needed a normal operations centre, working 24 hours a day, and the air movements organisation needed significant strengthening. Two Squadron Leaders would be upgraded immediately to Wing Commanders, one Flight Lieutenant would become a Squadron Leader, one Sergeant would become a Warrant Officer and five aircraftsmen would become Corporals. Moreover, three more officers, four senior NCOs and 25 airmen would be added to the establishment. Aden, Gan, Cocos, Mauritius, Pretoria and Ascension Island would all receive enhancements. The changes were readily agreed by the Air Member for Supply and Organisation (AMSO), Willy Merton, and VCAS, Wally Kyle. Clearly long term friendships paid a dividend.

The mood in the Ministry was not always so collaborative and Teddy failed to push through further establishment increases before finishing at Transport Command. In a letter of 9 September 1963, Jack Davis, who had taken over as AMSO on 1 August 1963, very courteously but firmly put the newest set of proposals on hold. Nevertheless, the formation of an Air Movements Wing was being formally discussed in the corridors of power.

AAFCENT

Air Chief Marshal Sir Peter le Cheminant reported that Teddy's personal staff officer at AAFCENT was the Frenchman Freddy Fuchs, a Free French Spitfire Squadron Leader who held Teddy second only to General de Gaulle in his esteem.

Sam Lucas was recruited as Teddy's ADC while he was still at Transport Command. The main requirement for the ADC was to be able to speak fluent French, and Sam proved to be one of very few Air Force officers suitably qualified. He reported that the great man asked him if he would like to become his ADC in Fontainebleau. 'No sir!' said Sam. At the time he was in a Lightning Squadron and simply did not want to give up flying. 'Good', said Teddy, 'you're probably the right man for it.' So against all his wishes, Sam became the ADC.

Strangely he was also interviewed for the role as Tom Pike's ADC in Versailles and was relieved that he didn't get that job: the man who was appointed (on the grounds that he was a Squadron Leader) had a tough time because, so it was said, Lady Pike kept firing the house staff.

Sam's abiding memories of his time in Fontainebleau are filled with the huge number of social events which they had to attend. Teddy really didn't enjoy standing around chatting about inconsequential matters, but would bear it provided his gin and tonic was steadily refuelled. Sam, who actually enjoyed the social part of the job, also enjoyed his gin and part of his role was to ensure that the house staff at Hotel Bellune, 4 Rue St Honoré, maintained a flow of booze for the two glasses positioned on either side of the elegant clock on the mantelpiece in the drawing room.

Being an ADC to Teddy Hudleston clearly endowed the incumbent with a strong desire to marry. Like Tim Cripps before him, Sam duly married the daughter of a German Colonel. Their wedding took place in the chapel of the château in Fontainebleau.

Life was pretty easy, but from time to time Sam had to stand his ground with the boss. There came an occasion when Teddy was due to fly to Berlin to stay with the GOC, Major General David Yates. Yates had enjoyed a gilded advance to senior rank in the same style as Teddy, having been a 34-year-old Brigadier on the General Staff of Alexander at Allied Force Headquarters in Italy in 1945. Teddy instructed Sam to bring some highly-classified documents about SACEUR's strike plan with him so that he could work on them in the plane. Sam objected. He pointed out that if their aircraft came down in the Soviet Sector, the Russians might get hold of them. Teddy persisted, but Sam stuck to his guns and eventually Teddy backed down. It must be said that his admiration for his ADC was amply reinforced by this bold but professional response.

In the picture of the line up at Hotel Bellune in March 1967, Teddy is clearly glowing with health, while everyone else looks rather pasty. The reason was that Teddy used any opportunity to play golf and Wednesday afternoons were generally devoted to sport. His Personal Staff Officer (PSO), Brian Spray, loved his golf too. The Commander's head would peer around the door of the staff officer's room shortly before lunch. 'Brian,' he would ask, 'is there much on this afternoon?' 'No sir,' would come the reply. 'Well, I think we can leave it to Sam then. I'll pick you up at two.'

But unlike his counterpart in Versailles, Sam enjoyed an excellent relationship with the boss's wife. 'She treated me rather like a son,' Sam reported. 'I used to go to the residence weekly to deal with staff matters. Lady H would instantly offer a glass of sherry and over the course of the next hour with several more glasses of sherry, she would assassinate the characters of all the senior NATO officers and their boring wives. Lady H was not boring.'

The personal staff at Hotel Bellune was now a small army of seven servicemen and women dedicated to supporting the Hudleston household. Staff Sergeant Scott was assisted by Sergeant Vella, two stewards, one stewardess, Sergeant Bigmore and Corporal (later Sergeant) Fife, who drove a formal black Citroen DS19 and deputised for Sergeant Bigmore when he was away.

The house was a lovely, classical 18th century mansion in the aristocratic quarter of Fontainebleau. Boasting two cottages and a large garden, the house lent itself to elegant entertaining. Visitors from around the world flowed through in a fairly constant stream, with many dinner parties characterised by vigorous debate in at least three, but often four or five languages. Nan, of course, was in her element because she was fluent in so many tongues, while Teddy had the capacity to surprise even his family because he had the knack of being able to find an elusive French or German word solely thanks to his classical education.

There is no doubt that Teddy was winding down. He knew that this was his last service job, so he could afford to take more time for personal enjoyment. He frequently stayed with his friends Edgar and Ann Ivens at their seaside house, Le Chaland, at Cap d'Antibes, and he went out of his way to tutor his wife's nephew, the author of this book, by taking him to see the battlefields of the Somme, playing squash and golf, or attending rugby internationals in Paris.

Nevertheless, this was the Cold War and no commander could abandon his duties. There was a genuine fear that the Soviet Bloc with 18 to 20 Divisions in East Germany would invade Western Europe. As Commander-in-Chief Allied Air

Forces, Teddy was in charge of Second and Fourth Allied Tactical Air Forces. The land commander had Northern Army Group and Central Army Group. The subtle difference about Teddy's appointment was that he was also appointed in 1964 as Deputy C-in-C Allied Forces Central Europe, answering to the French C-in-C, General Crepin. This meant that when the French removed themselves from the integrated military structure on 1 July 1966, Teddy became the de facto C-in-C while the politicians debated which nation would normally have the post in future. Ultimately the Germans secured it and he handed over to General Graf von Kielmansegg on 15 March 1967, the day that AFCENT Headquarters formally moved to Brunssum. But this meant that Teddy became the only British serviceman to command all Allied forces in Central Europe, more than 500,000 men, for almost nine months.

Two years older than Teddy, Johann von Kielmansegg had enjoyed a successful military career until the Gestapo arrested him on suspicion of being involved in the 20 July 1944 plot to kill Hitler. He was eventually released because there was no substantial evidence to support the charge. He was given command of the 111th Panzer Grenadier Regiment, leading them through the Battle of the Bulge until the end of the War. He was a prisoner of both the British and Americans, eventually being released in May 1946. As a civilian, he had a range of jobs, from truck driver to journalist until he re-joined the Army in 1955 as a Brigadier General and started to acquire a solid track record of international staff work at SHAPE, then ultimately as C-in-C Allied Land Forces from 1963. He was an amusing man and a warm-hearted host, who enjoyed reporting that he was descended from one of King George I's mistresses, Sophia von Kielmansegg. For the purists, historians now question whether she was George 1's mistress because she was his illegitimate half-sister. Whatever the reality, she was a great favourite of the King, who elevated her to two peerages as the Countess of Leinster and the Countess of Darlington.

Key senior officers who worked for Teddy in Fontainebleau included Major General Walter Walker, a Gurkha who was awarded no fewer than three DSOs and went on to be General Sir Walter Walker, KCB, CBE,DSO, and Commander-in-Chief Allied Forces Northern Europe. The major character, however, was General Johannes Steinhoff, who became Chief of the German Air Staff and ultimately went on to become Chairman of the NATO Military Committee. He was a patriot in every way, which did not mean that he was dewy-eyed about his leaders. He detested Goering, whose early career he admired, but who, in his words, became lazy, thereby losing the lives of many of his airmen. He had no respect for Hitler, whom he met on several occasions when being awarded greater and greater honours for his flying exploits.

An indicator of this great man's character is enshrined in an interview he gave shortly before he died in 1994 to Colin D. Heaton for *World War II* Magazine:

I was test-flying an Me-109 with my aide near our base at Foggia. This was before I had been exiled from Germany, during my first tour as Kommodore of JG. 77. Well, we were attacked at low level by a flight of P-38 Lightnings, about 100 American fighters in all, but the two of us figured, why not attack? We turned into them, and I flew through their formation going in the opposite direction, getting good strikes on a couple of them. I poured a good burst into this P-38 and the pilot rolled over, and I saw him bail out. I had this on gun camera also. Well, he was picked up and made a POW, and I invited him to my tent for a drink and dinner, as well as to spend the night. We drank some of the local wine... and drank and drank. I thought to myself, "What am I going to do with this guy?" Well, it was long after midnight, so I lay down in my tent and stretched my legs so I could reach his head. He woke up and said, "Don't worry, I won't run away, you have my word as an officer and a gentleman. Besides, you got me too drunk."We slept, and he kept his word, and I never placed a guard on him.

Steinhoff's flying career was astonishing. He flew over 930 combat missions, shot down 176 aircraft, was himself shot down twelve times and nearly died in a thirteenth incident in April 1945 in which the new jet he was flying crashed in woodland. It burst into flames and he was severely burnt, losing both eyelids. He was unable to close his eyes for the next 24 years until, on the instigation of Teddy and Nan Hudleston, Air Vice-Marshal George Morley, a British plastic surgeon, took skin from his arm and created new eyelids.

As if to emphasise their military independence, the French exploded their first nuclear device on Mururoa Atoll on 2 July 1966 and a second one on Fangataufa Island on 19 July. Not to be outdone, the Soviets performed a series of nuclear tests at Semipalitinsk in eastern Kazakhstan on 22 July, 5 August, 7 September and 19 October, with further tests in November and December. France responded with another test at Mururoa Atoll on 11 September, then continued with a series of tests in the following months. In a lower key, HMS *Resolution*, Britain's first nuclear submarine, was launched on 15 September. The USA flexed its muscles by increasing its bombing campaign in North Vietnam (348 aircraft in two missions on 13 and 14 October) and focusing on their burgeoning space programme, placing two vehicles in lunar orbit and several astronauts (Young, Collins, Lovell, Aldrin, Conrad and Gordon) in space. Within ten days of Lunar Orbiter One reaching the moon, Russia had launched its own spacecraft, Luna 11, to chase the Americans in lunar orbit and actually achieved a soft lunar landing with Luna 13 on 24 December. On 27 October and on 28 December China conducted its own nuclear tests at Lop Nor. There was no doubt about it at the time, and the perception still holds good almost fifty years later, that all of this activity was high level sabr-rattling, which was bound to sustain the concern about the threat from the Eastern Bloc.

On 1 March 1967 Teddy formally handed his command over to Air Chief Marshal Sir Augustus (Gus) Walker. He, and all of his successors, became Deputy C-in-C AFCENT, mirroring the appointment of a British officer as DSACEUR, and thereby retaining Britain's importance in the management of European defence.

CHAPTER 7

CIVILIAN LIFE

On 5 June 1967, after forty years and five months in the RAF,
Teddy retired. As a long serving and loyal senior officer, he was
offered a grace and favour house in Hampstead, which he
accepted with some relief. His salary as an Air Chief Marshal
was a mere £5,500 (about £70,000 in 2014 terms). In those
days, grace and favour properties were rent free, so this was an
enormous boost to the finances. Houses in Ingram Avenue today
sell for between £7 million and £9 million. The house enjoyed
a large garden with woodland behind and little traffic passing
through. By any standard, it was a very agreeable property for a
retired senior officer without much money to call home.

Nobody knew what Teddy would do. There were rumours,
of course, but the principal player wasn't giving anything away.
Many thought he was going to take over British European

Airways, which was going through a sticky time. Others were convinced that he was about to run MI5 or MI6, because additional security was arranged for the room he commandeered as a study. But the truth was much more prosaic. He swiftly became a non-executive director of Pilkington's Optics Division, and he agreed to become the permanent appeal secretary for King Edward VII Hospital Sister Agnes. For the first time since he had been a teenager, he had no responsibility for the management of people.

Sadly neither Pilkington's nor King Edward VII has records of Teddy's contribution in the late 60s and early 70s. The family understood that he was a great favourite with both organisations and he certainly seemed to enjoy job satisfaction, He was extraordinarily well networked and was not shy about deploying his contacts for the benefit of his paymasters. In those days, fundraising relied upon well written letters. Today what matters most is peer to peer, face to face. Teddy would have been brilliant at that too.

But he was a lonely man. Nan did spend time in Hampstead and was a powerhouse of energy and innovation for a range of service causes and for the Anglo Turkish Society, of which she became Chairman. Teddy supported her in all her initiatives but it must be said that they did not spend 'quality' time together. Nan continued to spend as much time at Cornhill with Johnny Collingwood, while Teddy frequently ate at the RAF Club instead of using the kitchen in Ingram Avenue. He would spend a few weeks with the Ivens in Cap d'Antibes every summer, again without Nan, who tended to take her holidays with Johnny in Spain.

Nevertheless, there was a form of rapprochement between the two. Teddy's letters were tender and informative and, in private moments of introspection, he acknowledged that he was as much the author of a shaky marriage as his wife, let alone Pip and Johnny.

Johnny Collingwood died at the end of April 1975, shortly before his 70th birthday. Nan was distraught. In a note which she kept and did not share with anyone else, she wrote that she considered suicide 'but didn't have the guts to go through with it'. She inherited the interest in Cornhill House and its remaining estate, together with woodland and two miles of fishing on the Tweed. She didn't care for it at all and determined to sell it all off as quickly as possible, although she did decide to retain Tor Cottage, a four-bedroomed substantial Victorian house on the edge of Cornhill Village, which Johnny had intended to give to the author as a wedding present. Teddy had refused to live in the house of his wife's former lover, but he was prepared to leave Hampstead for the smaller, less emotionally binding property at Tor Cottage. Sadly this proved to be a considerable error.

Tony's marriage to his Swiss-born wife, Danielle, was collapsing. With Nan's death in 1980, the whole operation went into terminal decline. This led to some very hard decision making, ultimately culminating in the decision to sell Tor Cottage so that Danielle and her children, and Sal and her children, could have some money. This completely disenfranchised Teddy, who had looked forward to continuing his rent-free retirement. He would not ask for another grace and favour house because he believed strongly that 'you cannot backtrack on an agreement with the Queen.' After much soul-searching, he bought a small flat in St Leonards on Sea. It was in his gift to sell the furniture at Tor Cottage and there is some irony in the fact that his daughter, Sal, used some of the money inherited from her mother's lover to pay for his furniture.

More surprising, but probably more understandable, Teddy swiftly decided to marry Brenda Withrington, the widow of an Army Colonel. Brenda was a very bright woman, who had taught sciences at Shrivenham. She was feminine, amusing and very good at keeping Teddy comfortable and contented. She was not tainted by, nor interested, in the historical workings of the Hudlestons, Collingwoods and Davises. Her sole interest was in looking after Teddy, which she did extremely well, providing him with the attention, amusement and female companionship that he wanted in his final years. They travelled, enjoyed the company of mutual friends and nestled securely in their waterfront flat overlooking a stony beach and a sea which was more often grey than blue. Children and grandchildren would visit for lunch, but few ever stayed.

During this time, Teddy cautiously drafted the outline of his biography. In fact, he started it on at least four occasions, using a series of lined notebooks and his scrawling manuscript, which became increasingly difficult to interpret. At one point, he decided that he should return to the government several files of a highly classified nature, which he should never have retained. But he did hold on to a body of material which is today lodged at the Imperial War Museum, available for the public to investigate.

It is sad to report that he never completed his drafts, which, in any event, lacked the all-important detail that would have brought the story to life. As soon as he wrote about the really interesting experiences, he retreated into Edwardian murmurings about 'a jolly good show,' or 'the chaps just got on with it'. For that reason, his diary, full of trenchant opinions and highly personal insights, has been an invaluable source, even though it covered little more than 1944/45 and 1956.

How does one sum up the life of an extraordinary man? He was intellectually sharper than almost all of his peers, a natural leader and manager, perceived by his father as 'old for his years', treated without affection by his mother, who yet managed to instil a very thorough Christian education and a love for the family ancestral home, which he didn't see until he was an adult. He was an excellent all-round sportsman and a good raconteur, who deftly avoided talking about personal affairs, often by adopting a blimpish demeanour which belied his acute brain and experience. Women enjoyed him, but he was more at ease with men and, however terrifying he seemed to people under his command, he had the knack of swiftly putting them at ease by conveying the message that they were making a valuable contribution. The majority of people who worked for him found him a hard but extremely fair taskmaster, who took an active interest in their views and career development.

The great acknowledged biographers were not prepared to write Teddy's story. He was not important enough for them to rate him alongside the renowned wartime commanders. And yet, at the height of the Cold War, he stepped seamlessly into the shoes of the departing French commander to become the Commander of Allied Forces Central Europe, responsible for the defence against the main thrust of a very credible and feared Soviet attack.

The public tends to want books about intrepid pilots and heroic dogfights. But who makes things work? Who wins the wars? The fact is that it is the commanders who create the conditions to make or break the peace. In a career of 40 years, Teddy spent just 17 as a junior and middle manager and 24 in Air Rank as the increasingly important decision maker. Clearly he had something special because nobody has every served longer as a one to five star airman. And that was in spite of his lack of operational experience as a Squadron Leader or Wing Commander with a fighter or bomber squadron. His ability to identify and solve problems was unparalleled. He mastered every brief and gave crisp reports which, as his rank and stature grew, became clear orders. At a very early age, his elders could see his capability and wisely deployed it.

The pool of potential Chiefs of the Air Staff for the twelve-year band from 1956 to 1968 contained seventeen candidates. Among them were the successful Boyle, Pike and Elworthy. Teddy respected Boyle and Elworthy personally and professionally, but he never thought Tom Pike was the man for the top. Other serious candidates would have been Broadhurst, Constantine, Kyle, Merton and Walker. In all of his many musings about the abilities of others, Teddy only ever picked out one man, his Cranwell contemporary Reggie Elsmie, as the fighting man who should have become CAS.

This very private Edwardian, dubbed by the newspaper obituaries 'The Quiet Australian', did not succeed in the same way as a family man. His relationships with his wife, his son and his daughter were strained. His stern upbringing and the War were clearly major factors, as was the determination of Nan's younger sister, Pip, to have Teddy for herself. Thus Nan was vulnerable to Johnny Collingwood's seduction, which only exacerbated the relationships. And throughout it all, Teddy and Nan presented a bold public face, largely to protect Teddy's potential to become CAS himself.

The top job was the one career goal which he wanted to achieve and for which most commentators have acknowledged he was amply qualified. Indeed, the Whitehall machine was quite taken aback when he was passed over. The decision lay in the hands of CDS and CAS and there is no apparent evidence that the politicians sought to interfere. The Prime Minister, Harold Macmillan, was Minister Resident in the Mediterranean during the War and often dined and debated with Teddy in North Africa and Italy. Tom Pike had less exposure, but would have met Macmillan often. The suggestion is that the Prime Minister did not feel strongly enough to intervene, seeing the appointment as an Air Force issue. Dickson's long term mentoring of Tom Pike and Boyle's preference for a man at the top with bags of operational flying experience put paid to Teddy's ambition.

He never gave a hint in public about his deep disappointment. He knew, as did all of those around him, that he was the man for the job. But good manners, duty and a profound sense of good sportsmanship prevented him from articulating any sense of injustice to the outside world. He was genuinely pleased when Sam Elworthy was appointed CAS, even though he was technically still a candidate himself. But a little bit of him withered. He did ultimately confide in his new wife, Brenda, which lightened the load of regret. He never let it sour his life thereafter, proving to be a wise mentor and guide for any who cared to ask for his advice.

In his last few years he started to lose his sight and sense of balance. Brenda was constantly on the alert because she knew that she would not be able to lift him if he fell. And, of course, he did fall, happily without personal injury, but with a loss of personal pride. The end was gentle. He died in his sleep in hospital in Brighton on 14 December 1994.

OUTSTANDING LEADERS OF THE RAF

THE YOUNGEST AIR COMMODORES

Air Chief Marshal Sir Augustus Walker, promoted on
24 March 1943, aged 30

Air Chief Marshal Sir Kenneth Cross, promoted on
12 January 1943, aged 31

Air Chief Marshal Sir Edgar Ludlow-Hewitt, promoted to
Brigadier on 17 October 1917, aged 31

Marshal of the RAF Lord Newall, promoted to Brigadier on
28 December 1917, aged 31

Air Vice-Marshal Donald Bennett, promoted on
18 December 1942, aged 32

Marshal of the RAF Lord Elworthy, promoted on
22 August 1944, aged 33

Air Vice-Marshal James Scarlett-Streatfeild, promoted on
27 February 1943, aged 34

Air Vice-Marshal John Weston, promoted on
3 March 1943, aged 34

Air Chief Marshal Sir Edmund Hudleston, promoted on
26 September 1943 aged 34

Air Chief Marshal Sir Hugh Constantine, promoted on
27 April 1943, aged 34

Air Marshal Sir Ronald Lees, promoted on
8 September 1944, aged 34

Air Marshal Sir Harold Martin, promoted on
15 October 1952, aged 34

Marshal of the RAF Sir John Salmond, promoted on
1 February 1916, aged 34

Air Chief Marshal Lord Dowding, promoted to
Brigadier on 23 June 1917 aged 35

Constantine, Hudleston, Scarlett-Streatfeild and
Weston were all contemporaries at Cranwell

THE YOUNGEST AIR VICE-MARSHALS

Air Vice-Marshal Donald Bennett, promoted on
6 December 1943, aged 33

Air Vice-Marshal James Scarlett-Streatfeild, promoted on
18 October 1944, aged 35

Air Chief Marshal Sir Edmund Hudleston, promoted on
10 November 1944, aged 35

Marshal of the RAF Sir John Salmond, promoted to
Major General on 22 June 1917, aged 35

Air Chief Marshal Sir Hugh Constantine, promoted on
16 January 1945, aged 36

Air Chief Marshal Sir Harry Broadhurst, promoted on
31 January 1943, aged 37

Air Chief Marshal Sir Alfred Earle, promoted on
29 April 1946, aged 38

Air Chief Marshal Sir Geoffrey Salmond, promoted on
1 April 1918, aged 39

Air Marshal Sir John Whitley, promoted on
12 February 1945, aged 39

Air Chief Marshal the Earl of Bandon, promoted on
14 March 1945, aged 40

Air Marshal Sir George Beamish, promoted on
15 June 1945, aged 40

Marshal of the RAF Sir Dermot Boyle, promoted on
26 April 1945, aged 40

Marshal of the RAF Sir Edward Ellington, promoted on
10 April 1918, aged 40

Air Vice-Marshal Hugh Champion de Crespigny, promoted
on 3 September 1939, aged 42

Air Marshal Sir John Higgins, promoted on
29 April 1918, aged 42

Air Chief Marshal Sir George Mills, promoted on
13 February 1945, aged 42

Air Marshal Sir Douglas Morris, promoted on
24 January 1955, aged 42

THE YOUNGEST AIR MARSHALS

Marshal of the RAF Sir John Salmond, promoted on
2 June 1923, aged 41

Air Chief Marshal Sir Edmund Hudleston, promoted on
1 April 1953, aged 44

Air Marshal Sir Peter Drummond, promoted on
1 June 1941, aged 45

Marshal of the RAF Sir John Slessor, promoted on
5 February 1943, aged 45

Air Marshal Sir Phillip Babbington, promoted on
18 November 1940, aged 46

Air Marshal Sir Paterson Fraser, promoted on
15 April 1954, aged 46

Air Chief Marshal Sir Rodric Hill, promoted on
29 November 1940, aged 46

Marshal of the RAF Viscount Portal, promoted on
3 September 1939, aged 46

Air Marshal Sir Arthur Coningham, promoted on
8 March 1943, aged 47

Air Chief Marshal Sir Hugh Constantine, promoted on
23 April 1956, aged 47

Air Chief Marshal Sir Kenneth Cross, promoted on
20 May 1959, aged 47

Marshal of the RAF Sir William Dickson, promoted on
2 May 1946, aged 47

Air Chief Marshal Sir Basil Embry, promoted on
19 April 1949, aged 47

Marshal of the RAF Sir John Grandy, promoted on
7 January 1961, aged 47

Marshal of the RAF Sir Andrew Humphrey, promoted on
18 March 1968, aged 47

Air Chief Marshal Sir Richard Peirse, promoted on
30 October 1939, aged 47

Marshal of the RAF Sir Thomas Pike, promoted on
9 November 1953, aged 47

Air Marshal Sir Robert Saundby, promoted on
15 February 1944, aged 47

Air Marshal Sir Ralph Sorley, promoted on
1 Janaury 1946, aged 47

THE YOUNGEST AIR CHIEF MARSHALS

Marshal of the RAF Sir John Salmond, promoted on 1
January 1929, aged 47

Marshal of the RAF Viscount Portal, promoted on
14 April 1942, aged 48

Marshal of the RAF Sir John Slessor, promoted on
1 January 1946, aged 48

Marshal of the RAF Sir Andrew Humphrey, promoted on
1 December 1970, aged 49

Air Chief Marshal Sir Richard Peirse, promoted on
7 July 1942, aged 49

Marshal of the RAF Sir Dermot Boyle, promoted on
I January 1956, aged 51

Air Chief Marshal Sir Harry Broadhurst, promoted on
14 February 1957, aged 51

Air Chief Marshal Sir Christopher Courtney, promoted on
1 January 1942, aged 51

Marshal of the RAF Lord Elworthy, promoted on
1 September 1962, aged 51

Air Chief Marshal Sir Basil Embry, promoted on
16 July 1953, aged 51

Air Chief Marshal Sir Wilfrid Freeman, promoted on
27 May 194+0, aged 51

Marshal of the RAF Sir John Grandy, promoted on
1 April 1965, aged 51

Air Chief Marshal Sir Michael Graydon, promoted on
31 May 1990, aged 51

Air Chief Marshal Sir Trafford Leigh-Mallory, promoted on
1 January 1944, aged 51

Air Chief Marshal Sir Edgar Ludlow-Hewitt, promoted on
1 July 1937, aged 51

Air Chief Marshal Sir Charles Medhurst, promoted on
1 May 1948, aged 51

Air Chief Marshal Sir William Mitchell, promoted on
9 September 1939, aged 51

Marshal of the RAF Lord Newall, promoted on
1 April 1947, aged 51

Marshal of the RAF Sir Thomas Pike, promoted on
1 November 1957, aged 51

Marshal of the RAF Lord Tedder, promoted on
1 July 1942, aged 51

Air Chief Marshal Sir John Thomson, promoted on
4 November 1992, aged 51

THE GREATEST NUMBER OF
YEARS IN AIR RANK

Air Chief Marshal Sir Edmund Hudleston, 24 years

Air Chief Marshal Sir Edgar Ludlow-Hewitt, 24 years

Marshal of the RAF Sir Edward Ellington, 23 years

Marshal of the RAF Sir Thomas Pike, 22 years

Air Marshal Sir Harold Martin, 22 years

Air Chief Marshal Lord Dowding, 21 years

Air Chief Marshal Sir Hugh Constantine, 19 years

Air Chief Marshal Sir George Mills, 19 years

Air Chief Marshal Sir John Steel, 19 years

Air Chief Marshal the Earl of Bandon, 18 years

Air Chief Marshal Sir Harry Broadhurst, 18 years

Air Chief Marshal Sir Walter Cheshire, 18 years

Marshal of the RAF Sir William Dickson, 18 years

Marshal of the RAF Sir John Grandy, 18 years

Air Chief Marshal Sir Arthur Longmore, 18 years

Air Marshal Sir John Whitley, 18 years

AUSTRALIANS AND NEW ZEALANDERS WHO ROSE TO SENIOR COMMAND IN THE RAF

Most of the information in this appendix is drawn from Air of Authority, a fabulous website without which this book could not have been written.

Barnett, Air Chief Marshal Sir Denis Hensley Fulton, KCB, CBE, DFC. Born 11 February 1906 died 31 Dec 1992.

Sir Denis Barnett was born at Dunedin, New Zealand, on 11 February 1906, the younger son of Sir Louis Barnett. He was educated at Christ's College, Christchurch, and before proceeding to Cambridge studied for a year at the University of Otago. At Clare College, Cambridge, he graduated BA in 1929 and MA in 1935. He received a permanent commission in the RAF in 1929 and has held numerous positions, both in the United Kingdom and overseas, including Air Ministry posts and command of the RAF Staff College at Bracknell, the Allied Air Task Force in the Near East, and Transport Command. During the Second World War he was awarded the DFC and CBE. He was made KCB in 1957 and has been honoured by

America and France as well — United States Legion of Merit (Commander), French Legion d'Honneur (Commandeur), and Croix de Guerre.

Bates, Air Vice-Marshal EC, CB, CBE, DFC. Born 9 June 1906, died 23 March 1975.

An Australian, he attended the University of Western Australia and was awarded a RAAF Cadetship in 1929. Following his pilot training, he was sent to the RAF in order to gain experience. Joining No 33 Squadron, initially at Eastchurch and later Bicester, he flew Hawker Harts. In November 1931 he moved to Netheravon and No 57 Squadron, still flying Harts. His final service appointment was AOA HQ Far East Air Force in November 1955. He retired on 27 January 1959 and became the Principal of the College of Air Training at Hamble.

Bennett, Air Vice-Marshal Don, CB, CBE, DSO born 14 September 1910, died 15 September 1986

Don Bennett was raised on a cattle farm in Queensland and his family hoped that he would pursue a career in medicine. Instead he enlisted in the RAAF and trained as a pilot at Point Cook. Commissioned on 11 August 1931, he was seconded to the RAF and joined No.29 Squadron in Siskins. He attended a flying boat pilot's course in 1932 and was then posted to No. 210 Squadron in Southampton. He spent two years as an instructor at the School of Naval Co-operation and Navigation at RAF Calshot then resigned his short service commission in order to return to the RAAF.

From 1936 to 1940, Bennett worked as a civilian pilot with

Imperial Airways but abandoned it all in order to join the RAFVR as a Pilot Officer on 25 September 1941. Within weeks he was a Wing Commander as Officer Commanding No 77 Squadron, then No. 10 Squadron. His Halifax was hit by flak on 27 April 1942 and he set course for Sweden. Realising that they weren't going to make it, he ordered his crew to bale out, remaining at the controls until they were all clear. He followed the crew and landed in heavy snow in Norway and made his way to Sweden with local help. A month after losing his aircraft, he was back in England and resumed command of his squadron. He received a DSO for his actions.

When his squadron was posted to the Middle East, he was summoned to Bomber Command to see Air Chief Marshal Sir Arthur Harris, the AOC-in-C and his old CO from flying boat days. Harris advised him that he had been instructed to form a special marking force in an attempt to improve the accuracy of his heavy bombs, and he wanted Bennett to lead the team. This was something Bennett himself had suggested to the Director of Bomber Operations about a year before. Bennett was promoted to Group Captain on taking command of this unit, which would be known as the Pathfinder Force. Setting up his HQ at RAF Wyton, Bennett was allocated one squadron from each group as his initial establishment, resulting in his unit being equipped with four different types - Wellingtons, Stirlings, Halifaxes and Lancasters. With the success of the new unit, following some early teething problems, Bennett's command was upgraded to Group status on 8 January 1943 and given the title - No 8 (PFF) Group with Bennett promoted to Air Commodore as its AOC. In December 1943 Bomber Harris recognised that Bennett ought to have the rank of Air Vice-Marshal because he was commanding a group, however small and specialised that may be, so Bennett was promoted Air Vice-Marshal at the dazzlingly youthful age of 33, thereby making him the youngest ever two-star airman.

During the remainder of the war No 8 Group continued to lead and mark targets for the Main Force, although he often found himself at odds with his fellow group commander at No 5 Group, AVM Ralph Cochrane, over marking techniques and the need to concentrate marking squadrons in a single specialist group.

He resigned his commission in 1945 in order to stand for Parliament, being elected Liberal MP for Middlesbrough West. His political career was short lived, and he lost his seat at the General Election shortly afterwards. He made further attempts to enter Parliament, unsuccessfully, eventually leaving the Liberal Party in 1962 owing to their support of the EEC, which he was against. After the war he returned to the world of civilian aviation, forming British Latin American Airways, later becoming British South American Airways Corporation as their Chief Executive from 1 August 1946 to 31 March 1948. He lost his job when he denounced the Minister for Civil Aviation, following the ministry's grounding of his Avro Tudor fleet in 1948. He then went on to form Airflight, using Tudors to fly oil into Berlin during 'Operation Plainfare', and in May 1949 he established Fairflight, which he sold in 1951. He continued to champion the cause of flying boats long after they fell out of favour and he was a leading advocate in the development of the Saunders-Roe Princess boats, only three of which were built but never entered service.

Boxer, Air Vice-Marshal Sir Alan, KCVO, CB, DSO, DFC Born 1 December 1916, died 26 April 1998.

A New Zealander, Boxer took a series of short-term jobs in order to help the family finances, his father having died when he was nine, whilst managing to take flying lessons in his spare time. With war clouds looming over Europe he decided to leave New Zealand in 1938 and join the RAF. Having already accumulated 175 hours of flying time, he found himself posted as a instructor following his service flying training. He remained in Training Command for two years, but eventually in 1942 he was posted to an operational unit, No 161 Squadron at Tempsford. Here he commanded the Hudson Flight and was involved in the delivery and collection of SOE Agents from occupied France, although many of his missions were long ranging to Scandinavia and Poland often lasting 13 hours. A spell as a staff officer at the Air ministry co-ordinating SOE flights was followed by a return to 161 Squadron, this time as CO.

After the war he attended both the RAF Staff College and the Army College at Haifa before being given an exchange posting with the USAF. Here he flew B29's on the West Coast of America including a six-month tour of duty taking part in operations during the Korean War. Following his return from the USA he spent a year at the Central Fighter Establishment before being appointed to the directing staff of the RAF Staff College.

After the Staff College he was tasked with reforming No 7 Squadron as a Valiant unit. Although the squadron officially reformed on 1 November 1956 at Honington, it was the end of the month before he was able to collect the first of its aircraft from the Vickers factory at Wisley. One of the tasks he performed with 7 Squadron was the transporting of an H-bomb to Christmas Island for the forthcoming tests. This necessitated him landing in the USA to re-fuel without being able to divulge the nature of his payload. Promotion to Group Captain brought command of the Victor base at Wittering. A staff post at HQ Bomber Command and attendance at the Imperial Defence College was followed by two SASO posts. The first at HQ No 1 Group and the second as the last person to hold the post at Bomber Command before it was amalgamated with Fighter Command to form Strike Command.

In 1967 he became the first RAF officer to hold the post of Defence Services Secretary, which involved liaising between the Ministry of Defence and Buckingham Palace. As such he was heavily involved with the Prince of Wales's investiture at Caernarfon in 1969. Retiring in 1970 he spent a brief period working as a planning inspector with the Department of the Environment but soon became despondent with the Civil Service and left to concentrate on his other two great passions sailing and conservation.

Broughton, Air Marshal Sir Charles, KBE, CB. Born 27 April 1911, died 1998.

Charles Broughton was born in New Zealand in 1911 and was educated at Christchurch Boys' High School. He commenced his Air Force career as a cadet at the RAF College, Cranwell, in 1930. He was commissioned in 1932 and posted to India from 1933 to 1936. He was a flying instructor for two years before the war and was then attached to Coastal Command from 1941 to 1943. The following three years he spent in the Middle East. He served in Flying Training Command, the Air Ministry, the Imperial Defence College, and Transport Command, apart from two further periods overseas at Washington D.C. and in the Far East. In August 1966 he became Air Member for Supply and Organisation until he retired on 12 October 1968.

Busteed, Air Commodore Henry, OBE, DFC Born 6 November 1887, died 1965.

An Australian born in North Carlton, Victoria, by 1910 Busteed was the first Australian to hold a pilot's licence and was one of the first three flying instructors at the Bristol School of Aviation at Larkhill. From June 1911 until 1913 he was Chief Test Pilot for the Bristol and Colonial Aircraft Company. He originally joined the Special Reserve of the RFC (Military) Wing, but in October 1913 he resigned his RFC commission and joined the RNR, immediately being attached to the RFC (Naval Wing). Called up in 1914, he was soon developing his own ideas, one of which was the launching of seaplanes from railway flat wagons, using the aircraft's engine to reach flying speed. Testing the idea himself, he rated the experience as 'great fun'. On 7 June 1915, he transferred to the RNAS.

Flying an impressed Albatross BII on 7 February 1915, Busteed suffered an engine failure on take off and ran into a dyke, causing the aircraft to overturn and slightly injuring him. In 1917 he was a member of the sub-committee which worked with Armstrong Whitworth looking into the design of arresting gear for aircraft carriers. Also in 1917, he supervised the trials in catapulting aircraft from ships. His final service appointment was

AOC No 34 (Balloon Barrage) Group in 1940. He retired on 1 August 1941.

Carr, Air Marshal Sir Charles Roderick, KBE, CB, DFC. Born 31 August 1891, died 15 December 1971.

Sir Roderick Carr was born at Feilding on the North Island of New Zealand on 31 August 1891 and was educated at Wellington Colleges in New Zealand. He served with New Zealand Forces, the RNAS and the RAF in the First World War. In 1919 he worked with the North Russian Expedition and the following year he was Chief of Air Staff in Lithuania. He was a member of Shackleton's Antarctic expedition in 1921-22 and in 1927 made the first RAF non-stop flight from England to the Persian Gulf. Sir Roderick was with the RAF in Egypt from 1929-33 and with the aircraft carrier HMS *Eagle* in Chinese waters 1936-39. He was mentioned in dispatches during his term as Officer Commanding No. 4 Group, Bomber Command, 1941-45. In the final year of the war he was Deputy Chief of Staff (Air) at Supreme Headquarters, Allied Expeditionary Force, and after a year in India he retired. He was a Commander of the Legion d'Honneur and Croix de Guerre (France) and Commander of the Orders of St. Anne and St. Stanislav (Russia). From 1947 to 1968 he was King of Arms for the Most Excellent Order of the British Empire.

Champion de Crespigny, Air Vice-Marshal Hugh V, CB, MC, DFC. Born 8 April 1897, died 20 June 1969.

Australian by birth, he joined the Suffolk Regiment and then transferred to the Special Reserve of the Royal Flying

Corps in 1915. He went on to be Officer Commanding No. 29 Squadron on the Western Front and then Officer Commanding No. 65 Squadron also on the Western Front. After the War he went to India where commanded No. 60 Squadron and then No. 39 Squadron and finally No. 2 (Indian) Wing. He served in World War II as Air Officer Commanding No. 25 (Armament) Group, as Air Officer Commanding Air Headquarters Iraq and then as Air Officer Commanding No. 21 (Training) Group. He retired in 1945.

After the War he stood as a Labour Party candidate for the British Parliament and then became Regional Commissioner for Schleswig-Holstein for the Control Commission for Germany. In 1948 he was succeeded as commissioner by William Asbury and stayed in Kiel as British consul until 1956. He later lived at Vierville in Natal, South Africa.

Clouston, Air Commodore Arthur E, CB, DSO, DFC, AFC
Born 7 April 1908, died 1 January 1984.

Having learned to fly in his native New Zealand, Clouston joined the RAF on a short service commission and was posted to No 3 FTS at Grantham (Spittlegate). Joining 3 FTS on the same course as K B B Cross (later Air Chief Marshal Sir Kenneth), he was promoted to the senior term after only 2-3 flying hours because of his previous experience. Posted to No 25 Squadron flying Fury I's at Hawkinge, he spent the next three years there before moving to No 24 Squadron at Hendon. No 24 was classed as a communications squadron and carried out a wide range of duties from refresher flying training to VIP transport using a multitude of aircraft types.

When Clouston's SSC ended in 1935 he was offered a permanent commission, but turned it down, having already decided to forge a career in civil flying back home in New Zealand. The plan changed when, having transferred to the RAFO, he was offered one of the two newly-created posts of civilian test pilots at the RAE Farnborough. During his time at Farnborough he carried out tests into the effects of wires on aircraft and countermeasures against them. In his own time he also managed to establish a number of distance records including a flight to Cape Town (from Croydon) between 14 and 20 November 1937, with Betty Kirby-Green, in a flight time of 17 hours 28 minutes and the following year he set a record for a return flight from London to New Zealand of 10 days 21 hours 22 minutes. Just prior to WW2, he was attached to Westlands in a private capacity by Air Vice-Marshal Tedder, to carry out tests on the new twin-engined fighter, the Whirlwind.

Recalled to duty on the outbreak of WW2, in the rank of Acting Squadron Leader, he continued research flying, including tests into the possibility of using flares to illuminate enemy bombers to enable night fighters to make interceptions. In order to gain a better understanding of the problems involved in night fighting, he requested an attachment to a operational squadron, serving with 219 Squadron from Redhill for a month. Further tests in the night fighting sphere followed his return to Farnborough when he was tasked with carrying out trials with the Turbinlite, designed by Air Commodore Helmore and fitted into the nose of Douglas Boston.

Clouston commanded No 224 Squadron, a Liberator anti-submarine unit based at Beaulieu. After nearly a year in the job, he was promoted Group Captain and appointed CO of the still incomplete Coastal Command station at Langham in Norfolk. Here he was responsible for two Beaufighter strike squadrons, No 455 (RAAF) and No 489 (RNZAF). At the end of the war, he was posted to Germany to command the airstrip, B151, later renamed Buckeburg and expanded, the base would become the headquarters of the British Air Forces of Occupation.

At Buckeburg he was offered a permanent commission in the RAF, which he accepted. At the same time he was offered the post of Director-General of Civil Aviation in New Zealand. Replying that he was interested but would need Air Ministry approval, the New Zealand government formally announced his appointment, which resulted in the Air Ministry refusing to release him. Possibly as a consolation, he received a secondment to the RNZAF for two years as CO of RNZAF Ohakea.

In 1950 he was appointed Commandant of the Empire Test Pilots School, a post he held for three years. Promoted Air Commodore, he returned to the Far East as AOC Singapore for three years before once again returning the world of aircraft testing as Commandant of the Aeroplane and Armament Experimental Establishment at Boscombe Down.

Coningham, Air Marshal Sir Arthur (Mary), KCB, KBE, DSO, MC, DFC, AFC, born 19 January 1895 and assumed to have died on 30 January 1948.

During the First World War, Coningham was at Gallipoli with the New Zealand Expeditionary Force, transferred to the Royal Flying Corps, where he became a flying ace. Coningham was later a senior Royal Air Force commander during the

Second World War, as Air Officer Commanding-in-Chief 2nd Tactical Air Force and subsequently the Air Officer Commanding-in-Chief Flying Training Command.

Coningham developed forward air control parties directing close air support, when he was commander of the Western Desert Air Force between 1941 and 1943, and as commander of the tactical air forces in the Normandy campaign in 1944. On 30 January 1948, he disappeared along with all the other passengers and crew of the airliner G-AHNP Star Tiger when it vanished without a trace somewhere off the eastern coast of the United States in the Bermuda Triangle.

Drummond, Air Marshal Sir Peter (Roy) Drummond, KCB, DSO, OBE, MC. Born 2 June 1894, died 27 March 1945.

An Australian from Perth, Drummond rose from private soldier in World War I to Air Marshal in World War II. Drummond enlisted in the Australian Imperial Force in 1914 and saw action during the Gallipoli campaign the following year. He joined the Royal Flying Corps in 1916 and became a fighter ace in the Middle Eastern theatre. Transferring to the RAF on its formation in 1918, he remained in the British armed forces for the rest of his life.

Between the wars, Drummond served for two years in the Sudan and for four years in Australia on secondment to the Royal Australian Air Force (RAAF), including a tour as Deputy Chief of the Air Staff. Based in Cairo at the outbreak of World War II, he was Air Marshal Sir Arthur Tedder's Deputy Air Officer Commanding-in-Chief RAF Middle East from 1941 to 1943. Drummond was twice offered command of the RAAF during the war but did not take up the position on either occasion. Britain's Air Member for Training from 1943, he was lost in a plane crash at sea in 1945.

Edwards, Air Commodore Sir Hughie, VC, KCMG, CB, DSO, OBE, DFC. Born 1 August 1914, died 5 August 1982.

Born in Fremantle on 1 August 1914, Edwards was destined to become the most highly-decorated Australian airman of the Second World War. Hughie Edwards was forced to leave school at the age of 14 because the family finances could no longer support him. He obtained a post as a shipping office clerk but, like many others, lost his job with the onset of the great depression. He then found himself a job in a racing stable, which gave him a lifelong interest in horse racing. He moved on to work for a brief time in a factory and began his military career as a private soldier in March 1933 in the 6th Heavy Battery, Royal Australian Artillery. Transferring to the RAAF in 1935, he gained his 'wings' in June 1936 and was shortly afterwards transferred to the RAF. Posted initially to No 15 Squadron flying Hinds, within six months he was moved to No 90 Sqn as Squadron Adjutant. Shortly after his arrival the Squadron began to re-equip with the new monoplane bomber, the Blenheim. During a break from his admin duties he was flying a Blenheim when it became uncontrollable. Unfortunately as he baled out his parachute snagged on the aircraft and in the ensuing crash he severed a nerve in his leg resulting in a long spell of hospitalisation and non-flying duties. He was injured again on 25 September 1940, whilst carrying out a night reconnaissance operation in Blenheim IV, T1796, of No 13 OTU at Bicester.

He finally returned to operations with No 139 Sqn at Horsham St Faith flying the Blenheim Mk IV. Taking over command of No 105 Sqn at Swanton Morley again flying Blenheim IVs, he soon set about his task with vigour attacking shipping and coastal targets at very low level. During the mission of 4 July 1941, he was leading nine aircraft from his own squadron and six from 107 Squadron against docks and factories in Bremen. He attacked under extremely fierce enemy fire, flying through the balloon barrage and strafing targets after he had released his bombs. His aircraft was hit several times and his gunner had his knee shattered, but Edwards managed to escape the fire and fly his Blenheim back to England. For this operation, he was awarded the Victoria Cross. A few days later he led 105 Squadron to Malta to relieve other No 2 Group units on the island. From Malta the squadron undertook operations against Axis shipping in the Mediterranean area. Returning to the UK, he left the squadron to join a lecture tour of the United States and on his return he took up the duties of CFI at Wellesbourne Mountford.

It was not long before he returned to operations and unusually he regained the reins of his old squadron, No 105, by now equipped with the De Havilland Mosquito. He was awarded the DSO following the 2 Group attack on the Phillips works at Eindhoven on 6 December 1942. Promotion to Group Captain took him to Lincolnshire and command of the bomber station at Binbrook, which was the home of fellow Australians No 460 Squadron. Elevation to the post of 'Station Master' did not deter him from taking part in operations, usually by 'skippering' new inexperienced crews. With the end of the European war in sight, he was posted to the Far East where he filled a number of posts including Group Captain – Ops, SASO at AHQ Netherlands East Indies and AHQ Ceylon as well as station commander at Kuala Lumper. He was awarded the CBE for is work in the Far East.

Remaining in the post-war RAF, Edwards received further awards in the form of an OBE (1947) and a CB (1959). Following his retirement from the RAF he returned to his native Australia, where he became Australian Representative for Selection Trust until 1974 when he was appointed Governor of Western Australia, being sworn in on 7 January 1974. Ill health persuaded him that he must retire early. He was succeeded by Air Chief Marshal Sir Wallace Kyle. He retired to Sydney, where he died abruptly on his way to the races in August 1982.

Elworthy, Marshal of the Royal Air Force, Baron Elworthy of Timaru, KG, GCB, CBE, DSO, LVO, DFC, AFC. Born 23 March 1911, died 4 April 1993.

Born in New Zealand but educated in England at Marlborough College, Elworthy served as commander of a squadron of Blenheim bombers and then as a station commander during World War II until he was promoted Air Commodore at the age of 33 on becoming SASO at 5 Group. In 1957 he was appointed Commandant of the RAF Staff College for two years before moving to the Air Ministry as Deputy Chief of the Air Staff. In August 1960 he took over as C-in-C HQ British Forces Arabia, which ultimately metamorphosed in the C-in-C HQ Middle East Command. He became Chief of the Air Staff in 1963 and implemented the cancellation of the TSR-2 strike aircraft and the HS681 military transport aircraft programmes. He also became Chief of the Defence Staff in which role he oversaw the evacuation from Aden in November 1967 and the growing crisis in Northern Ireland in the late 1960s.

Evill, Air Chief Marshal Sir Douglas, GBE, KCB, DSC, AFC, DL. Born 8 October 1892, died 22 March 1971.

Born in Broken Hill, New South Wales, Evill was a first cousin of Arthur Longmore, who advised him to take flying lessons. On 13 June 1913 he applied to join the RNAS, but it was December 1914 before he was accepted. Whilst serving as SASO Bomber Command, he was selected as a member of the mission led by Air Vice-Marshal Christopher Courtney to Germany, where he had the opportunity to examine at first hand the developing Luftwaffe, experience, which prove useful a couple of years later. He became a serial SASO from 1936 to 1942, working at both Bomber Command and Fighter Command before becoming Head of the RAF Delegation to Washington in February 1942. He was Vice Chief of the Air Staff from 1943 to 1946. In retirement he became Honorary Air Commodore to No 3617 (County of Hampshire) Fighter Control Unit as well as a member of the council of King Edward VII's Hospital for Officers.

Faville, Air Vice-Marshal Roy, CBE. Born 5 August 1908, died 18 June 1980.

Having gained a degree in engineering at home in New Zealand, Faville travelled to England and joined the RAF in 1931. From 1960 to 1964 he was General Manager for Richard

Costain (Middle East) Ltd in Libya and from 1968 to 1970 Secretary of Torch Trophy Trust.

Hayr, Air Marshal Sir Kenneth, KCB, KBE, AFC. Born 13 April 1935, died 2 June 2001.

Born in Auckland in New Zealand, Kenneth Hayr was a member of No 3 (City of Auckland) Squadron, ATC, rising to the rank of Cadet Warrant Officer. He joined the RNZAF and was sent to Britain to attend the RAF College, Cranwell, which he represented at tennis. He became a Senior Flight Cadet and was awarded the R M Groves and Hicks Memorial Trophies. Graduating from Cranwell in 1957, he was posted to No 66 Squadron, flying Hunters. He later converted to the RAF's latest interceptor, the Lightning. Following a spell at the Central Fighter Establishment, which later became the Fighter Command Trials Units, he converted onto yet another type when he was given command of the Phantom OCU. a fighter pilot for the most part of his career, his next command found him converting onto both a new type, the Harrier, and a new role, ground attack.

Hayr attended the RAF Staff College in 1972, after which he was a Wing Commander on the air staff of No 38 Group. He returned to operational work when he assumed command of RAF Binbrook in Lincolnshire, home to the Lightnings of No 5 and 11 Squadrons. Promoted to Air Commodore, he was appointed Inspector of RAF Flight Safety before attending the Royal College of Defence Studies. He served as Assistant Chief of the Air Staff (ACAS) (Operations) from 1980 to 1982. During this period he was responsible for much of the planning of the RAF's part in the re-capture of the Falklands Islands.

In 1985, he moved to Cyprus, as Commander, British Forces Cyprus and as such he also held the appointment of The Administrator of the British Sovereign Base Areas. Returning to Britain he was Deputy C-in-C Strike Command until being appointed DCAS (Commitments) at the Ministry of Defence.

On retirement he returned to New Zealand and took up the Chairmanship of the New Zealand Aviation Heritage Trust Board, but he continued to split his time between Britain and New Zealand in order to continue his love for flying by performing displays in various vintage aircraft. It was in such an aircraft, a Vampire, that he was killed during the 2001 Biggin Hill air display.

In 1996, the Inspectorate of Flight Safety moved into new purpose-built accommodation at Bentley Priory and the facilities new lecture theatre was named 'The Hayr Theatre' in honour of Sir Kenneth who was the first Inspector in 1976 (prior to that date the post had been that of Director).

Hobler, Air Vice-Marshal John, CB, CBE. Born 26 September 1907, died 13 January 1996.

Born in Australia, Hobler was a founder member of the Central Queensland Aero Club in 1929. On 14 May 1940, he was flying Battle I, P2246 against targets around Sedan, when he hit by flak making a forced landing behind enemy lines. He and his crew managed to evade capture. Having been seriously burned during this encounter, he was evacuated back to Britain and joined the Air Staff at No 1 Group. From 1942 to 1945 he served in Bomber Command and at the end of the War was sent to the RAF overseas Staff College in Haifa. He spent two years on the directing staff of that College before being appointed Deputy Director of Plans. From October 1958 to May 1961 he was AOC No 25 Group and his final appointment was AOA HQ Far East Air Force.

Hughes, Air Marshal Sir Rochford, CBE, AFC, DFC. Born 25 October 1914, died 17 September 1996.

Sidney Weetman Rochford Hughes was born at Auckland, New Zealand. He was educated at Waitaki Boys' High School (1929-32). From 1933 to 1937 he was on the editorial staff of the *New Zealand Herald*. He was selected for No. 1 Pilot Training Course at Wigram in 1937 and transferred to the RAF in the following year. He served in RAF Sunderlands in Far and Middle East until 1941 and was twice decorated for gallantry. In 1942 he commanded the Middle East Air-Sea Rescue and Reconnaissance Flight in the Western Desert and, following a term of staff duties at headquarters, Middle East, he commanded 511 Squadron in the United Kingdom in the first two years after the war. While on exchange with the United States Air Force he served as Chief of Operations, All Weather Flying Division. He later commanded the RAF Experimental Flying Department at the Royal Aircraft Establishment, Farnborough, for three years and a tactical fighter base in Germany for four years. His final appointment was as C-in-C Far East Air Force.

He stayed in the Far East following his retirement from the RAF acting as Air Adviser to the Government of Singapore a post he held for three years. Returning to New Zealand, he sat on the Boards of a number of companies such as Mazda Motors NZ (Chairman 1972 - 87), NZ Steel (Director 1973-84),

General Accident (Director 1975–84) and Reserve Bank NZ (Director 1974–77) to name just a few. He was also a Liveryman of the Guild of Air Pilots and Navigators.

Jameson, Air Commodore Patrick, CB, DSO, DFC. Born 10 November 1912, died 1 October 1996.

A New Zealander, Jameson learned to fly whilst working as a clerk before travelling to Britain, where he joined the RAF in 1936. Following training he was posted to No 46 Squadron, and became a flight commander by 1940. Commanded by Squadron Leader K B B Cross (later Air Chief Marshal Sir Kenneth), the squadron was advised that it was to reinforce the RAF in France and Pat Jameson together with his CO went over to France to recce the available airfields. Much to their surprise, as soon as they returned from France the squadron was sent to reinforce the British forces operating in North Norway around Narvik. They worked in extremely trying conditions and were eventually told to destroy their aircraft and proceed by boat back to HMS *Glorious*. Cross and Jameson were determined not leave their precious aircraft and secured permission to attempt landing them on the deck of the carrier. Jameson led the first three aircraft and after making a successful landing, which was repeated by the other two pilots, he sent the signal that it was possible to land Hurricanes on a carrier, so the rest of the squadron followed suit.

Things did not go well. While returning to Scotland, the *Glorious* was sighted, attacked and sunk by the *Scharnhorst* with the loss of all the aircraft (including the Gladiators of No 263 Squadron), and almost the whole of the ship's company and the personnel of the two squadrons. Jameson rescued a marine after the sinking and together with Cross was able to find a raft, which eventually held 37 survivors. They drifted in this raft for three days and two nights until picked up by the Norwegian trawler SS *Borgund*, by which time only seven of the original survivors remained alive. Following this ordeal, Jameson spent six weeks in Gleneagles Hospital.

By the end of WW2 he had shot down nine enemy aircraft with one probable and another shared, two damaged and two destroyed on water. Following retirement, he suffered from tuberculosis resulting from his wartime service, and when he recovered he returned to New Zealand.

Jarman, Air Commodore Lancelot, DFC. Born 20 February 1906, died 1983.

Born and educated in New Zealand, Jarman attended the University of New Zealand before joining the RAF on a short service commission in 1929. Flying duties in Britain (No 12 Squadron equipped with the Fairey Fox) and Palestine (No 14 equipped with the Fairey IIIF), was followed in December 1931, by sitting the first exam taken by Short Service Commission holders to undertake specialisation training, successful completion of which would lead to the award of a Permanent Commission.

He then held a number of engineering posts until he returned to flying duties in 1939 with No 214 Squadron equipped with the Harrow and later Wellingtons. Moving to No 9 Squadron as a flight commander, he then became Chief instructor at three OTUs before being appointed to command

RAF Lichfield, the home of No 27 OTU. In 1943, he took over command of RAF *Wyton* and qualified as a 'Pathfinder'. In 1945, he left the UK to become SASO of No 205 Group in the Middle East.

Returning to the United Kingdom, he commanded a number of RAF stations as well as holding a staff appointment in Maintenance Command before moving overseas on secondment to the RPAF. Before returning to Britain, he was attached to the USAF and during this attachment he was based at Nellis AFB to observe tests of T33 and F86E. During this period, he also acted as an observer at atomic tests at Yucca Flats and Nevada. His two final appointments in the RAF were as Administration Officer in the Cabinet Office and at HQ Coastal Command. When he retired from the services he became a Director of the Engineering Industries Association (1958-1973). At some point he changed his name to Elworthy-Jarman, although this name was never used in the Air Force Lists.

Kingston-McClaughry, Air Vice-Marshal Edgar J, CB, CBE, DSO, DFC. Born 10 September 1896, died 13 November 1972.

The younger brother of Air Vice-Marshal M W A McClaughry (see below), Kingston-McClaughry was born in Adelaide, Australia and like his brother qualified as a mining engineer before World War I. With the outbreak of the war, he joined the Army as an Engineer serving in Egypt and transferring to the RFC in December 1916. Following training he was posted to No 23 Squadron flying Spads in France and was shot down. While recovering he became an instructor, after which he was posted to No 4 Squadron, Australian Flying

Corps, under the command of his brother, as a flight commander. Between 12 June and 24 September, when he was shot in the thigh and invalided home, he claimed 21 enemy aircraft destroyed although some of his fellow officers considered some of these to be a little over optimistic.

Appointed to the planning staff of the Allied Expeditionary Air Force, he was involved in the preparation of the detailed plans for the employment of air resources for 'Operation Overlord'. In January 1944, he became Chairman of the AEAF Bombing Committee and in July, following the actual invasion, he was attached to Montgomery's staff as Leigh-Mallory's representative. After 'Operation Charnwood', the bombing of Caen, in 1944 when heavy bombers were used in a tactical role, he was asked, along with Professor Zuckerman, to carry out an inquiry into this attack.

Towards the end of 1944, Kingston-McClaughry was posted to AHQ India and was Air Member, C-in-C India Reorganisation Committee. He spent nine months as SASO AHQ India before going to No 18 Group as AOC. In June 1948 he became SASO at Fighter Command and eighteen months later he was posted as AOC No. 38 Group. His final service appointment was Chief of Air Defence at the MoD.

Kyle, Air Chief Marshal Sir Wallace, GCB, KCVO, CBE, DSO, DFC. Born 22 January 1910, died 31 January 1988.

Kyle was born in Western Australia, where he received his early education at Guildford School before entering the RAF College at Cranwell, which he represented at cricket, squash and tennis and where he attained the rank of Flight Cadet Corporal.

After being commissioned, he was posted in 1929 to No 17 Squadron for two years, then to No 442 (Fleet Spotter Recce) Flight. He took command of his first Squadron in June 1938 at No 3 Flying Training School and 139 Squadron in 1940. For most of the rest of the War he was a station commander at RAF Marham and RAF Downham Market. On 26 April 1949 he was appointed as ADC to the King, and he remained the monarch's ADC when the Queen came to the throne in 1952.

In 1951 he was Assistant Commandant at the RAF College Cranwell and from June 1952 to February 1965 he spent all but two years in the Air Ministry in a range of jobs, culminating in his appointment as Vice Chief of the Air Staff, taking over from his old school friend, Teddy Hudleston. His last two service jobs were AOC Bomber Command, then AOC Strike Command.

From 1975 to 1980 Kyle was the Governor of Western Australia, having succeeded Air Commodore Sir Hughie Edwards VC, who retired early on health grounds. In 1995, his widow renamed the South Wing of the RAF Benevolent Fund's Princess Marina House in Sussex the 'Kyle Wing' in Sir Wallace's honour. Sir Wallace had been the first chairman of the home.

Latton, Air Commodore Kenneth. Born 6 June 1941, died 19 October 2001.

A New Zealander, Latton represented the RAF College at Rugby and was awarded Air Ministry Prize for War Studies and Humanities, the John Anthony Chance Memorial Prize, the Royal United Services Institute Award, the Queen's Medal and the Sword of Honour. Following graduation from Cranwell he undertook his advanced training at Valley and in April 1963, he became the first *ab initio* pilot to solo and graduate on the Gnat, which had just replaced the Vampire. He commanded 226 OCU at Lossiemouth before becoming the Tornado Joint Operational Training Project Officer. He was back in Lossiemouth in 1984 as the Officer Commanding and in May 1989 he was AOC and Commandant at the Central Flying School. His last military appointment was as an Air Commodore in charge of Flying Training at HQ RAF Support Command. He retired at his own request and became Principal of Oxford Air Training School. He was elected a Warden of the Guild of Air Pilots and Air Navigators in 2001.

Lees, Air Marshal Sir Ronald, KCB, CBE, DFC. Born 27 April 1910, died 18 May 1991.

Australian by birth, Sir Ronald attended St Peter's College in Adelaide joining the RAAF in 1930. He was transferred to the RAF in 1931. Although he handed over command of 72 Squadron in July 1940 on promotion to Wing Commander, he returned to fly with the unit whilst on leave in September 1940. The following excerpt is taken from the diary of a fellow pilot, R Deacon-Elliott:

'Wing Commander Lees was there - for a short while, anyway. I recall how hectic it had been for those operating from Hawkinge. The CO, Squadron Leader Collins, was shot down for a second time and unfortunately this time badly wounded in his knee and hand. He never returned to the Squadron and Flight Lieutenant Ted Graham assumed command. Wing Commander Lees was shot down early in the day's fighting. He crash landed on Hawkinge and it was only with great difficulty he was released from the cockpit. It appeared a cannon shell struck his canopy frame "welding" it to the frame of the windscreen. Later when attacking a gaggle of ME 110s he was shot down again. This time being well and truly hit, both his aircraft and he himself in the thigh which led to a spell in hospital. This was bad luck – all of us including the "troops" were very disappointed as we had hoped he would be with us for a whole week.

From 1942 to 1942 he had a range of appointments in North Africa culminating in the role as SASO of No 242 Group in Algiers. He was appointed as Air ADC to the King in 1943 and remained as the Air ADC to the Queen on her accession to the throne. With the advent of peace, he was posted as Officer Commanding RAF Bassingbourn. In September 1952 he became AOC No. 83 Group, then from August 1955 he served in the Air Ministry as ACAS (Ops).

Longmore, Air Chief Marshal Sir Arthur, GCB, DSO, DL.

Born in St Leonards, New South Wales and educated at Benges School, Hertford and Foster's Academy, Stubbington before entering Dartmouth, Longmore was interested in flying from its very earliest days. When the opportunity arose he applied for and was accepted as one of the first four officers to undergo pilot training by the Admiralty, gaining RAeC Certificate No 72 on 25 April 1911. Shortly after this in November 1911, he became the first man to fly an aircraft from land onto water in England, a feat he carried out in a Short biplane in Sheerness Harbour. One of his first tasks at the CFS was to teach Captain Paine, the school's first Commandant, to fly in order that he could take up his new post. He also taught Major Hugh Trenchard to be a military pilot. He commanded 'E' Flight of three (should have been four, but one did not fly) aircraft during the Royal Flypast at Spithead on 18 July 1914. On 28 July 1914, he successfully launched the first torpedo from an aircraft, whilst flying Short Type 81, '121'.

In 1916, he returned to normal naval duties as a Lieutenant Commander aboard the battle-cruiser Tiger. He was directly involved in the Battle of Jutland, during which he acted as air adviser to the Flag Officer, Battle Cruisers. His appointment to the staff of C-in-C, Mediterranean put him in overall control of all RNAS units in the area, including Malta, Italy, The Aegean, Egypt and later Gibraltar.

During his tour as the Commandant of the RAF College, the College Hall Officer's Mess was completed. On 28 January 1936 he was a mourner at the funeral of HM King George V. Appointed AOC, Middle East, he was involved in the early campaigns against the Italians. Amongst these was the Italian and German assault on Greece. Here he took the unilateral decision to send RAF units from the Middle East in order to support the Greeks, a decision, which received the full backing and support of Winston Churchill. When the expected reinforcements from Britain, to replace those units sent to Greece, did not arrive he found his command seriously under equipped. He made vigorous complaints about the lack of reinforcements, which soon made him an 'enemy' of Churchill, with a consequent loss of confidence. Recalled to London in May 1941 to discuss the supply problem, he was relieved of his command and his deputy, Arthur Tedder, was appointed in his place. After retiring from the Services, Longmoor stood for Parliament as Conservative candidate for Grantham, but was defeated by the Independent candidate. He then joined a voluntary organisation, Yachtsmen's Emergency Service, and was involved in providing transport for the invasion fleet building up off the South coast in 1944. In 1943, he was recalled to service to undertake a planning review for post-war activities. From 1954 to 1957 he was Vice-Chairman of the Commonwealth War Graves Commission and he continued to sail as a member of the Royal Yacht Squadron.

Magill, Air Vice-Marshal Graham, CB, CBE, DFC. Born 23 January 1915, died 1 December 1998.

A New Zealander from Cambridge, Graham was educated at Hamilton Technical High School and became an electrical engineer. He joined the RAF in 1936 and by 1940 was flying Vickers Wellesley bombers from Khartoum in the Sudan with No. 47 Squadron. On 26 June 1940 he flew Wellesley K7785 on a raid to Gura and on his return to base the undercarriage collapsed on landing, resulting in the aircraft being struck off charge. In 1943 he took command of No. 180 Squadron flying American B25s. He was awarded the DFC during this time. He moved on to the Operations Staff at No. 2 Group from 1943 - 1945. He was subsequently mentioned in despatches and awarded a bar to his DFC.

After the War Magill spent some time on the staff of HQ Middle East in Egypt, then commanded the Ferry Control Wing at RAF Benson. He spent time on the staff of HQ Allied Air Forces Central Europe in Fontainebleau before returning to England to command RAF Upwood. He became Commandant of the Royal Air Force College of Air Warfare in Lincolnshire and then Director General of Organisation in the MoD in 1964. His final appointments were as AOC no 25 (Training) Group, then AOC No. 22 (Training) Group.

Manning, Air Commodore Edye, CBE, DSO, MC. Born 14 February 1899, died 26 April 1957.

An Australian, Manning was studying Medicine at Edinburgh when war broke out and he immediately joined the 15th Hussars, serving in France and Belgium. With the advent of static trench warfare in 1915, he decided to transfer to the RFC, gaining RAeC Certificate No 2253 on 9 October 1916. He was wounded in combat whilst serving in No 3 Squadron in July 1916 during the Battle of the Somme.

As CO of No 6 Squadron, he was in charge of the evacuation of the British High Commissioner and his wife and staff from Suliemanieh in Kurdistan, for which he received the DSO. In 1928 he voluntarily went on half pay in order that he might attempt a flight from England to Australia. He set off in a Westland Wigeon and despite a seized engine and a blown cylinder head gasket he reached Tunis, only to suffer further delays before being able to continue. Eventually he set off again, only to crash at Lebda and although he was uninjured, the aircraft was a write-off and he was forced to give up the attempt.

Retiring in 1935 at his own request, he returned to Australia, joining the Sydney Stock Exchange, but with the prospect of war looming again, he was recalled to service rejoining the RAF in the Far East. In March 1941 he was appointed officer commanding No. 221 Group as a Group

Captain, then was replaced in January 1942 but remained with the Group as Senior Officer in charge of administration in the rank of Air Commodore. Prior to the Japanese attack in December 1941 he was responsible for the establishment of a string of airfields stretching from Lashio to Mingladon.

Martin, Air Marshal Sir Harold, KCB, DSO, DFC, AFC. Born 27 February 1918, died 3 November 1988.

When Martin arrived in Britain in 1939, he had no intention of joining the RAF. In fact, he was sent to England by his family in Australia to 'experience some life' before settling down to become a doctor. The declaration of war in September 1939 halted these plans and he volunteered for the RAF on 28 August 1940, with hopes of becoming a fighter pilot. That ambition was frustrated when he was posted to No 455 Sqn flying Hampdens in No 5 Group. Martin soon developed his skills in low flying, which even included the bombing run which he usually carried out at around 4000 ft, so he could see the target more clearly and because the AA fire would be directed at the aircraft flying higher. He always insisted that his aircraft be maintained in first-class condition, even helping the ground crew if necessary.

When 455 was transferred to Coastal Command, he moved across the airfield at Swinderby and joined No 50 Sqn, initially flying Hampdens, but soon converting onto the new Manchester and then Lancasters. He had completed 13 sorties with 455 and he went on to complete a further 23 with 50 before being 'rested' as an instructor.

It was whilst on his rest tour that he was selected by Guy

Gibson to join the new squadron he was then forming. His main task in 617 was to supervise the training of the other crews in the difficult skill of low flying at night. Martin piloted one of the nine Lancasters led by Guy Gibson himself in the first wave of aircraft, which attacked the Möhne Dam. Following his own bomb run, he then helped Gibson distract the AA fire from the other aircraft as the carried out their bomb runs, for which he was awarded the DSO.

Martin stayed with 617 after the Dams Raid and was involved in training new crews as the squadron undertook a range of 'specialist' operations. On the night of 15/16 September, he took part in a mission against the Dortmund-Ems Canal using the new 12,000lb High Capacity bomb, during which the squadron's new CO was killed when his aircraft was hit flak. Taking over the lead, Martin continued on to the target with the rest of 617, although only his and one other bomb actually landed on target. On his return, he was immediately promoted to Squadron Leader as temporary OC. Fortunately for him at the time, he was soon relieved by Leonard Cheshire and between them they set about developing their low-level marking techniques, first using the Lancaster and then Mosquitoes.

Following his period with No 617, Martin was moved to Group HQ as a Staff Officer. Never one to be a 'mahogany pilot', he managed to get transferred to No 515 Squadron in No 100 Group and was involved in night intruder operations in support of the Bomber Command's Main Force. By the time he was finally taken off operations in late 1944, he had completed 83 sorties, 49 in bombers, and been awarded both the DSO and the DFC, both with Bars.

After the war he set a new speed record for the England to Cape Town route when he covered the 6700 miles, flying a Mosquito, in 21 hours 31 minutes. In 1951 he was asked to select three crews to train on the B-45C Tornado in order to undertake a number of special operations, but having selected his crews, he failed a medical test and was replaced by another officer. Following retirement from the RAF, he joined Hawker Siddeley International Ltd as an adviser, principally in the Middle East.

Maynard, Air Vice-Marshal F. H. M., CB, AFC, Legion of Merit (US); England; born at Waiuku, south of Auckland on the North Island of New Zealand on 1 May 1893; died 26 January 1976.

Maynard started his service career as an engineer with the Royal Naval Division before training as a pilot with the RNAS in 1915. He served with them as a pilot in No. 1 Squadron, flying Sopwith triplanes throughout the remainder of the War. He was credited with shooting down six enemy aircraft. For much of the time between the two World Wars he was a staff officer in the Middle East, Iraq and England although he commanded No.4 FTS in 1923 and 12 Squadron from 1929 to 1931. He attended both the RAF Staff College in 1924 and the Imperial Defence College in 1931. In January 1940 he was appointed AOC RAF, Mediterranean. He went on to be Air Officer in Charge of Administration, Coastal Command, 1941-44 and finally AOC No. 19 (Reconnaissance) Group, Coastal Command, 1944-45.

From 1946 to 1951 he was Manager of the Conservative Central Board of Finance. His son Nigel also joined the RAF and rose to become Air Chief Marshal Sir Nigel Maynard, making himself and his father one of the very few father and son combinations to achieve air rank.

McClaughry, Air Vice-Marshal Wilfred A, CB, DSO, MC, DFC. Born 26 September 1894, died 4 January 1943

An Australian originally named Kingston-McClaughry, he was the elder of two brothers, both destined to become Air Vice-Marshals. He dropped the 'Kingston' from his surname in order to avoid confusion with his brother Edgar (see above). Educated at Queen's School in North Adelaide and the University of Adelaide, McClaughry joined the Australian Militia Forces in 1913 and served in World War I with the 9th Australian Light Horse Regiment before transferring to the Royal Flying Corps in 1916. He was appointed Officer Commanding No. 71 Squadron, which became No. 4 Squadron AFC. After the War he joined the Royal Air Force and became Officer Commanding the Air Pilotage School in 1921. He was appointed Officer Commanding No. 8 Squadron in 1924 and then spent three years as a staff officer at Headquarters Wessex Bombing Area. He went on to be Station Commander at RAF Heliopolis in 1934, then Station Commander at RAF Mersa Matruh the same year, before becoming Air Officer Commanding British Forces Aden in 1936. He became Director of Training at the Air Ministry in 1938 and served in World War II as Air Officer Commanding No. 9 (Fighter) Group during the Battle of Britain and then as Air Officer Commanding AHQ Egypt. He was killed in an air accident in Cairo in 1943. Lady Tedder, the first wife of Air Chief Marshal Sir Arthur Tedder, died in the same accident.

McGregor, Air Marshal Sir Hector Douglas, K.C.B., C.B.E., D.S.O. Born 1910, died 1973.

Hector McGregor was born at Wairoa, New Zealand, on 15 February 1910. He was educated at Napier Boys' High School and joined the RAF when he was 18. When the Second World War broke out he was commanding a fighter squadron and won the DSO. In 1941 he was on the Special Planning Staff and in 1943 he became Deputy Director Operations, Intelligence and Plans, Mediterranean Allied Air Forces. He spent 1948-49 with the Air Ministry before being posted for a two-year term with NATO Standing Group in Washington D.C. From 1951 to 1953 he was Officer Commanding 2 Group in Germany. He then spent three years with the Ministry of Supply, where he was Director of Guided Missile Development for two years and Assistant Controller of Aircraft for one. From 1957 he was Chief of Staff (Air Defence) at SHAPE in Paris. He was knighted in 1960 and received a United States Legion of Merit award in 1945. In 1959 Sir Hector became Air Officer Commander-in-Chief of Fighter Command. He relinquished this post in June 1962 when he was appointed Commander-in-Chief of Britain's Far East Air Force in Singapore.

McKee, Air Marshal Sir Andrew, KCB, CBE, DSO, DFC, AFC. Born 10 January 1902, died 8 December 1988.

McKee was born in New Zealand and educated in Christchurch. He travelled to England in 1926 and joined the RAF in January 1927. On completion of his flying training, he was posted to 27 Squadron in India for almost three years. During the war he commanded 99 Squadron, 9 Squadron and

RAF Marham and was appointed AOC 205 Group on the day that Hitler committed suicide, 30 April 1945. After spending some time as the Commandant of RAF Hornchurch and the RAF Flying College, he became AOC 21 Group. After two years as SASO Bomber Command, he undertook his final active appointment as AOC-in-C Transport Command from 15 October 1955 until his retirement on 13 June 1959.

Maclean, Air Vice-Marshal Cuthbert Trelawder, CB, DSO, MC. Born 1886 at Wanganui, New Zealand, and died 25 February 1969.

Mclean was educated at Wanganui Collegiate School and Auckland University College. During the First World War he served in the armed forces, and in 1915 he was seconded to the Royal Flying Corps and transferred to the RAF three years later. He was Officer Commanding British Forces in Aden from 1929 to 1931, when he spent three years at the Air Ministry as Director of Postings. From 1934 to 1938 he was Air Officer Commanding the RAF in the Middle East. He then took over as AOC 2 Bomber Group in May 1938, finally retiring on 27 December 1940.

Park, Air Chief Marshal Sir Keith, GCB, KBE, MC, DFC. Born 15 June 1892, died 5 February 1975.

Born at Thames in the North Island of New Zealand, Keith Park studied mining at the University of Otago and later went to sea as a purser. He fought at Gallipoli as an NCO in the New Zealand Artillery and was awarded a field commission for distinguished service. He transferred to the British Army and was posted to the Somme, where he was seriously wounded and was invalided out of the Artillery. Two months later he joined the RFC and became a Flight Commander in 48 Squadron, then took over the Squadron as a temporary Major in April 1918. By the end of the War, he had an MC and Bar, a DFC and the French Croix de Guerre.

During the twenty years between the wars, Park had staff appointments in the Middle East, commanded 111 Squadron and RAF Northolt, and spent a little over two years as the Air Attaché in Buenos Aires. On 1 January 1937 he was appointed Air ADC to the King and eleven days later started the year-long course at the IDC.

On completing the senior staff course, he took command of RAF Tangmere before being appointed SASO at HQ Fighter Command, where he was under Dowding's command and was directly involved in the setting up of the Control and Reporting system which would become so vital in the summer of 1940. There were critics, of whom the most vociferous was his opposite number at No 12 Group, Trafford Leigh-Mallory, who felt that Park should concentrate his fighters in force rather than small units. Park's tactics attempted to destroy and separate German bombers before they could reach their targets. Leigh-Mallory, on the other hand, attacked in force after German bombers had completed their mission. With the benefit of hindsight, it can be seen that the Battle of Britain was won because both methods combined to make a major impact. Probably the biggest fault in the system was the intermittent lack of co-ordination between Nos 11 and 12 Groups, exacerbated by Leigh-Mallory's determination not to collaborate with Park.

Park took over as AOC in Egypt in 1942 and successfully managed the air defence of Malta. In November 1944 Leigh-Mallory, disappeared whilst en route to the Far East to take up the post of Air C-in-C, Air Command South East Asia. The aircraft had flown into a mountain in the Alps and was found in June 1945. The person chosen to replace him was Keith Park.

He retired to his native New Zealand in 1946 and served on Auckland City Council. Many commentators believe he was one of the greatest commanders in the history of aerial warfare.

Paxton, Air Vice-Marshal Sir Anthony, KBE, CB, DFC. Born 7 August, died 25 September 1957.

Born in Sydney, Paxton was sent to England to complete his education at Dulwich College and, on leaving school, he travelled to Mexico and became British Vice-Consul in Sonora. In 1916, he travelled to Vancouver and enlisted in the RFC and received his commission in England in 1917. He was swiftly posted to No. 2 Squadron AFC on the Western Front.

Between the wars, he completed a variety of staff and operational appointments, including time spent as a flying instructor. He commanded No. 25 Squadron at Hawkinge from 1933 to 1935 and was then sent to join the air staff in Iraq. In 1940 he was SASO at 21 Group and later became SASO at HQ Flying Training Command. There followed two appointments as AOC, first at 85 Group, then at 2 Group. His final role was Director-General of Personnel. He retired in July 1950 and died at the youthful age of 61 in September 1957.

Rae, Air Vice-Marshal Ronald, CB, OBE. Born 9 October 1910, died 19 June 1994.

Rae was born in Sydney and served in the Australian Citizen Force RAAF, from 1930 to 1931 as an Officer Cadet. He transferred to the RAF in 1932.

He flew as a pilot with 33 Squadron and 142 Squadron before taking an Armaments course and being posted to Singapore as an Armament Officer. He spent several years in the Far East, travelling widely around the uninhabited islands of the Pacific, Ceylon, Borneo, Burma, Hong Kong and Malaya. He met his wife Rosemary in Singapore, where her father, Charles Howell, was the Attorney General and they married in 1939. He became the Officer Commanding RAF Tengah (in Singapore) in 1942 but was taken as a prisoner of war in Java in 1943. He was mentioned in despatches for his service in the Far East.

After the war he became the Officer Commanding the Central Gunnery School at RAF Leconfield for two years. He attended the RAF Staff College and subsequently moved through a range of posts, twice as a Station Commander (North Luffenham and Oakington) and staff jobs in the Air Ministry, working in the Chief of the Air Staff's department and as Deputy Air Secretary. His final task was as AOC 224 Group in Singapore from June 1959 until his retirement in October 1962. At some point he changed his name from Rae to Ramsey-Rae. He died on 19 June 1994.

Russell, Air Vice-Marshal Herbert B, CB, DFC, AFC. Born 6 May 1895, died 15 June 1963.

A New Zealander, Russell was commissioned into the

Royal Field Artillery having attended the Royal Military Academy. He transferred to the RFC in 1915, initially as an Observer with No 2 Squadron. However, at the end of 1915 he began pilot training and was awarded his Royal Aero Club Certificate (No.2168) on 12 December.

Joining No 23 Squadron, he flew on numerous operations until 26 June 1916, when he was shot down in flames following combat with enemy aircraft over Fampoux, east of Arras. Russell was badly injured but survived, after a lengthy stay in various German hospitals. His observer, Lt J. R. Dennistoun, died of his injuries on 9 August 1916. After a stay in various prison camps, Russell was sent to Switzerland on 9 December 1917, as part of an exchange of severely wounded POWs, and was repatriated to the UK on 24 March 1918.

Tacon, Air Commodore Ernest, CBE, DSO, LVO, DFC, AFC. Born 16 December 1917, died 9 September 2003.

Born at Napier on the north Island of New Zealand, Tacon was educated at St Patrick's in Wellington, where he was a keen sportsman. He joined the RNZAF in 1938, and in May 1939 he was transferred to the RAF, as a result of an agreement that the RNZAF would supply six trained pilots a year to the RAF. Posted to No 233 Squadron at Leuchars, he flew Ansons, until converting to the Lockheed Hudson on the outbreak of war. After eighteen months with 233, he was involved in ferrying aircraft across the Atlantic, converted No 407 Squadron onto the Hudson at RAF North Coates and No 59 Squadron at Thorney Island before going out to Canada to set up a new OTU in Nova Scotia.

From Canada, Tacon returned to his native New Zealand, where he was given command of No 1 Squadron for two months before he took over No 4 Squadron RNZAF in Fiji. Returning to Britain in early 1944, he converted to the Beaufighter and was given command of No 236 Squadron. Whilst commanding No 236, he acquired a reputation for extremely aggressive, successful attacks against enemy shipping. On 12 September, he was leading 40 Beaufighters from the North Coates and Langham strike wings when his aircraft was badly hit, setting his fuel tank alight and causing his cannon ammunition to start exploding. Unable to release the escape hatch, he decided to dive into the gun post that was firing at him and rolled the aircraft on its back and began to dive at it. Suddenly there was a violent explosion and he found himself outside the aircraft and immediately pulled the ripcord on his parachute, landing on the island of Texel. Badly burned, he was captured and taken to the local jail, but not until he had been physically assaulted by some German sailors. His burns were treated and he eventually ended up in Stalag Luft I at Barth, until being freed by the Russians in 1945.

Returning to Britain, he was given command of a transport squadron at the end of 1945 and in 1946 he transferred permanently to the RAF. He became the first CO of the King's Flight after WW2 and had eight months to 'rebuild' the Flight before the King's tour of South Africa in 1947. Various appointments followed as detailed above, until he retired in early 1971, when he returned to his native New Zealand, running the Intellectually Handicapped Children's Society (IHC) and later worked as a manager with Air New Zealand.

Williamson, Air Vice-Marshal Peter, CB, CBE, DFC. Born 28 February 1923, died 8 October 1982.

Australian by birth, Williamson joined the RAF rather than the RAAF, having been informed that to join the latter, he would have needed to return to Australia, which at that time of the war was not a practical option. He was posted to No 153 Squadron, which was flying Defiants but soon received Beaufighters and it was with this type that the squadron moved to North Africa. He remained with 153 until it disbanded in 1944, when he returned to Britain and joined No 219 Squadron as a flight commander and later CO. His final tally for the war was nine destroyed and one damaged. He retired from the RAF having been diagnosed with bone marrow cancer, and died at the early age of 59.

BIBLIOGRAPHY

Richard J Aldrich: *Witness to War*

Field Marshal Lord Alanbrooke: *War Diaries 1939 – 1945*

Dr. Mahmoud A. Ali, Department of Political Science Applied Science Private University Amman – Jordan. Article published in the International Journal of Humanities and Social Science Vol. 2 No. 24 [Special Issue – December 2012]

Malcolm Barrass: Website Air of Authority

Chaz Bowyer: *Men of the Desert Air Force*

Marshal of the Royal Air Force Sir Dermot Boyle, GCB, KCVO, KBE, AFC, personal papers held at the RAF Museum, Hendon

Stephen Bungay: *The Most Dangerous Enemy*

Neil Cameron: *In the midst of things*

Canadiansoldiers.com: *Operation Husky*

Tom Carver: *Where have you been?*

Ronald W Clark: *Tizard*

Michael Coles, 2006 article to celebrate the 50th anniversary of Op Musketeer: *'Suez. A Successful Naval Operation Compromised by Inept Political Leadership'*

Lieutenant Colonel Stephen Cote, USMC: *Operation Husky: A Critical Analysis.* May 2001

Tim Darling: *'Excerpts from my grandfather's WWII Journal' published online*

Marshal of the Royal Air Force Sir William Dickson, GCB, KBE,

DSO, AFC, Personal papers held in the archives at Churchill College, Cambridge

Dwight D Eisenhower: *First Annual Report from the Supreme Allied Commander 2 April 1952*

Adrian Fort: *Archibald Wavell*

Garland & Smith: *US Army in the Second World War; Sicily and the surrender of Italy*

Dr Ian Gooderson: *Air Power at the Battlefront*

Lavinia Greacen: *Chink*

Stephen Ashley Hart: *Colossal Cracks*

Group Captain E.B. Haslam: *The History of RAF Cranwell*

HMSO: RAF Middle East; *The official story of Air Operations in the Middle East from February 1942 to January 1943*

Hudleston Papers at the Imperial War Museum: *ECH 1, 2 and 3*

Thomas Keneally: *Australians*

Keith Kyle: *Suez*

Harold MacMillan: *War Diaries 1943 - 1945*

Francis K Mason and edited by **RC Sturtivant**: *Hawks Rising*

Maurice Matloff and Edwin M Snell: *Strategic Planning for Coalition Warfare 1941 - 1942*

Eric Mensforth, CBE: *The Future of the Aeroplane*

Air Commodore Edward J Morris, CB, CBE, DSO, DFC, DFC (USA*): It's a great life if you don't weaken*

Nigel Nicholson: *'Alex'*

Vincent Orange: *Coningham – A biography of Air Marshal Sir Arthur Coningham*

Vincent Orange: *Dowding of Fighter Command*

Vincent Orange: *Park*

Vincent Orange: *Tedder 'Quietly in Command'*

Hermione Ranfurly: *To War with Whittaker*

Laurence Rees: *Behind Closed Doors*

David Rosier: *Be Bold 'Air Chief Marshal Sir Frederick Rosier, GCB, CBE, DSO'*

Hilary St George Saunders: '*The Royal Air Force 1939 – 1945*'

Glen Segell: *A Historical Phase Appreciation of Weapon Procurement*

JC Slessor, *Air Power and Armies*

Stockwell papers: (Stockwell 8/2/2) at King's College Library

Michael Thornhill: *Road to Suez*

Barry Turner: *Suez 1956*

Jeffery Williams: *The Long Left Flank*

World War II Magazine (Weider History Group)

Philip Ziegler: *Mountbatten*

http://www.flightglobal.com/pdfarchive/view/1928/1928%20-%200029.html

Mead, Richard (2007). Churchill's Lions: A biographical guide to the key British generals of World War II. Stroud (UK): Spellmount. ISBN 978-1-86227-431-0.

The Historical Subsection, Office of Secretary, General Staff, Supreme Headquarters, Allied Expeditionary Staff. May 1944. *History of COSSAC (Chief of Staff to Supreme Allied Commander)*
http://www.history.army.mil/documents/cossac/Cossac.htm

SHAPE: The New Approach, 1953 – 1956
http://www.nato.int/nato_static/assets/pdf/pdf_archives/20121126_SHAPE_HISTORY_-_THE_NEW_APPROACH_1953_-_1956.pdf

The Sicilian Campaign 1943
http://www.bestofsicily.com/ww2.htm#Prelude_to_War

Unpublished Sources:

Letters of Johnny Collingwood to Nancy Hudleston 1948 – 1975

Nan Hudleston diaries and notes

Senior Appointments:

http://www.gulabin.com/armynavy/pdf/Royal%20Air%20Force%20Senior
%20Appointments.pdf

Flightglobal.com

National Archives

AIR6 / 110, 111, 112, 116, 117,126, 127, 128, 198, 130, 131, 134, 150

AIR8/2342

AIR25/ 1093, 1399, 1422, 1425, 1426, 1429

DEFE4/ 104, 105, 106, 108, 111, 113, 114, 118, 119, 121, 125, 126, 128,
129, 130, 132, 133, 134, 135, 136, 139, 140, 141, 143

INDEX